The Developing Ego
and the Emerging Self
in Group Therapy

The Developing Ego
and the Emerging Self
in Group Therapy

Dorothy Flapan, Ph.D.
Gerd H. Fenchel, Ph.D.

𝓐

Jason Aronson Inc.
Northvale, New Jersey
London

The following chapters were published previously under slightly different titles and are reprinted with permission from Brunner/Mazel, Inc., New York:

Chapter 1: "The Developing Ego in Group Psychotherapy," *Group* 10(4):195–210, 1986; *Chapter 9:* "Resistance in Group Psychotherapy," *Group* 9(2):35–38, 1985; *Chapter 10:* "Countertransference in Group Psychotherapy," *Group* 8(3):17–30, 1984; *Chapter 11:* Acting Out in Group Psychotherapy," *Group* 11(2):94–107, 1987; *Chapter 12:* "Group Members' Contacts without the Group Therapist," *Group* 7(4):3–16, 1983; *Chapter 13:* "Terminations," *Group* 11(3):131–143, 1987.

---

10 9 8 7 6 5 4 3 2 1

Library of Congress Cataloging-in-Publication Data

Flapan, Dorothy.
   The developing ego and the emerging self in group therapy
Dorothy Flapan and Gerd H. Fenchel.
   p.   cm.
   Includes bibliographies and index.
   ISBN 0-87668-980-2
   1. Group psychotherapy.   2. Ego (Psychology)   3. Self.
I. Fenchel, Gerd H.   II. Title.
   [DNLM: 1. Ego.   2. Psychotherapy, Group.   WM 430 F585d]
RC488.F57 1987
616.89'152 – dc19
DNLM/DLC   87-22956
for Library of Congress   CIP

Manufactured in the United States of America

Contents

Preface

Our purposes in writing this book are threefold: (1) to teach mental health professionals how to conduct analytic group psychotherapy, (2) to convey to individual practitioners how their work may be complemented by placing their patients in a therapy group in conjunction with individual psychotherapy, and (3) to present a body of knowledge integrating clinical experience with contemporary theories of psychoanalytic psychotherapy.

The analytic therapy group affords the clinician the opportunity to see psychoanalysis "in action." In the analytic group the emphasis is on observing individuals relating to one another with their habitual modes of coping. Group provides the practitioner with more than verbal reports by the person; it presents an unexcelled opportunity to see how each member utilizes other group members and relates to reality. Group members act, react, and interact, giving the group therapist an opportunity to observe and infer from these observations the nature, intent, and quality of the interactions.

When we started formalized group therapy training, the questions raised by students made it necessary for us to clarify our theoretical thinking and integrate it with our clinical approach. Both of us taught group therapy courses and participated in the clinical training of group therapists. We grappled with several questions:

1. Does a more general theoretical system underlie both individual psychotherapy and group psychotherapy?
2. Does group psychotherapy have something unique to offer that complements dyadic psychotherapy?
3. Are group dynamic concepts compatible with a psychoanalytic approach?

The following assumptions serve as a foundation for our basic theoretical propositions:

1. There are generic principles underlying psychoanalytic psychotherapies, whether dyadic or group.
2. A developmental psychoanalytic point of view enables the practitioner to assess self and ego development and make appropriate interventions.
3. Using both ego psychology and object relation theories enables the clinician to confront intrapsychic problems.
4. Narcissistic defenses are clearly delineated in interactional patterns and can be addressed specifically and effectively in the interactional process.
5. The participation of the group therapist in the interactional framework stimulates more spontaneous responses, which are helpful in restructuring personality.

Thus, certain aspects of the group process provide unique opportunities for therapeutic progress. In the analytic therapy group, the therapist is more self-revealing than in individual analytic therapy just by virtue of the ongoing interaction with the group members. This deidealizes the therapist and makes less likely the development of transference for the gratification of individual needs.

The acceptance or rejection of the social reality of the group becomes a major focus for discussion. Because the group members do not know how to deal with the other members—which is a social reality – they project their own expectations, thoughts, and feelings based on past experiences. When they cannot make contact the way they have anticipated and find that they are rebuffed, they have to modify their perception – which results in modifying identifications and modes of interaction.

In analytic group therapy we examine maladaptive patterns, as well as value systems, and point out the person's weaknesses and strengths. From the very beginning, the struggles of a person entering a group give us an indication of what therapeutic goals can be set and met. These goals, however, are continually revised by the group member and the therapist, based on experiences both inside and outside of group. When the patient's and therapist's goals for the patient coincide, and the patient has achieved them, the therapeutic contract is terminated and the patient leaves the group. At this point, ideally, the patient has more wisdom and self-knowledge and can integrate such knowledge into his/her life.

This book is based on 30 years of experience conducting groups and 17 years of teaching group psychotherapy to individual practitioners and students. Dorothy Flapan, after working for several years with groups of nursery school-aged children, worked under the supervision of Bruno Bettelheim at the Orthogenic School of the University of Chicago with a group of emotionally disturbed preadolescent girls. She subsequently served as a social psychologist at the Family Study Center of the University of Chicago for several years, conducting groups of married couples in an experimental project to develop empathy between spouses.

After a period of leave for childrearing, she worked with Peter B. Neubauer for several years at the Child Development Center of the Jewish Board of Guardians and, together with him, wrote *Assessment of Early Child Development*. Dr. Flapan is also the author of *Children's Understanding of Social Interaction*. She taught at Teachers College, Columbia University, and Hunter College before joining the Washington Square Institute, where she conducts a clinic group in addition to her private therapy groups. As Director of the Group Psychotherapy Department, she has been responsible for 18 clinic groups as well as the two-year training program in group therapy.

Initially, Gerd H. Fenchel learned about group psychotherapy as a cotherapist in inpatient groups in a hospital setting. Subsequently, he was influenced by his studies of group behavior with Morton Deutsch and by the enthusiasm for this method expressed by Asya Kadis, at that time Director of Group Psychotherapy at the Postgraduate Center for Psychotherapy and Mental Health. He became more deeply involved in the study of this method and began conducting private therapy groups, as well as clinic groups at the Alfred Adler Mental Hygiene Clinic.

Based on these experiences, Dr. Fenchel evolved a group therapy program at the Long Island Consultation Center. From this, he became directly involved in training group psychotherapists at the Long Island Consultation Center and founded there the Institute of Group Psychotherapy. At a later date, he introduced group psychotherapy at the Washington Square Institute, informally training individual practitioners there.

This book is divided into three parts: Thinking about Group Therapy, Beginning Groups, and Working with Groups. The first part discusses theory, the second part presents practical considerations regarding the beginnings of therapy groups, and the third part relates to specific interventions by the therapist during the middle and final phases of therapy.

Throughout the book, clinical examples illustrate theoretical concepts; bibliographical references permit the reader to follow up those topics of further interest.

This book is intended for both practitioners and group therapists-in-training. Over the years, there has been increasing interest in group therapy by psychiatrists, clinical psychologists, school psychologists, social workers, psychiatric nurses, guidance counselors, religious leaders, youth workers, and other professionals. We hope our book will be useful for all these varied professionals engaged in the practice of group therapy.

Acknowledgments

First and foremost, the book could not have been possible without our patients. We have enjoyed working with them through good and bad times. We have taught them and they, in turn, have taught us much about the human psyche. Once the usual clutter of resistances and transferences have been worked through and a dialogue established, we never cease to be amazed at the wisdom that many patients exhibit.

We are grateful for the conferences and symposia given by the American Group Psychotherapy Association (AGPA), which have stimulated much of our thinking. The attempts of presenters such as S. Scheidlinger and M. Pines to integrate group therapy with psychoanalytic thought always proved stimulating.

The interchanges with our students at the Washington Square Institute also proved invaluable. Their queries and discussions raised issues that usually needed clarification.

Finally, Dr. Fenchel wishes to acknowledge a debt to his analysts. Alfred Farau taught him to have basic respect for the patient as a human being and demonstrated how one must look flexibly at the human condition without too much prejudice. Asya Kadis, with her boundless energy and skillful handling of group themes, developed his enthusiasm for groups.

Part I

Thinking about Group Therapy

Chapter 1
The Developing Ego

How does analytic group psychotherapy help a group member improve ego functions and solidify identity—often better than individual psychoanalysis can? Individual psychotherapy is limited to an interaction between two persons and therefore is skewed toward aspects of the personality structure that operate within the dyadic system. The analyst is dependent on what the analysand reports and cannot determine the objective validity of these reports. In contrast, the group therapist directly observes interactional behavior. Unlike the dyadic situation, the group offers each member the opportunity to interact with many individuals and may therefore evoke more self and ego aspects.

The group modality is used for a variety of purposes with particular populations and to achieve various therapeutic goals. For example, peer groups or consciousness-raising groups do not fully exploit the therapeutic potential; rather, such groups focus on support and on enhancing self-esteem. Groups for particular populations, such as medical patients, the elderly, incest victims, and individuals with eating disorders, deal with symptoms or specific patterns of behavior and therefore have limited therapeutic goals.

Analytic group psychotherapy offers the potential both for

developing ego functions that have been inhibited and for reintegrating aspects of the self. To bring about a new and lasting personality integration is a complex undertaking that requires the skills to evaluate the group members' ego functions and deficiencies, as well as a heightened sensitivity to their interaction within the group.

The growing number of patients with ego and self pathology has forced clinicians to modify the classical psychoanalytic approach (conflict and defense) in favor of a developmental approach that focuses more sharply on developmental lags and deficits. Although every individual has unconscious conflicts and fantasies, the manner in which these are expressed will be determined by the developmental history. Even though the underlying cause may be similar, each individual employs different defenses and coping behaviors.

One person may use aggression to keep people "off his back," while another is charming and seeks narcissistic alliances. Both individuals will present difficulties in becoming therapeutically engaged and will require special therapeutic approaches. The aggressive patient holds his fragile self together in the service of separation; this defense must be respected. The charming patient employs whatever resources are available at the moment and must be allowed to use the group narcissistically for a while. Only after such patients become more integrated in the group "holding environment" can confrontation and analytic exploration be undertaken. Each patient will use the ego functions that have developed, even though this functioning may not appear to be adapted to reality. Ego strength is measured by the degree to which there is adaptation to reality and integration of ego functions.

THE EGO

The term *ego* refers to the organization of a variety of functions governing perception, intentionality, and motility that can be either inner- or outer-directed and that have adaptation as their chief aim.

Theoretical Basis

Although Freud used the terms *ego* and *self* interchangeably, he came to refer to the ego as a system of functions that related chiefly to the environment. With his revision of the theory of anxiety (1926), he began to emphasize the organizational aspects of the ego system. Among various ego functions he listed were providing a stimulus barrier, controlling motility and perception, thinking, and forming defenses.

Continuing her father's work, Anna Freud (1936) included such ego functions as the testing of inner and outer reality, controlling motility, remembering, and the integrating and binding function, also known as the synthetic function.

Along similar lines, Hartmann (1964) viewed ego functioning as a process of organizing and integrating, correlating aspects of mental functioning with one another and with outer reality and striving toward equilibrium among various adaptive trends. He viewed motility, intentionality, and judgment as subordinate to the goal of adaptation. Ego functions develop within the context of reciprocal interaction with the "average expectable environment." During the course of this development, just enough frustration occurs to stimulate attempts at mastery and, with this mastery, feelings of accomplishment. According to Hartmann, under optimal conditions, the mother acts as a buffer (stimulus barrier) for the infant; this function becomes internalized in the child as *self-soothing*. Within this climate, internal conflicts do not interfere with developmental progression, and ego functions develop more or less without conflict.

Other analysts stressed the integrating capacity of the ego. Nunberg (1948) wrote of the ego's "synthetic function," and Waelder (1960) suggested that every psychic act functions in relation to drive gratification, conscience, and adaptation to reality. That organization is an integral part of adaptation was later stated by Sandler and Joffe (1969) and Loewald (1977).

A survey of the literature indicates that psychoanalysts have had some difficulty deciding which functions are to be considered ego functions. Discussing ego deviation in childhood schizophrenia, Beres (1956) listed seven functions; in their study of normal,

neurotic, and schizophrenic adults, Bellak, Hurvich, and
Gediman (1973) described twelve ego functions that could be
defined and appraised by quantitative performance. Blanck and
Blanck in 1979 included under the total organizing function
drives, affects, self and object images, and the external world
experience.

We believe that ego organization can be studied only within
the context of developmental sequences, and further, that nor-
malcy is the result of development and organization, whereas
pathology is the result of malformation in the organizing process.
Data from developmental observations support this belief. For
example, Spitz (1959) observed "psychic organizers" at various
developmental levels. The absence of an organizer affects the
next developmental phase.

Ego Development in Analytic Group Therapy

According to Slavson (1964), the group modality provides patients with an experimental setting in which their perception of
reality is continually revised through interacting, experiencing
the quality of the interaction, and reality testing. The "holding
environment" for such explorations is initially created by the
group therapist, who encourages an atmosphere of openness,
respect, and courage in which the events in the group can be
investigated. Under conditions of safety, the therapist encourages spontaneous interaction in the here-and-now and more
introspective regression in the service of the ego. Object-
directed aggression – that is, the expression of anger – was considered by Slavson (1964) to be the most important therapeutic
vehicle.

One of the most important elements in analytic group therapy
is the observation of how individuals attempt to structure their
boundaries. Aggression is discharged to create and maintain
interpersonal boundaries in order to prevent merger (Saravay
1975). It becomes the therapeutic task to confront rigid boundary
structuring and, in so doing, to destructure and restructure such
characterological behaviors. This is especially possible in groups,
according to Saravay, because the need to establish an emotional

bond with strangers leads to the opening of previously closed boundaries, resulting in temporary structural regression. Such a process is analogous to the developing child's gradual differentiation of self from object and akin to Mahler and co-authors' description (1975) of the separation-individuation phase.

Clinical observations of borderline patients and patients with severe narcissistic pathology have further contributed to the understanding of ego deficits and defenses. Liff (1978) sees the goal of group therapy as progressively, sequentially "thawing out the frozen internalized entropic scripts" (p. 190). The group leader must observe reciprocal interactions—that is, both how members transmit messages and how the messages are received. Patients must become aware of reciprocal impact. "Playing it safe" does not promote ego development. Pathological boundaries must be confronted in the heat of emotional interaction, and the crystallized transferences must be addressed by the therapist: "Both the therapist and group members share the responsibility for moving the group as a whole into life-affirming channels from predominantly internalized pathways that are life-negating" (p. 191).

The group therapist's role as an ego-organizer, who regulates the opening and closing of interpersonal boundaries in the service of ego growth and self-differentiation, has also been described by Saravay (1978). He viewed the leader as a common object of transference wishes and believed that the group therapist's interpretations promote new identifications and subsequent redifferentiation of the group members' egos and superegos (1985).

Most clinicians agree that the pathology of the borderline patient is based on deficient ego functions arising from a disturbance in early object relationships with the caretakers. Pines (1975) described such "difficult" patients as having painful affects, being full of strife and anger, and refusing to learn the "lessons of life." The group therapist who is exposed to their anger should view it as a struggle with authority designed to created much-needed autonomy. Such anger must be respected. The group leader must take the role of the negotiator, who enables each member to retain a discrete identity and to observe himself

within the context of his own life. In this way, the group leader
acts as an *integrator*, akin to the synthetic function of the ego,
maintaining a sense of identity while reconciling commonalities
and differences in group members and acknowledging the anxiety that is inherent in the attempt to achieve adaptation to
reality. Stormy outbursts alternate with anxious moves toward
reconciliation; this pattern characterizes the rapprochement period described by Mahler and colleagues (1975). The therapist
and the group alternately assume the role of the mother in
symbiosis to infuse confidence so that the patient can sustain
separateness at a later time.

We previously stressed the importance of the ego in its organizational aspects in the service of adaptation. Pines (1985) has
reviewed how analytic groups aid in establishing "coherence,"
which is similar to the organizational, structure-building, and
synthetic functions of the ego. Coherence, or a firm identity,
makes it possible to remain open to change throughout the life
cycle; Pines equates this with personal maturity. He believes
that while individuals may emerge from individual psychoanalysis less neurotic, they are not necessarily more mature; from
group analysis, on the other hand, the patient may emerge still
neurotic, but having achieved maturity.

Pines distinguished between group cohesion and coherence.
Group *cohesion* represents emotional bonding, which may also
turn into a resistance; *coherence* is defined as "separate parts
brought together in harmony with one another." In analytic
groups, the process of communication is identical with the process of therapy.

On the basis of this communicational network a form of
psychological organization develops in a group based upon
mutual experience, relationships and understandings. The
shared history of the interpersonal relationships in the
group and of the shared work together lays down this
dynamic group matrix. An analytic group seems to follow a
spiral course, returning again and again to some of the same
eternal issues of love, hate, hopes and disappointments, of
dependency and interrelatedness, of individuation and to-

getherness, of the relationships of the self and other in childhood and in the present. [p. 27]

As these themes are repeatedly explored and reacted to affectively, the analytic work of the group can lead to better recognition and acceptance of these patterns in both past and present. A mature ego is open to exchanges and learns by experience. Rigid and primitive superego structures prevent new ways of perceiving and learning. "Where we can open up those areas dominated by the superego to renewed dialogue, negotiation and experiences, the ego principle can reclaim those territories" (p. 28).

Pines states that the exercise of ego functions is grounded in such principles as reciprocity and complementarity, synchrony and role reversal. The group situation, unlike the dyadic interaction, fosters a give-and-take dialogue not influenced by the therapist's intentionality. It is a form of social reciprocity that characterizes all forms of human behavior, and its rhythm is reminiscent of the mother–child interaction. The same rhythm is experienced in groups in alternation between introspective and interactive experiences. Recognition of similarity is an opening up of interpersonal boundaries as well as internalized object relationships. Through identification, one extends oneself to the world and acquires new experiences, new recognitions, and new appraisals – the building blocks of identity (Loewald 1977).

EGO FUNCTIONS IN GROUP THERAPY

During the course of orderly development, an individual alters his perception of reality from a narcissistic, omnipotent one to a more realistic one. The individual whose development has been interfered with, however, will be in conflict with himself and with the world. A patient's behavior in a therapy group will reflect this state of internal and external conflict. Adaptation to the group requires that the patient exercise the available ego functions. During the course of group therapy, these functions can be observed and evaluated as a basis for appropriate interventions.

The psychotherapeutic experience becomes a major reality-retesting endeavor.

Although various authors list a number of different ego functions, we suggest the following eleven for diagnostic assessment in groups: (1) adaptation to reality, (2) judgment, (3) drive control, (4) object relations (relationships with others), (5) thought process and communication, (6) defenses, (7) affect differentiation, (8) autonomy, (9) mastery and competence, (10) regulation of self-esteem, and (11) frustration tolerance.

Adaptation to Reality

Adaptation to reality requires a coherent internalized structure which allows one to negotiate life situations. There is also a perceived sense of reality, which stems from the secure knowledge of whether stimuli originate from within or outside the organism. A decision (judgment) has to be made as to the cause of the sensations and the appropriate reaction to what is perceived. Failure of this structure results in perceptual distortions, identity confusion, and irreconcilable ego states. Such is the case when an individual is unable to respond appropriately to others because the responses are focused exclusively on internal conflicting issues.

Factors in evaluation of adaptation include how the patient perceives and reacts to the presence or absence of group members; deals with problems in the areas of friendships, love relationships, work, and financial responsibilities; and adapts to changes in the self or others.

Judgment

Judgment is assessed based on observations of how the patient negotiates life. Is he/she able to establish lasting friendships with suitable persons, as well as sound work relationships? Is she/he able to take care of personal and financial needs? Can he/she make "good" decisions?

The discriminating function of judgment is a central aspect of all secondary process thinking and involves *anticipation* and *appropriateness.* The concept of anticipation is closely linked to the concept of *signal anxiety*, a signal to the ego to set defenses in operation to avoid painful experiences. It implies anticipating sequences of events (causality) and then directing one's actions based on these anticipations. One must be able to delay the initial impulse in order to scan various possible responses and select an appropriate action.

Judgment is vulnerable to irrational desires, wishful thinking, and sudden impulses. Defensive constellations and cognitive styles can also produce inappropriate responses.

In groups, during the heat of interaction, people often respond quickly and inappropriately, showing poor judgment. It takes reflective assessment subsequent to interaction to assimilate what was going on and to integrate it. Those with rigid, defensive styles, such as obsessive-compulsive persons, often ignore or misperceive emotional cues from others.

> During one group session, Jane confronted Jill, expressing her anger at Jill for making condescending remarks to her. Instead of reflecting or exploring the interaction, Jill angrily responded that she had had enough of Jane and didn't want to talk to her any more. The group members supported Jane's accusation, but Jill refused to talk about it. Jill's response showed poor judgment and was not in accord with the group's standards of exploring members' interactions.
>
> When the group therapist empathized with Jill, she admitted feeling hurt and was then more willing to talk about her many attempts to befriend Jane and about feeling rebuffed by her. The ability to respond differently the next time would evidence developing judgment.

Drive Control

This ego function concerns the ability to delay responses that occur either because of tension or because of the need for immediate gratification. Drive control is intimately linked to other functions, such as affect differentiation and frustration tolerance. The strengthening of this capacity involves coping with anxiety, moods, and disappointments, as well as expressing inner wishes and urges in a harmonious, modulated manner. In groups, the lack of drive control may be expressed in acting out, being provocative, demanding gratification, or ignoring the needs of others.

Chuck regularly monopolized the group's attention with his tales of romantic adventure and frustrations. He presented himself as a victim. Although the group was usually fascinated by Chuck's tales of woe, they did not react benevolently to his complaint that he was not given enough time to talk in the group. They repeatedly told him that he took up more than his share of group time in each session and that his complaints were not reality based but, rather, concerned his inordinate need for attention and love. It took a year for Chuck to comprehend that it was not that the group had treated him badly, but that his needs could not be satisfied in the way he wanted them to be. After that, he became more restrained in the group and more considerate of the needs of others.

Object Relations

The capacity for adaptation to group relations is considered by Slavson (1964) to be an index of health. Disturbed persons, plagued by murderous and regressive impulses, seek a nonthreatening environment. They feel intruded upon by others, fear self-disclosure, and are impelled by mood swings ranging from grandiosity to depression (Pines 1975). In such instances, the group member demands that another person fulfill all his/her needs in order for the other to be experienced as a good object. When this does not happen, the other is reacted to as a hated person. Although such an individual may go through the motions of living with a partner, the affective state is one of withdrawal, discomfort, rage, and guilt. The developmental stage of individuation was not completed, and the individual can never be sure whether he/she is submitting to another person because of fear that love will be withdrawn, or whether he/she is meeting and making reasonable demands.

Sally, a bright, attractive young woman, entered the group in a narcissistic cocoon. She commented about others but was not self-revealing and did not interact. She communicated that she was a "princess" who looked down on the other group members. She did not appear to be affected by the comments of the women in the group, but she did listen attentively when confronted by the men, whom she respected more. Gradually, as she interacted and received responses from other members of the group, she became able to participate equally with both sexes.

Thought Process and Communication

Verbal communication, when explored, tells us how a person thinks—that is, whether the mode of thinking follows secondary-process logic and causality, or whether it tends to follow the peculiar logic of primary process and drive discharge. Thinking is "trial action"; when firmly established as an ego mode, thought and speech are used for the purpose of communication and are understood by the recipient. Blocked speech and tangential thinking manifest vagueness; in these situations, speech is employed to hide feelings and fantasies rather than to communicate.

John, a borderline patient, seldom said anything during group sessions. He would react with hostility when confronted by group members. Then one day, he reported to the group that he had experienced the "crazies." In the twilight of his room, he had seen little bugs with helicopter wings swarming all over. He had felt frightened and anxious. The therapist interpreted that the bugs were related to group members who asked John questions. During the next group session, John disclosed a dream that was less frightening. In the dream, the group members formed a fire brigade and emptied his apartment. It was suggested that he feared that if his participation in the group improved, his creative talent would be taken away from him.

John's initial hostility and abstention from participation could be explained by his state of panic and the delusional quality of his thinking. John experienced the interpretation of his dream symbols and their relationship to his anxiety within the group as supportive, allowing him to express and test his fears within the group.

Defenses

When one feels threatened and overwhelmed, the "signal function" of anxiety becomes inoperative. Whether because of a low anxiety threshold, the need to maintain tenuous self-esteem, or an overextension of ego boundaries, one may defend oneself irrationally. Slavson (1964) recognized that such states make a group member unresponsive to others and prevent the person from acquiring insight. "In fact, the major impediments to insight are impelling ego defenses and character rigidities" (p. 164).

Defenses and perception often go hand in hand. Defenses may allay anxiety about conflict and painful affects, or they may indicate where the patient tends to erect barriers—that is, how much space is needed between the patient and another person to preserve the integrity of the self. In the hierarchy of defenses, splitting and denial develop first and are more primitive. More sophisticated defenses are repression, projection, reaction formation, and sublimation.

The defense of *splitting* occurs either when emotions are suppressed from ideas, thoughts, and fantasies, or when two contradictory emotional states are stimulated by the same person, thought, or idea. Another primitive defense mechanism, *denial*, is manifested when an unwanted piece of external reality is denied by fantasy or behavior. By means of *repression* the ego removes from consciousness unwanted impulses or derivatives including memories, affects, and fantasies. *Projection* is employed when one attributes a wish or impulse of his own to some other person or even nonpersonal object in the external world. The more sophisticated defense of *reaction formation* is used when one of a pair of ambivalent attitudes is repressed, with subsequent overemphasis of the other. The most common and healthy mechanism of *sublimation* is instituted by the ego via a substitute activity conforming to the demands of the environment, giving a measure of unconscious gratification to an infantile drive derivative that has been repudiated in original form.

The elasticity or rigidity of a defense is an indicator of how necessary the particular defense is for shoring up a fragile self or for preventing panic. Patients who cannot use symbolic communication exhibit rigid boundary regulations. When group members fail to notice changes, such as the addition of new members, the absence of members, marriages, or deaths, defensive perceptions may be at work.

Roger had a firm belief that all women were "out to get him." He therefore aggressively defended himself in order not to be hurt by them. Lois, who was frightened by the group and believed that the men were denigrating the women, came to one group session wearing perfume and a new dress. Roger did not notice the change in her. He addressed himself to Lois's conflicts from the previous session and provoked her frustration and anger. When group members pointed out to him the change in Lois, his level of communication changed and he became complimentary. Lois was pleased by Roger's recognition.

Affect Differentiation

The mature person expresses a range of affects appropriate to the eliciting situation. Between the poles of pleasure and unpleasure are many situations that are appropriately responded to with varied shadings of emotions. This function is dependent on an accurate appraisal of reality as well as on flexible internal controls.

The patient with crude and explosive affect must learn to reappraise what he has perceived and to offer a more moderate response. The patient whose emotions seem stereotyped and invariant must learn to search for what these defensive reactions cover.

Larry usually sat in the group smiling and agreeing with everybody. For a long time, group members, having become aware of the defensive quality of his smile, confronted him and expressed their curiosity that he didn't respond with a variety of emotions to the exchanges within the group. Finally, when Michael one day challenged the importance of Larry's new job, Larry expressed anger for the first time in the group. Michael then apologized.

Autonomy

One's degree of autonomy is behaviorally expressed by the degree to which one can master obstacles and achieve competence. The concept of ego autonomy has been variously explained. Hartmann (1939) developed the concepts of primary and secondary autonomy. Certain ego apparatuses, such as perception, intention, object comprehension, thinking, and language, are inborn and develop in a "conflict-free" ego sphere. Secondary autonomy is an attitude that initially arises in the service of defense and then becomes a structure that functions independently of drives. Secondary autonomy is a relative concept, viewed on a continuum defined by the extent to which it is removed from conflict.

While Hartmann emphasized an independence from ego–id conflicts, autonomy may also be defined as being relatively independent from both external conflicts and environmental influence. Autonomous functions are believed to be fueled by "neutralized" energy, becoming automated functions that participate in mental structure building. Some such functions, not central to the main ego, include habits, skills, interests, learning, intentionality, and motility.

If autonomy connotes relative independence from internal wishes and from the influences of the external environment, then it is readily inferred that the ego is capable of synthesis—that is, integrating various and contrasting aspects of experience. Regulation of tension and order among aspects of mental functioning is attained when we can abstract and conceptualize. These processes both remove us from the immediacy of experience and aid us in dealing with it by *symbolization*. Deri (1984) suggested that the capacity for symbolization has a dual function—that of observing external reality and keeping it partially hidden—thus functioning as a stimulus barrier. The aim of symbolization is the creation of order and intentionality. The greater the ease with which intentionality is expressed, accuracy of self-and-other perception established, and preciseness of communication exhibited, the more we can conclude that these functions have become autonomous.

Mastery and Competence

Mastery and competence are the degree to which individuals channel their energies to deal with new situations, overcome obstacles, and actualize their potentials. Inherent in this concept is the idea that we can expedite changes in the external world that are to our advantage. Competence can be described as the capacity to interact successfully with the environment. Motor and cognitive skills, plans, and intentional actions are all brought to bear to attain a goal.

Individuals who have lacked a relatively secure childhood, with curiosity inhibited and active behaviors discouraged, often exhibit ego passivity rather than efforts at mastery. Curiosity about oneself and others is one of the chief ingredients in analytic groups. Exploration of anxieties and encouragement to take small steps in the direction of spontaneity aid group members in striving for mastery and developing competence.

   Albert presented himself to the therapy group as a bright, competent fellow. His other-directed behavior was that of a "wise guy," challenging others to fight. He was emotionally inhibited, denied any weaknesses, and had assumed the burden of "knowing all the answers" and being able to deal with all obstacles. When group members insisted that he relate to them differently, he became shy and depressed.

Albert disclosed that while he thought he had made a good impression on his job, he had recently been told that his work was unsatisfactory. When the group explored this further with him, it appeared that he tended to make good first impressions and then slacked off in his performance when obstacles were presented. Instead of asking for help, he preferred to "slide through." The group tried to impress upon him the fact that nobody knows everything and that, with sufficient help and learning, it was possible to master difficulties and problems. Albert listened to them, accepted their advice, and improved his performance on the job.

Self-Esteem

One's self-esteem and the image one has of oneself are intimately related. Some self-perceptions are unconscious and are based on early identifications or counteridentifications with the important persons in our lives. Other self aspects—more closely linked to "identity"—are conscious and refer to the various psychological and social roles we play out daily.

Fenichel (1945) defined self-representations as the sum of one's realistic and distorted self-images, including bodily states (i.e., physical sensations). Jacobson (1964) conceptualized the self as the totality of the psychic and bodily person. Horwitz (1984) suggested that self aspects in groups are revealed in three areas: (1) the mirrored self, (2) peer relatedness, and (3) a sense of belonging. Horwitz's *mirrored self* is defined as the responses one receives from others and the reactions one transmits to them. Such mirroring integrates diverse parts of the self.

Self-esteem is related to reality testing and is also strongly influenced by the superego. Jacobson (1964) linked self-esteem to the wishful concept of the self. Slavson (1964) and Mahler and colleagues (1975) stated that the vitality of self and ego depend on the love and care received by the infant. Chein (1972) defined the subjective self by three variables: (1) a dim awareness of who and what we are, (2) a strong motivation to be what and how we would like to be, and (3) a more or less dim awareness of how others see us. Discrepancies among these three variables may interfere with identity formation, and arousal of anxiety sets into motion self-esteem regulation.

In analytic therapy groups, self-esteem is frequently threatened. It is the therapist's responsibility to initiate interventions aimed at protecting group members' self-esteem (Gustafson and Hartman 1978, Harwood 1983).

Lucille criticized the group members for not being sufficiently interested in one another. She pressed various members to become more involved with her, repeatedly stating that she could not understand how people could show such lack of interest.

Lucille had been born "on the wrong side of the tracks" and had interpreted the group members' more casual way of relating as an unwillingness to engage someone "inferior to them." When her demands for acceptance provoked others to attempt to squelch her, the group therapist sided with Lucille's good intentions. He praised her for wanting a more loving environment and actively tried to change the group atmosphere to make Lucille more comfortable. Lucille eagerly accepted the therapist's compliment, and it sustained her while she examined whether she could express herself in a less intense way.

Frustration Tolerance

Frustration tolerance is the ability to tolerate anxiety and disappointments and to postpone expected satisfactions. It involves the harmonious expression of inner wishes and emotional strivings. Postponement of emotional gratification becomes possible as memory traces of gratification and gratifying objects continue to accumulate. With delay of discharge, thought is imposed on action, which leads to the capacity to weigh consequences and consider alternatives. The person with low frustration tolerance possesses few techniques for reducing fear and anxiety while maintaining other functions. Such a person has difficulty sublimating, and even mild fear and anxiety may result in a breakdown of controls.

Charlene, an attractive young woman, usually saw herself as a victim. She made minimal efforts in her job and complained about supervisors and peers. She experienced herself as emotionally drained, lacking energy for self-gratification on weekends. She therefore decided to leave her job, and when she was offered a position with more responsibility, she was both delighted and afraid.

During one group session, she related a nightmare in which she was the defenseless victim of uncontrollable forces. The group was astonished to hear this from someone they saw as quite competent. Charlene apparently felt that the position would be overwhelming, that she would have to shoulder too much responsibility, and that she would fail and be fired. It became clear that Charlene, in a panic, had exaggerated the task, perceiving it as full of frustrations. Because of her low frustration tolerance, anxiety failed to function as a signal, and so she was rendered helpless. The group encouraged her to delay accepting the position and to examine in group the reality of her perception of the situation. In subsequent sessions, she examined the situation step by step, and her feeling of helplessness abated.

ASSESSING EGO FUNCTIONS

Differentiation between assessments of ego functions and of self aspects is facilitated when one observes group members' reactions to, and modes of dealing with, a difficult task. In a heterogeneous group of long standing, the group atmosphere was disturbed when a new cotherapist was introduced. The cotherapist was a mature woman whom some of the group members had known in another context. Though the group therapist had been aware of this, he did not know that the previous contact had left disagreeable, unresolved feelings.

This clinical vignette of a group session will discuss the reactions of three group members—Joyce, Karen, and Sara—in terms of ego functions and self-esteem regulation.

Group Session

   Joyce, acting as instigator, attempted to incite Kate, Sara, and Karen to rebel against the group therapist and force him to evict the new cotherapist. She felt betrayed by the therapist, whom she thought had informed the cotherapist of her personal problems. She said she had discussed this with friends at work, and they had agreed with her. Joyce perceived the new cotherapist as cold and unfriendly, and she believed that she had a right to chose her therapists. She wanted support for her stance from the other female group members; when she appeared to receive it, she smiled smugly. She said that she could not be honest and revealing with this cotherapist in the room. When the therapist confronted her with the fact that she had broken confidentiality by talking with friends at work, she denied it and protested her innocence.

   Joyce is an ambitious young woman of humble origin who would like to achieve a position of status and wealth. From the outset she has not liked being in the group, reiterating that the group members are "not good enough" for her. She would not have chosen them as friends. Consequently, she has been unwilling to interact or to join the others in self-disclosure. Following is a summary of Joyce's ego functions:

1. She is unable to adapt to reality; transference distortions and low self-esteem impel her to fashion her own reality.
2. Her judgment is impaired, with evidence of paranoid trends and revenge feelings.
3. She maintains superficial control over her drives and is impelled to discharge them.
4. She maintains narcissistic object relationships; she exploits people and relates on a need-gratifying, oral level.
5. Under the influence of narcissistic insult, her secondary process becomes impaired.

6. She tends to use the defenses of denial, projective identification, and splitting.
7. Although she is able to control affects intellectually and verbally, she expresses them explosively and with little differentiation.
8. In terms of autonomous functions, her mastery and synthetic function are impaired when self-esteem is threatened; pathological self-esteem regulation occurs.

Joyce is an immature woman who has developed along narcissistic lines. An unmodulated ego ideal impels her. She has not come to terms with her childhood disappointments and relates to others with a strong sense of entitlement. When her surroundings are in harmony with the ego ideal, she can be pleasant and productive. When there is disharmony, however, her ego functions become impaired.

Karen complained that the room was cold; she wished for a warm blanket. She remained fairly quiet during Joyce's tirade. After a while, she addressed the cotherapist sweetly, superficially apologizing for having forgotten her name. She then joined Joyce and Sara in complaining that the group therapist had done something terrible by bringing the cotherapist into the group. Karen admitted that she was "just a normal neurotic," but insisted that she was nevertheless justified in becoming furious. In an intellectualized tone, devoid of affect, she remarked that the cotherapist reminded her of "a yente" (gossip). When the group therapist pointed out her "sneaky insult" (forgetting the cotherapist's name) and her disparaging remarks, she angrily responded, "I would like to shove a knife up your ass!" Toward the end of the session, Karen asked how the cotherapist felt, and the cotherapist answered that she felt uncomfortable.

Karen espouses liberal causes and carries a banner for the world's underdogs. Although competent in her vocation, she lacks Joyce's ambition. Karen's family background is severely disturbed, but she is usually mild mannered and wishes to project an image of a loving mother. She suffers from depression and, at times, panic attacks. A summary of Karen's ego functions follows:

1. She does not adapt to reality; she cannot integrate feelings of rage and sympathy.
2. Her inappropriate affect interferes with her judgment.
3. When threatened, she has tenuous control over her impulses.
4. She relates to people as need-gratifying objects that are to provide her with warmth and security. She does not differentiate between herself and others.
5. Her secondary process is not firmly established.
6. Her customary defenses include denial, intellectualization, splitting, and projection.
7. Her synthetic functions are only partially successful.
8. Her unneutralized aggression preempts attempts at mastery; loss of objectivity and distorted perception impair her autonomous functions.

Karen functions on a borderline level. Severe developmental impairment coupled with unfortunate life circumstances produce a rather passive ego and dysphoric mood swings. She tends to cling to support figures (mostly women friends) and uses her energies to make herself comfortable in the status quo.

Sara is a young, competent professional woman, the middle child of a large, achievement-oriented family. She had a rather intense relationship with her father, who treated his daughters differently from his sons.

At the beginning of this session, Sara remained quiet. When Joyce described how unfriendly and cold the therapist appeared to be, Sara seized the opportunity provided for her. She casually mentioned that she had met the therapist at a social occasion; then she retired into silence. When Joyce and Karen joined in the resistance, Sara felt courageous enough to enter the fray. She took up Joyce's complaint that she had not been asked whether she accepted the cotherapist in advance and felt that her rights had been violated. Looking at the therapist, she asserted that she knew from experience that arguing with him was useless; nevertheless, since all the women in the group shared the same feeling about the cotherapist, he, as the group leader, should remedy this situation.

The therapist asked Sara what she wanted him to do. Sara, squirming in her seat, said she did not know. In response to her discomfort, the therapist then asked Sara to do something about the situation. Sara turned to the cotherapist and asked in a low voice whether she would leave the group. Sara admitted that, like Joyce, she had spoken to people outside the group about this event.

The breach of confidentiality was addressed. The therapist stated that he would not tolerate further acting out of this nature but would prefer instead to talk about it. He wondered whether the women felt competitive with the cotherapist. Sara said that she did not think so; rather, she experienced the cotherapist as a peer and would not allow a peer to assume a superior position.

Following is a summary of Sara's ego functions:

1. She adapts to reality but tends to act out under the sway of transference.
2. Her judgment is altered by impulsive affect.
3. She has a strong, infantile impulse life.
4. Although her object constancy is more or less established, she exhibits provocative behavior when she feels slighted.
5. Her secondary process is firmly established.
6. Intellectualization, projection, and reaction formation are her typical defenses.
7. Although Sara is able to be tender as well as aggressive, her affect is not well controlled, and her affect discrimination is poorly established.
8. Her attempts at synthesis are only partially successful.
9. Her adaptation is best when reaction formation is effective. Otherwise, she fluctuates between exaggerated assertive-

ness and helplessness; her autonomous functions are generally well preserved.

Sara is an assertive, professional woman. Although she can be competent and efficient, she is often immature. Her responses to transference are impetuous and exaggerated. It is difficult for her to accept anyone else's authority, and because Sara can only be a moralistic authority figure, her relationships with people are fraught with ambivalence.

Discussion

The foregoing episode demonstrates how the group modality lends itself to an assessment of ego functions and self-esteem regulation within an ego-psychoanalytic framework. Of the three group members, Karen was probably the most functionally impaired, maintaining herself at a minimum level of adaptation. Joyce presented herself as well adjusted, but her narcissistic development made it difficult for her to become integrated in the group. Sara functioned more autonomously and possessed more sophisticated defenses. The interplay between transference and self-esteem regulation, and their effect on ego functions, has been described. The women allied themselves to fight for their cause; the men did not participate in this fight and preferred to distance themselves from the women.

Upon examining the participant's attitudes toward the group, one is impressed by Joyce's denigration. Joyce did not like being part of this group. She viewed herself not as in need of help, but rather as in search of advice on how to improve herself. She could not introspect, voiced no complaints about her parents (her father was an alcoholic and had made advances toward her girlfriends) and reported her childhood to have been wonderful. She admired the male therapist as an accomplished person from whom she could wrest the secret of success. She perceived the group members as unsuccessful and therefore of no use to her. Although she would generally take a provocative stance toward other female group members, she joined them for the first time in the session described. She would arouse the group's ire by coming late to sessions or missing sessions, always for "good" reasons.

Karen could not be engaged in exploratory therapy. Having had a damaging childhood, she needed a supportive environment to maintain minimal functioning. She assumed the role of loving mother in the group, rushing to the defense of any member who seemed to need her help. She never confronted personal issues, nor did she allow other group members to help her master developmental tasks. She needed the group only as a holding environment and thus increased the other members' resistance.

Sara was a fairly well-functioning but immature woman. As one of six children, she had not received parental attention, except in response to transgressions. Her entrance to the group was peculiar indeed. She would sit silently eating a quick dinner, playing the role of the narcissistic child who does not want to be disturbed. When the group helped her to participate, she seemed shy and embarrassed. She reacted strongly against limits, zealously guarded her space, and accused others of lack of interest.

Sara frequently withdrew from group participation when she sensed that members did not approve of her acting out. She was able to accept some limits set by the therapist, but would not submit to her peers. When she felt slighted, she would explode with paranoid reactions. As she struggled, she slowly emerged as a more adult person who was able to introspect and to substitute reason for infantile rage.

REFERENCES

Bellak, L., Hurvich, M., and Gediman, H. (1973). *Ego Functions in Schizophrenics, Neurotics, and Normals*. New York: Wiley.

Beres, D. (1956). Ego deviation and the concept of schizophrenia. *The Psychoanalytic Study of the Child*, 11:164–255.

Blanck, G., and Blanck, R. (1979). *Ego Psychology II*. New York: Columbia University Press.

Chein, I. (1972). *The Science of Behavior and the Image of Man*. New York: Basic Books.

Deri, S. (1984). *Symbolization and Creativity*. New York: International Universities Press.

Fenichel, O. (1945). *The Psychoanalytic Theory of Neurosis*. New York:

W. W. Norton.

Freud, A. (1936). *The Ego and the Mechanisms of Defense.* New York: International Universities Press.

Freud, S. (1926). Inhibitions, symptoms and anxiety. *Standard Edition* 20:87–156.

Gustafson, J. P., and Hartman, J. (1978). Self-esteem in group therapy. *Contemporary Psychoanalysis* 14:311–329.

Hartmann, H. (1939). *Ego Psychology and the Problem of Adaptation.* New York: International Universities Press.

———— (1964). *Essays on Ego Psychology.* New York: International Universities Press.

Harwood, I. (1983). The application of self-psychology concepts to group psychotherapy. *International Journal of Group Psychotherapy* 33:469–487.

Horwitz, L. (1984). The self in groups. *International Journal of Group Psychotherapy* 34:519–540.

Jacobson, E. (1964). *The Self and the Object World.* New York: International Universities Press.

Liff, Z. (1978). Group psychotherapy for the 1980s: psychoanalysis of pathological boundary structuring. *Group* 2:184–192.

Loewald, H. (1977). Instinct theory, object relations and psychic structure formation. In *Papers on Psycho-analysis,* pp. 207–218. New Haven: Yale University Press, 1980.

Mahler, M., Pine, F., and Bergman, A. (1975). *The Psychological Birth of the Human Infant.* New York: Basic Books.

Nunberg, H. (1948). The synthetic function of the ego. In *Practice and Theory of Psychoanalysis.* Vol. 1, pp. 120–136. New York: International Universities Press.

Pines, M. (1975). Group therapy with "difficult" patients. In *Group Therapy 1975: An Overview,* ed. L. Wolberg and M. Aronson, pp. 102–119. New York: Stratton Intercontinental.

———— (1985). Psychic development and the group psychoanalytic situation. *Group* 9:24–37.

Sandler, J., and Joffe, W. (1969). Towards a basic psychoanalytic model. *International Journal of Psycho-Analysis* 50:79–90.

Saravay, S. (1975). Group psychology and the structural theory: a revised psychoanalytic model of group psychology. *Journal of the American Psychoanalytic Association* 23:69–89.

———— (1978). A psychoanalytic theory of group development. *International Journal of Group Psychotherapy* 28:481–507.

———— (1985). Parallel development of the group and its relationship to the leader: a theoretical explanation. *International Journal of Group*

Psychotherapy 35:197–207.

Slavson, S. R. (1964). *A Textbook in Analytic Group Psychotherapy.*
New York: International Universities Press.

Spitz, R. (1959). *A Genetic Field Theory of Ego Formation.* New York:
International Universities Press.

Waelder, R. (1960). *Basic Theory of Psychoanalysis.* New York: International Universities Press.

Chapter 2
The Emerging Self

One's self-concept will affect one's reactions to experiences, one's behaviors and feelings about those behaviors, and one's evaluation of both past and anticipated future experiences. For example, one might respond to a situation by saying, "Oh, I couldn't do *that*," or "I *never* imagined I would say such things," or "That's not *like* me. Why did I act that way?" One's self-concept thus provides continuity with both the past and the future. And as one's self-image changes, one may modify perceptions and evaluations of past experiences, as well as anticipation of and plans for the future. A therapy group provides an ideal environment for developing new ways of thinking and feeling about oneself.

In our conceptualization, the following comprise the self-image:

Physical aspects: Body image and body experience (including physical pleasures and discomforts), gender identity, and attitudes and feelings about these physical aspects.

Personal characteristics: Adjectives one thinks of as describing oneself (for example, caring or hostile, proud or ashamed, responsible or irresponsible). Most prevalent mood states, such as joyful or sad, optimistic or pessimistic. Character traits; that is, characteristic ways of relating and responding to others, and anticipation of others' reactions.

Social roles: One's concept of interaction with others in terms of work identity, social group memberships, marital status, age, sex, race or religion; and feelings and attitudes about these.

Self ideals: One's values, standards, goals, and aspirations, as well as how one sees oneself measuring up to these ideals.

Group therapy can be effective in changing self-image and self-feelings, since these thoughts and feelings are continually being brought into awareness by the ongoing group process. The feeling of belonging engendered by a therapy group may enable a member to expose and look at previously concealed or denied aspects of the self, as well as to risk trying out new behaviors. This, in turn, may open new ways of thinking about the self and relating to others. As they become aware of their interactions with one another and with the therapist, group members gradually come to know themselves better. In group, they can explore the motivations for their actions, look at their reactions to other members, see and hear how others respond, and observe their impact on these others. How others see them may affect self-image and how others evaluate them may affect self-feelings.

A group member who grew up in a hostile, uncaring environment will usually have experienced fragmentation, narcissism, and depression. If the individual was always forced to accommodate to parental needs, no strong sense of a genuine self will have developed. Instead there will be an "as-if" personality, or what Winnicott (1960) refers to as a *false self*. Such a person will reveal in group only what he anticipates will be accepted or approved by others, while inside there may be a sense of emptiness and futility or dishonesty. There may be feelings of alienation, as well as self-consciousness, shyness, and vulnerability. In the process of trying to please other group members, there may be much pretense, with a marked difference between the public, displayed self and the private, experienced self.

In some instances, no clear self-image will even exist. For example, Bill, when urged by his therapy group to "be himself," responded, "Who is myself? This is my problem when people tell me to be myself. There is an unreality about what I do. I don't feel I am anchored firmly onto anything."

Members may struggle in the therapy group to separate ideas and concepts incorporated from early caretakers, from ideas developing in the current group experience. Members are frequently put into the position of asking themselves, "How is that affecting me? And why?" At times the question may even become, "What did *I* do that provoked such a response?" And through the interactions in group, members may gradually be able to rework the earlier experiences and come to know better, or view differently, their feelings and intentions, as well as strengths and weaknesses, and to integrate the previously denied, conflicted aspects of the self with the emerging image of and changing feelings about the self.

Changes may occur in external behaviors, feelings about the behaviors, self-image in relationship to others, standards and ideals for oneself, and feelings of self-worth.

RELEVANT LITERATURE

Psychologists, sociologists, and philosophers gave attention to the concept of "self" much earlier than did psychoanalysts. In 1890, William James wrote that, "In its widest possible sense, a man's self is the sum total of all that he can call his." Some years later, Cooley (1902) conceptualized the "looking-glass self," which referred to seeing oneself as reflected by others, as though the others were mirrors. In a somewhat different vein, Mead (1934) wrote about the "I" and the "me," the "I" being one's spontaneous, nonreflective action, and the "me" being the reflective looking back on one's own actions and "taking the role of the other" toward oneself.

Many years later, Chein (1972) stated that the self is the object of many enduring, interrelated, and interdependent concerns and motives that are always fueled in the service of adaptation for self-preservation. He defined the self experience within three parameters: (1) a dim awareness of who and what we are; (2) a strong motivation related to what and how we would like to be; and (3) a more or less dim awareness of how others see us. The potentially wide range of discrepancies among these three parameters may make for disturbing elements to identity. The anxiety aroused by such discrepancies sets into motion what is commonly called *self-esteem regulation*. The experiential self organizes one's identity as a unique person and provides a sense of continuity and stability.

Psychoanalysts

Hartmann (1964) referred to the self as the ego's mental representation of who we are and saw this as a way of defining and expressing ourselves, while Jacobson (1964) distinguished among the ego as a topographical mental structure, the self as the totality of the psychic and bodily person, and self-representations as self-images based on momentary feelings of pleasure or unpleasure.

Some time later, Loewald (1971) described the self as follows:

> While the self is not an agency of the mind, it is also not a content. If the self is somewhat like Freud's *Gesamt-Ich* (total ego), then self would be the mind as cathected in its totality. *Self, mind, personality, identity* are terms referring to a totality seen from different perspectives. [p. 351]

Kohut (1971, 1977) presented the concept of early mirroring, in which the child is "the gleam in the mother's eyes." The self develops in relation to the mother, who becomes the empathic selfobject, anticipating and ministering to the infant in a timely, sensitive manner. When parental empathy is not forthcoming, however, narcissistic structures become stabilized.

Annie Reich (1960) suggested that under severe stress, self-esteem regulation may assume bizarre manifestations. These pathological attempts to maintain the self should not be confused with the more healthy parts that self-esteem regulation protects, although some people are almost exclusively focused upon self-esteem regulation and are thus unable to allow the healthy parts to develop.

Jacobson (1964) defined self-esteem as the harmony or discrepancy between the self-representations and the wishful concept of the self. Healthy self-esteem is ideationally and emotionally expressed when aggressive or sexual impulses are modulated and not in conflict with self-representations.

Group Psychotherapists

Battegay (1967) has noted that the group, by encouraging spontaneity and independence, activates the genuine self. On the other hand, group therapy, as a behavioral and interactional mode of psychotherapy, may be experienced as stressful by those who have self-boundary problems. Winthrop (1974) expressed his concern that an individual may "lose himself" in the group and give up his individuality via merger.

In contrast, Stone and Whitman (1977) stated that the "group may serve as an accepting arena for display of grandiose and exhibitionistic drives as well as provide a sense of belonging to a wonderful ideal group." They discussed the "internalization of the group-as-a-whole and the leader in maintaining a cohesive feeling of self" (p. 355). More recently, Stone (1983) pointed out the following:

> The interpersonal setting of group psychotherapy is particularly suited for patients with deficits to utilize others as selfobjects in the development of a cohesive self. Group members use one another or their inner image of the group as a whole to stabilize their self-esteem and potentially develop more enduring structure, less vulnerable to narcissistic hurts. [p. 13]

While warning that groups often have a tendency to diminish individuality, threaten the stability of a fragile self, and cause regressive, primitive mental processes, Harwood (1983) advocated that the therapist's role be that of guardian of the "nuclear self" in the group. It becomes the group leader's "awesome responsibility" to distinguish between sometimes bizarre self-esteem regulation and resistance. According to Harwood, the group therapist must ensure the safety of the emerging self of each group member in order to protect its growth and development.

More recently, Horwitz (1984) and Modell (1985) have suggested that the structural theory of personality does not provide a sufficient account of the self-concept, because it deals only with intrapsychic processes and not with the person's phenomenological existence in the world. To the structural concept of personality, they believe, must be added the dimension of interpersonal relationships to account for the parts of the self that respond to feedback from others. This has its effect on the structural system, which then modifies the feedback that is projected back to the external world. Such reciprocal interaction is ongoing. In this way, structural and interpersonal theories contribute to our understanding of the self-concept. The two conceptual frameworks provide two different perspectives from which one can view the self.

> Although almost everything can be viewed either in the context of a one-person or a two-person psychology, let us not forget that there is an underlying unity to the thing observed; it is only the need of the observer to find the appropriate context. [Modell 1985, p. 88]

We believe that the continuity of the structural self is maintained by character traits. Although these traits account for a certain consistency of personality, they may be either adaptive or maladaptive in a given situation. When an individual experiences intensely affectionate interactions, as in a love relationship or in group therapy, conflict is generated and a loosening of former identifications occurs. This may lead to a reorganization of structure, permitting dormant self-aspects to surface.

GROUP EXPERIENCES THAT AFFECT THE SELF-IMAGE AND SELF-FEELINGS

Among group-specific experiences that affect the self-image and self-feelings are (1) the "mirror phenomenon" and triadic relationships; (2) resonance (that is, responding to a group theme or group mood); (3) direct confrontations and challenges; (4) comparison of oneself with, and differentiation of oneself from, other members; (5) experimentation with new ways of relating to others.

The Mirror Phenomenon and Triadic Relationships

Foulkes (1964) wrote about the "mirror phenomenon," referring to group therapy as a hall of mirrors in which each member is confronted with various aspects of his social, psychological, and physical image in his direct interactions with other members of the group. According to Foulkes, the individual "gets to know himself" by the effect he has on others and the picture of him they reflect. These phenomena could perhaps be dissected into psychoanalytic concepts, such as projection and identification, but Foulkes preferred to put them together and give them a collective name, emphasizing the mirror aspect.

Proceeding with this conceptualization, we tend to think of the group as a hall of distorted mirrors, since each may see some self-aspects that are exaggerated in other members and some self-aspects that are minimized in others. In seeing distorted aspects of oneself in another, one may become more vividly aware of these aspects in oneself. Pines (1982) described the mirror phenomenon as "the steady to-and-fro rhythm of externalization and internalization, me in you and you in me" (p. 13).

In the mutual mirroring and reflection among the group members, both positive aspects and negative aspects are experienced. Members may see how others are affected by their behavior or see something of themselves in another, or they may hear something about themselves from another. For example, when

Beverly told Lenny that he looked and sounded angry, he initially denied feeling any anger toward her. But as she persisted and as others seemed to agree, he realized that he really was angry at her, but that he had not until that moment been aware of the feeling, nor of the fact that it showed in his face and posture.

Group members may see in another person what they fear and hate in themselves and may verbally attack that person, until they realize that their reaction is to the mirror image of themselves.

Besides telling someone directly how they perceive him/her, members may show their perceptions in their reactions. Ben, for instance, was very gentle and overly protective with Tina because he saw her as frightened and fragile; his behavior reflected this image back to her. Natalie, on the other hand, said she had recently become aware that people were reacting to her in negative and self-protective ways; she realized from these reactions that "I am very argumentative and very critical."

In addition to the mirror phenomenon, group therapy offers the opportunity for *triadic relationships,* an interaction in which the third person, in observing the interaction of two other group members, may recognize aspects of herself in one of the two, while at the same time having the opportunity to see how the second person responds to the first. In fact, in observing the interaction of two group members, the third person may at times even recognize and become aware of denied aspects of herself. Pines (1982) stated, "The person sees himself, or part of himself—often a repressed part of himself— reflected in the interaction of other members. He sees them reacting in the way he does himself, or in contrast to his own behavior."

A benefit of group therapy is that members may feel less unique or "strange" and more related to others as they recognize the similarities between themselves and other group members. In fact, after observing in others' interactions what had been concealed, denied, or repressed, a member may become more willing to let these aspects of the self emerge openly in the therapy group.

Resonance

Resonance refers to the phenomenon in group therapy whereby what one person is talking about in the group session – feelings, attitudes, experiences – will reverberate in other members and be echoed by them, producing a series of rebounding echoes. Each "returns" or "sends back" to the others a personal reflection of what is being said. As each member responds, the theme or feeling or focus is intensified and enriched. What one person is talking about will "resonate" in other members, and what began as an individual, personal reaction will become generalized to other members.

   Frank, a salesman, began one session by talking about his new job, which had the potential to offer him financial success, but which evoked in him much fear and anxiety. To succeed meant to be admired by other people (including his wife and his parents), and he felt uncomfortable with that, having always seen himself as "a bum."
   The therapist asked whether anyone else in the group could relate to the theme of not being able to accept success. Helen, a recently appointed assistant principal in a secondary school, immediately volunteered that she could not understand how she had gotten her position since she feels she knows so little. Her only explanation was that there must have been some political reason. Peggy, a middle-manager in a national organization, laughed and reported that she had recently received a promotion and an unusually large salary increase but had not told the group because she thought someone had made a mistake, and she kept expecting to be informed of this mistake!
   As these three interacted with one another, and as others joined in with similar experiences or feelings, they saw how each was sustaining feelings of unworthiness, and they

laughed as they pointed out to one another the ways in which they denied or could not accept their successes.

Direct Confrontation and Challenge

One does not find oneself by being always submissive and in harmony with others. It is in moments of opposing, confronting, or challenging another that individuality and differentiation are achieved. When group members act *against* one another, they become more aware of their hidden selves. At the same time, the group members who are being confronted or challenged may correct some of their own distortions and misperceptions.

In one group session, Fred directly confronted Bill with his behavior and Fred's feelings about it: "You *always* get sleepy in group, and I don't like it because I want your attention." Bill said that he was surprised because he did not think Fred ever paid any attention to him, and he certainly had never imagined that his opinion mattered to Fred. This comment from Fred stimulated Bill to make a conscious effort to be attentive and active in group and not to withdraw.

Evelyn, another group member, would never assert herself or say what she thought or wanted, always "giving in" to others and then withdrawing. In her own words, she "wiped herself out." When Bob, a new group member, directly challenged this behavior, she felt she had to respond to him, and a bit of interaction between Bob and Evelyn continued for several sessions, with the consequence that Evelyn became more real to group members *and* to herself.

As these case examples imply, challenges and confrontations alone do not bring about changes in self-image or self-feelings. With the assistance of the therapist and the other group members, each member must engage in much "working through," moving from the external, observable behaviors to the intrapsychic conflicts that have caused the behavior.

Therapy groups also provide the opportunity for individuals to confront the group-as-a-whole and to ask directly how they are perceived by others, as well as what others think or how they feel about what they see.

> Larry, who had been in group for many months, said, "I feel like I'm not part of the group. I want to know how other people see me." (It had taken some time for him to be willing to take this risk.) The others responded by pointing out how guarded and self-protective he was–as if he was afraid to let anyone get to know him. Some suggested it was because he was holding in "so much anger." He admitted that at times he did feel *very* angry in group, but he had not thought it showed, and he had been careful *not* to express it verbally. With other members' observations of him out in the open, Larry subsequently dared more often to express disagreement with, and anger at, others and remarked that he was beginning to see himself as "more like the others."

Group interactions can challenge pretenses based on "shoulds." Group members may say, "You don't seem real to me" or "That doesn't sound genuine." One member may suggest to another, "Let us look behind your mask." With such challenges from other members and from the therapist, there may emerge various affects or behaviors that had previously been hidden, denied, or repressed.

The therapy group also provides an opportunity for confrontations regarding a person's misperceptions or distortions.

> Harriet kept complaining that other group members were hostile and nongiving until, finally, they pointed out to her that every time someone tried to help her, she took this as a criticism or hostile attack.

Comparing Oneself with, and Differentiating Oneself from, Others

A group member who has no clear sense of self will feel bound by others' definitions and responses. The person may feel empty, worthless, and vulnerable. Such an individual cannot consider others' needs (except in ways that protect the self from attack, ridicule, criticism, or rejection) and is constantly hiding from the possibility of humiliation.

One gets a firmer grasp of who one is when one can individuate from others, and group provides an arena in which to compare oneself with, and differentiate oneself from, others. Group members may see that they can be similar in some ways to other members and different in other ways. In comparing themselves, they may increase their self-awareness and perhaps their appreciation of themselves as unique, even though they share certain qualities with other members of the group: "I am similar to Betty in being reserved and soft-spoken, but I am different in many other ways. I am more than this one characteristic." Or a member may compare his own reaction to others' reactions to another member. For instance, Manny said to Ginny, "They all were sympathetic to you, but I didn't see you that way," and began to wonder aloud why his perception was so different.

In the therapy group, each member is helped by the therapist to acknowledge similarities to the others *and* differences from them. While seeing aspects of themselves in others and aspects of others in themselves, each can also explore in what ways he is unique. In this way, each sees a multifaceted self, relating in a variety of ways to the various others. The relationship with *each* of the other members is unique. And as the members interact, they may get new, unexpected responses and discover novel aspects of themselves.

Further, as group members oppose one another, they differentiate themselves and become aware of themselves as unique and separate from the others. If one must always agree with others, there is no way to discover one's own way of seeing and responding to situations.

The therapist can enable members to admit that what they attack in another is also what they dislike in themselves and can help members to see their differences as well as their similarities. In addition, the therapist contributes to members' differentiating themselves and developing more self-esteem by recognizing both their accomplishments within the group and their willingness to take risks. The therapist's support of Larry's revelation of his anger, which he had previously kept hidden from the other members, is an example of such a contribution.

Experimentation

The therapy group provides an opportunity for experimentation, for playfully trying out various ways of relating, so that undiscovered or unrecognized aspects of the self can emerge. Within the group, a member can "try out" unaccustomed roles and ways of relating to see what effect these new behaviors have on others. In watching and then joining the interaction of two other members, a third member may risk entering an unfamiliar situation in which there are no fixed patterns for relating; he may thereby unexpectedly discover novel responses in himself.

Group members have an opportunity to see that there are various ways of coping with the same problem and to compare these with their own habitual ways or even try them out.

> As Jack became aware that his reactions were quite different from those of other group members, he experimented with new approaches. Sarah, using questions and comments, began to "help" Jack and subsequently some of the other men; this in turn contributed to changing her self-image and feelings of self-worth.

A member may attempt a variety of experiments to obtain different responses, and in experimenting begin to see novel aspects of the self. In one group, Ruth purposely tried to control her habitual impatience and made an obvious, conscious effort to empathize with two members who had often supported her; she was pleased when both of them acknowledged what she was doing.

Sometimes, after group members see that it is safe to risk disclosure or confrontation, they will also take the risk.

> Marian challenged Steve, who "always put her down." She questioned his perception of her and forcefully presented

how she saw herself changing in group. After a heated exchange between the two, Steve agreed that she *was* changing. Several weeks later–after some similar exchanges with other members of the group–Marian volunteered, "I feel more real in here. I have less artificial politeness, fewer shoulds."

As group members experiment with helping other members–even those they had considered more competent–there comes an increasing feeling of self-worth and an appreciation of what they are capable of doing.

When members are willing to experiment and risk themselves, they become more "real," more genuine, in their interactions in the group. They see that it is progressively less necessary to pretend and to be governed by all of the "shoulds" that had persisted from childhood. There is gradually less denial, less artificial courtesy, and less covering-up in the group interaction. As Virginia said in one session, "I get angry when I do too much for other people and not enough for me, and I am finally becoming unwilling to do all the stuff in here I had been doing before. I want something for *me*. I'm tired of feeling that I'm giving everything for everybody else."

THE ROLE OF THE THERAPIST

One of the therapist's basic tasks is to develop a setting that feels safe, so that group members are willing to take risks and expose all sides of themselves. Each individual has different selves (some conscious and dominant and others latent, unconscious, or hidden) that come out in various contexts. Although members will attempt in the therapy group to display only those parts of themselves that are comfortable, the dynamic interaction of the group and the interventions of the therapist stimulate other aspects that they have been afraid to show. One of the therapist's tasks is to illuminate the hidden opposites. The working-through process begins when the group member is aware of these various aspects and attempts to integrate them. The maturity toward which the group works would allow each member to exhibit the repertoire of selves in a less defensive and more appropriate manner.

The therapist contributes in many ways to an environment that facilitates changes in the members' self-perceptions and self-feelings. The therapist's communication of an accepting, noncritical attitude sets the mood for the group and provides a model for the group members in their interactions with one another. At times the therapist may encourage or stimulate a playful atmosphere in which new interactions can develop and emerge.

In addition, the therapist seeks to facilitate specific types of interaction that can positively affect the self-image and self-esteem of the group members. For instance, the therapist may question whether a group member sees aspects of herself mirrored in one of two interacting members. Or the therapist may act as a negotiator between two members who are relating as a mutually destructive dyad, each seeing in the other what they fear and/or hate in themselves. The therapist enables both to admit that what they are attacking in the other is also within themselves. At the same time, the therapist has raised the relationship from a dyadic to a triadic level.

The therapist is sometimes in a position to facilitate the resonance that is potential in a group interaction by asking whether other members can relate to the topic or feelings. In this way, a group member can see that she is not unique or "strange" in having particular thoughts, wishes, or feelings.

In addition to the members' challenging or confronting one another, the therapist may also at times confront a group member or offer feedback. For example, the therapist may pay particular attention to what a member has just done. Or the therapist may suggest that a group member compare herself with, and differentiate herself from, another member in order to become aware of the similarities and differences between them.

There are also times when the therapist will suggest that a

member try out, or experiment with, new ways of responding, to "see how it feels."

The therapist made such a suggestion to Shirley, who had always presented a strong, intellectualized masculine front. The following week, Shirley began the group session by presenting a shocking incident. However, instead of "stone-walling" her way through, as she usually had, she allowed her vulnerability to show and cried as she talked—the first time she had ever allowed the group to see tears. Group members responded in a completely new way to her; they were sympathetic and supportive.

To their surprise, Shirley accepted all of this and expressed appreciation, topping it by saying to the therapist, "See! I tried a *new* role." The experience eventually resulted in her developing new relationships with some of the group members and presenting herself as a softer person.

The group therapist may also contribute to a member's self-awareness and self-esteem by recognizing one of the member's accomplishments within the group, such as risk-taking or a new self-revelation or a beginning attempt at empathy with another member.

Through the group experience, members can modify their self-images and self-feelings. The group can provide affirmation and validation of these changes, with the therapist taking a significant role in this process.

Group members see themselves become more active, more assertive, better functioning, and more accepting of themselves and others. They may "get in touch" with what they want (or do not want) and be better able to express it. Or, they may become more tolerant of themselves and of others.

At the same time, as group members become more secure about their own worth, they may no longer have to work so hard to avoid criticism and to emphasize their differences from the others. They recognize they can be the same basic self, regardless of who is present. They do not have to obscure themselves while working to please others. Nor do they have to deny themselves in order to become more like the others. They confront other members, having become more genuine in their interactions, with freer access to their own authentic feelings.

REFERENCES

Battegay, R. (1967). *Der Mensch in der Gruppe*, Vol. 2. Bern: Hans Huber, 1975.

Chein, I. (1972). *The Science of Behavior and the Image of Man*. New York: Basic Books.

Cooley, C. H. (1902). *Human Nature and the Social Order*. New York: Schocken Books, 1964.

Foulkes, S. H. (1964). *Therapeutic Group Analysis*. London: Allen & Unwin.

Hartmann, H. (1964). *Essays in Ego Psychology*. New York: International Universities Press.

Harwood, I. (1983). The application of self-psychology concepts to group psychotherapy. *International Journal of Group Psychotherapy* 33:469–487.

Horwitz, L. (1984). The self in groups. *International Journal of Group Psychotherapy* 34:519–540.

Jacobson, E. (1964). *The Self and the Object World*. New York: International Universities Press.

James, W. (1890). *The Principles of Psychology*, Vol. 1. New York: Holt, Reinhardt & Winston.

Kohut, H. (1971). *The Analysis of the Self*. New York: International Universities Press.

_____(1977). *The Restoration of the Self*. New York: International Universities Press.

Loewald, H. (1971). Book review: Heinz Kohut, the analysis of the self. In *Papers on Psycho-analysis*. New Haven: Yale University Press, 1980.

Mead, G. H. (1934). *Mind, Self and Society*. Chicago: University of Chicago Press.

Modell, A. (1985). The two contexts of the self. *Contemporary Psychoanalysis* 21:70–90.

Pines, M. (1982). On mirroring in group psychotherapy. In *Group Therapy Monograph #9*, pp. 9–45. New York: Washington Square Institute.

Reich, A. (1960). Pathological forms of self-esteem regulations. In *Annie Reich: Psychoanalytic Contributions*, pp. 288–311. New York: International Universities Press.

Stone, W. (1983). The curative fantasy in group psychotherapy. In *Group Therapy Monograph #10*, pp. 10–35. New York: Washington Square Institute.

Stone, W., and Whitman, R. (1977). Contributions of the psychology of the self to group process and group therapy. *International Journal of Group Psychotherapy* 27:343–359.

Winnicott, D. W. (1960). Ego distortion in terms of true and false self. In *Maturational Processes and the Facilitating Environment*, pp. 140–152. New York: International Universities Press, 1965.

Winthrop, H. (1974). The group as a surrogate for the individual. *Bulletin of the Menninger Clinic* 38:239–249.

Part II
Beginning Groups

Chapter 3
Preparing Patients

The average person has little knowledge and many misconceptions about group therapy – what the group task and the nature of the group process is, what is expected of the group members. Consequently most people have many fears and anxieties about even the thought of becoming a member of a therapy group.

Various methods are used to allay the misconceptions and fears of prospective group members. Therapists can provide printed information, offer public lectures, make available a typed protocol or an audiotape or videotape of a group session, require a preliminary short-term group experience, or use an individual interview as a means of preparing for group therapy.

We have concluded that the most useful of these preparatory approaches, for both the prospective group member and the therapist, is the individual interview. The interview can serve many purposes. It aids the prospective group member in clarifying the reasons for entering group therapy. In addition, it can be used by the therapist to describe how group therapy functions and to inform the person about some of the differences between individual and group therapy. Moreover, the individual interview enables the therapist to evaluate the appropriateness of group therapy as the modality of choice for the particular individual. No less important is the fact that the interview can reduce some of the fears of and anxiety about entering a group. It prepares the person to maximize both the initial use of the therapy group and the long-term benefits derived from the experience. Knowing what to expect will facilitate entrance into a group. The situation will not seem as "strange" as it might have were there no preliminary session. As a consequence, uneasiness and resistance may be minimized during the early phase of the group process, thereby enabling the person to become an actively participating member at a faster rate.

SOURCES OF PATIENTS

Patients come to the group therapist from various sources – from the therapist's own practice of individual therapy, from colleagues who practice only individual therapy, from physicians who are not psychotherapists, from training institutes that require group-therapists-to-be to have a therapy group experience, from individuals who have attended conferences on group therapy, and from the general public who may have read about group therapy.

The Therapist's Own Individual Patients

After the patient has worked in individual therapy for a period of time on intrapsychic problems, either the therapist or the patient may suggest that it would be beneficial for the patient to have a group therapy experience to "try out" his ego strengths and self-knowledge. The therapist may see a group setting as useful for working through the patient's entrenched character or personality problems. Group therapy is usually strongly recommended by the therapist and is generally not chosen by these patients on their own initiative.

The therapist already knows the patient from his practice and has evaluated the advisability of group therapy. Based on knowledge of the patient, the therapist can point out what relevance the group endeavor may have for the patient's "therapeutic life." He can use as many interviews (or parts of individual therapy sessions) as necessary to discuss group therapy and to prepare the patient for entry into the group. This preparation may be extended over a period of weeks or months, or in some instances even years. Thus, the therapist can allow the patient's motivation for and interest in group therapy to develop gradually.

As much time as necessary can be taken to describe what group therapy is and how it differs from individual therapy, and to acquaint the patient in a general way with the group he will be entering. The therapist presents the "rules" of the group so that the patient's anxieties can be addressed. When necessary, the therapist may take an extended period of time to explore with the patient some of the fears, anxieties, and defenses that will be stimulated in the group. He may also take time to focus on the importance of early childhood experiences and memories of group experiences, satisfying as well as unpleasant.

In addition, the therapist may want to discuss the fact that in the group, he will no longer be experienced as the exclusive property of the patient, but rather will be shared with other group members. It is probably helpful for the therapist to emphasize that material from the individual therapy sessions will remain separate and apart from the group sessions, and that he will respect the patient's right to privacy; it will be the patient's right and responsibility to reveal certain issues.

Referrals from Colleagues

Group therapists often receive referrals from colleagues who are continuing to see the patient for individual therapy. The group therapist may request a summary history of the patient from the referring individual therapist. In addition, the therapist will want to see the person for an interview, or perhaps even two or three interviews, before the decision is made to accept or reject the individual for group therapy.

Self-referred Patients

Some individuals request group therapy because they feel they cannot afford the fee for individual therapy. Others who are in individual therapy with another therapist or who have completed individual therapy are interested in having a different kind of therapeutic experience. Some acknowledge that they are having difficulty in interpersonal relationships and seek group therapy to deal with this problem. Group-therapists-in-training refer themselves for group therapy because it is mandatory.

As is the case with referrals from colleagues, the group therapist will see the self-referred prospective group member for at least one interview in order to evaluate the appropriateness of group therapy and to prepare the person for entry into a group. For the therapist-in-training, the group is presented as a serious therapeutic endeavor to be experienced not primarily for the purpose of fulfilling the requirements of a training program, but for its therapeutic benefits to the trainee.

INDIVIDUALIZING THE INTERVIEW

The various topics that can be discussed in these interviews will be presented in this chapter. The range and order of topics will vary with each individual, however, depending on whether the prospective group member is already in individual therapy with the group therapist, has been referred by a colleague, or is a self-referral. We will describe our approach, based on what we have found useful in preparing potential members for our therapy groups, which are five- to eight-person groups that meet once a week for one and a half hours and that have an alternate session without the therapist present.

Our approach is psychodynamic and explorative, not just supportive. We adjust the presentation to the needs of the interviewee. Although the same general material is covered, each group therapist has his own style of beginning to establish a relationship with a patient, and each patient has idiosyncratic needs. In some instances the preparation may extend to two or three sessions or even more.

Some people need to talk at the beginning of the interview about themselves and their needs and hopes, and have in mind exactly what they want to present and what questions they would like to have answered. This will give direction to the order of topics taken up in the interview. Others come to the initial interview feeling bewildered and anxious; they tend to wait for the therapist to guide them. In any case, an attempt is made to accomplish all of the intended purposes by the end of the allotted period.

ASSESSING MOTIVATION AND INTEREST

In the individual interview with either a colleague-referred or a self-referred patient, the therapist attempts to explore the prospective patient's reasons and motivations for entering group therapy, as well as the expectations and goals. To obtain this information, the therapist might ask the following questions:

1. Can you tell me about your interest in beginning group therapy at this time?
2. How do you think group therapy can be helpful to you?
3. What would you hope to get from being in a therapy group?

The answers to such questions provide some indication as to initial motivation and perceived needs. Whatever an individual's diagnostic category, symptoms, or other characteristics, motivation is a primary consideration and may largely determine the outcome of the group therapy experience.

Take, for example, the individual who says that he is seeking group therapy because his wife thinks he should or because his individual therapist told him it would be good for him or because it is a training requirement. Such responses must be followed up by further exploratory questioning. If the patient is acting *only* to please someone else who is pushing him into group therapy or to fulfill a requirement, and not because he thinks group therapy has any value for him, he might not participate in the group in a manner that would be beneficial for him or for the group. In fact, he might not participate at all, but rather might be present as a passive, or even hostile, observer. Or he might actively sabotage the group for himself and for the other group members.

However, a patient's claim that he is looking into group therapy only because someone else suggested it still merits exploration and examination. Some individuals respond to a suggestion to join a therapy group even though they had not originally considered such a possibility—and they may have considered the idea for weeks or months after the suggestion was made before acting on it. Also, they may have some interest and yet not want to assume full responsibility for having taken the initial step.

If, on the other hand, the prospective patient has known people who have had a group therapy experience and has seen changes in them and wants to achieve similar results for himself, he is a more promising candidate. It is often a positive prognostic sign if the patient has read articles that have aroused an interest in and desire for group therapy.

DESCRIBING GROUP THERAPY

As part of the initial interviews, the therapist can ask questions designed to determine what the individual already knows about group therapy:

1. What kinds of things have you heard about group therapy?
2. What have you read about group therapy?
3. What do you think it would be like to be in a therapy group?

Prospective members may indicate that they do not have a clear idea about what group therapy is, and in fact may even state that they know *nothing* about it. Often the only conception people have of group therapy is what is portrayed, often humorously, in the movies or on television.

Some prospective group members expect group therapy to be similar to a small class, with the therapist in the role of teacher.

Others who have had some kind of small-group experience in a high school or college class expect the therapy to be similar to a focused-discussion group. Many have heard of, or even participated in, encounter groups or consciousness-raising groups and anticipate that group therapy will be like these groups. It is therefore important in the initial interview to assess the prospective member's anticipations and expectations, and to try to communicate what group therapy is and what it is not.

As part of informing the prospective member about group therapy, the therapist should differentiate between individual therapy and group therapy, indicating that the therapies are different in their techniques and in their primary emphases and goals, although there may be some overlap. For example, it is pointed out that individual therapy is a one-to-one situation in which the entire focus is on the individual patient and in which an intense relationship can develop between the patient and the therapist. The therapist should explain that most of the material that is dealt with in individual therapy is what is *reported on* by the individual patient, whether these are "reports" about current life experience, about the past, or about dreams and fantasies. The patient and the individual therapist then use this material to better understand the patient's psychodynamics and inner conflicts.

The prospective group member is informed that in the group therapy situation, each member not only relates to the therapist but also relates to, and interacts with, all of the other members of the group. Although there is some reporting by group members about current life experiences and about the past, there is also the more important ongoing interaction between the members of the group. The group therapy session becomes like a laboratory, in which members can observe their impact on others and others' impacts on them. Each behavior and interaction can be immediately examined and an attempt be made, through mutual questioning and responding, to understand it at that moment.

It is thus explained to the potential member that the primary focus in group therapy is more on *interpersonal* relations than on the *intrapsychic* dynamics and conflicts that are the primary focus of individual therapy. Individuals interact in a meaningful way, examine their reactions to one another and to the therapist, and attempt to understand themselves at the same time that they are trying to empathize with other group members.

The therapist might use the initial interview to elicit attitudes or preconceptions that could interfere with therapy and to try to modify these in order to help the person remain in the group and to gain more from it.

Janet, a young woman who had been referred by an individual therapist, said that she had been in a therapy group many years ago. She had found that she was able to "let out" all her anger and to attack others, but she did not like it when others attacked her. She "did not see what anyone gets out of just expressing all this anger and attacking one another"—although she was capable of doing it. If that was all there was to group, she surely would not be there very long!

The interviewer pointed out that part of Janet's group therapy experience would be to look at herself and to try to understand why she becomes angry at another person. The interviewer suggested that Janet ask herself some questions. Is it *what* he is saying? Or is there something about the *way* he is saying it that reminds you of yourself in some way? Or does he bring back old memories that are not pleasant? Also, why are you *attracted* to this other person? What is it about him that attracts you—his way of talking? Or the way *he* responds to *you*? And what makes you upset when you see him talking to someone else in an animated way? Regardless of what is going on, the therapist noted, it is not *just* that group members react, but that they try to understand what they are reacting to and what evokes the reaction.

This was a new idea to Janet, and she began to conceive of group therapy in an entirely different and more positive way. She now realized that it was not just that everyone in group therapy attacks everyone else, but that the members gain an understanding of how they relate to others and how others relate to them by trying to figure out what is going on. With this new outlook, Janet no longer predicted that she "would not stay long" in group.

During the initial interview, the therapist also points out that most of what happens in a group session goes on between group members; the group therapist is there to raise questions, set limits, provide guidelines, and at times make "connections" or interpretations. However, the group therapist does not determine the topics to be discussed each week, as a teacher might do, nor plan activities and exercises as in some other types of groups.

The therapist might make the point that the combination of individual and group therapy is often advantageous. Group therapy can stimulate the person to talk more about feelings in individual therapy or to bring up feelings and memories not previously discussed, while individual therapy can influence interactions with other members in the therapy group. Also, if the prospective member has one therapist for individual therapy and another for group therapy, either may request a consultation with the other at any time. As a result, both are better able to work therapeutically with the patient to bring about the desired changes.

EDUCATING ABOUT THE THERAPY GROUP

As part of the preparation for group, the therapist gives the prospective member factual information about the group. Among the first points mentioned is the number of members in the group, which is usually between five and eight. It is explained that in larger groups, such as groups of ten to fifteen, many individuals remain sideline observers rather than participants, and that there may be more of a tendency for the members to subgroup, breaking up into dyads and triads. With eight or fewer members, everyone is able to participate in the interaction. Further, if a member is not engaging in the ongoing interplay with the others, it soon becomes noticeable to all, and the group members may then try to encourage the silent one to join in the

interaction, or may at least question that person's lack of participation.

We also explain that, insofar as it is possible, an effort is made
to form a heterogeneous therapy group. The rationale for this is
discussed: One might feel comfortable and find it easier to relate
in a homogeneous group, but there would be little carryover to
the "real world," where individuals are quite different from one
another. In addition, it seems that there is more interstimulation
and confrontation in heterogeneous groups and group members
are stimulated to recall forgotten experiences and reactions.

Consequently, the group is set up to be as diverse as possible.
Each group comprises both men and women who range in ages
and who also differ in terms of marital status, educational backgrounds, work and life experiences, and even the problems that
brought them into therapy. What the group members do have in
common is their interest in understanding and improving their
interpersonal relationships. They share the common human emotions, which do become aroused in the interaction of group
therapy. Often more emotion seems to be aroused *and* expressed
in group therapy than in individual therapy.

Prospective group members tend to respond immediately to
the idea of heterogeneity. They realize that it would be much
easier for them at first if everybody in group were like them;
there would be a feeling of familiarity, and they could more
readily talk to one another. However, they also come to realize
that they would not gain as much from the group experience in
the long run, and that in a heterogeneous group there would be
many perspectives and more active inquiry and confrontation.

The therapist informs the potential group member that the
group will meet once a week for a one-and-a-half-hour session
(rather than the 45 minutes of an individual session). We also
describe our "after-sessions," which we consider part of the group
process, a continuation of the group session. We explain that at
the end of the hour-and-a-half group session, the therapist leaves,
and the group continues for an unspecified and unstructured
time. The duration of the after-session may vary from week to
week, depending on the involvement of the group members.

The main benefit of such an after-session is that it points up the

ways in which participation differ when the therapist (the authority figure) is and is not in the room. Some members are quite
active while the therapist is present to protect, to set guidelines,
to raise questions, to support, and to structure the situation
when necessary. When they are alone with peers, however, they
may become silent and inactive. Others are quiet while the
"authority figure" is present but become dominating participants
after the therapist leaves. A supposedly quiet member may even
act as group leader in the after-session; others may find it easier
to bring up problems or feelings in the after-session and will then
discuss them the following week in the regular group session,
knowing that they have the understanding and support of fellow
members. Discussion of a topic in the after-session can serve the
important function of facilitating its being brought out in the
main session. All group members understand and accept that
whatever goes on in the after-session is to be brought back into
the regular session for further discussion. The therapist is thus
informed of the content of the after-sessions and, when relevant,
can deal with it in the regular session.

DEALING WITH THE PATIENT'S ANXIETY

As previously indicated, the preparatory interview can also
serve the purpose of helping the prospective member deal with
some of the anxiety about joining a group. The person is encouraged to verbalize concerns, doubts, and fears, as well as to
express fantasies about the group and its members and about the
first group session.

Prospective group members generally fear the unknown. The
information received during the initial interview helps to allay
some of this anxiety. The prospective member is also encouraged
to ask questions about group therapy.

Most prospective group members are anxious about others'
reactions to and evaluations of them, as well as about how they
will present themselves to the group. "What will happen when I
start group? What will the others *do* to me?" Prospective members may express fears about being confronted or challenged by

other group members, or they may anticipate being unfavorably evaluated or compared with other members. Some prospective group members are concerned about being questioned in *any* way. Discussing these fears and concerns can ease some of the anxiety.

The interview provides the opportunity for the colleague-referred or self-referred person to have contact with the therapist before entering the group, so that there is at least some initial feeling of familiarity and support. It also allows the group therapist to anticipate how this person might react upon entering the group.

If the prospective member is joining an ongoing group, the therapist usually explains that the entrance of each new member is unique, since both the group's behavior and the individual's behavior are unpredictable. The same group will react differently to the entrance of each individual. For example, sometimes the group will focus on an incoming member and ask questions about what she is looking for from group or what her problems are. Alternatively, the group may continue with unfinished business from the previous week and not pay much attention to the new member. The group may begin talking about its history and past members, thereby temporarily keeping the new member "outside." The point is also made in the interview that each of the group members has had the experience of entering the ongoing group, so that they have some appreciation of what the incoming member is experiencing.

The therapist emphasizes that there is no one right way to enter a group. Some individuals will be active as a way of dealing with anxiety and may try to monopolize the first session; others will try to become invisible, just observing and listening to the others for several sessions. A few new members will participate by commenting and questioning as though they were long-term members of the group.

If the patient is going to become a member of a newly forming group, the therapist can indicate that none of the members have had experience in the therapy group, and that most will be anxious during the group's first sessions.

The therapist also tries to make clear that adjustment to the group is a gradual process; it does not occur at the first session. Twelve weeks is considered a reasonable trial period.

Evaluating the Prospective Member

The initial interview of a colleague-referred or self-referred patient is used to evaluate the prospective member in order to determine whether group therapy is an appropriate treatment modality. The therapist looks for indications that prospective group members are willing to risk exposing themselves in the group even though they are aware of their own anxiety about the exposure. The interviewee may say, "I'm so nervous, and I dread going in there." Yet as dangerous as it feels, and even though there is anticipation that the group members may be rejecting, the prospective patient has the courage to take the risk. From the kinds of questions the person raises and from the responses to the interview questions, the therapist can also assess the patient's motivation, needs, concerns, readiness for group therapy, and potential fragility.

As part of the evaluation process, the therapist obtains a brief social history of the prospective group member. The therapist thus asks about various group experiences—in social groups, clubs, organizations, cliques, work groups, groups of friends, and so on—starting with the present, which is less threatening, and moving back through time to the early experiences in the family group. The intention is to identify the roles that the patient has taken in various groups: Has the patient been an initiator or a follower? Active or passive? Compliant or provocative? Has he tended to avoid groups, or has he been a compulsive "joiner"? Has he tended to stay in groups a short time, or a long time? This history may provide a brief overview of the characteristic style of relating to and functioning in groups.

Through questioning, the therapist also attempts to determine whether the patient has some awareness of problems in interpersonal relationships or communication. For example, one person may mention having trouble with co-workers, while another may

reveal problems with family or with intimate friends. Someone
else may say, "I want to find out *why* people react to me the way
they do" or "I want to find out what *I* am doing."

The therapist attempts to find out whether the prospective
member has had any experiences with close pairings. The individual may be asked to describe one or two close friends at the
present time or during college or high school days. This information indicates a capacity to relate, as well as the types of friends
selected and the length of the friendships, and provides some
initial information about the style of relating intimately or *not*
relating intimately.

After discussing friendships and group experiences during
college, high school, and elementary school years, the individual
is asked about the first group of which he was a member–the
family group. Patients are asked which "group member" they
felt closest to and most distant from, and what types of interaction went on between the "members" in this primary group. Most
people have not considered the family in this way; they have not
thought about who related to whom in the group and what role
each member played. These questions present an uncustomary
way of looking at the family, thus providing a new perspective
and sometimes even new insights. In addition, this line of questioning may offer some preview of the transferences that will
develop in the therapy group.

Asking during the interview how the patient feels about a male
or female therapist may bring out attitudes, feelings, or experiences with authority figures of each sex. If no previous report is
available from an individual therapist, the group therapist might
want to use the interview to obtain some historical and background information.

As part of the evaluation process, the therapist also tries to
determine whether the prospective group member has some
control over aggressiveness and hostility. A member who is
extremely aggressive or hostile disrupts the group, as did the
patient in the following example.

Alice had been referred specifically for group therapy.
Her psychiatrist insisted that a preparatory interview was

unnecessary because he had treated her individually and it was clear to him that group was appropriate for her. She therefore directly entered a group.

Within one month, Alice had antagonized and alienated *every* member of the group. Perhaps because of her resentment about having been referred to a group, she slashed each member verbally, until everyone had been a victim of her tongue; then she said, "I'm leaving." She had tried, unsuccessfully, to destroy each member individually, and then hoped to wipe out the whole group by abruptly leaving. She had attacked both the men and the women for not being "liberated enough" to agree with her way of thinking; at the same time, she could see no point of view but her own.

The group members tried to persuade her to stay and to discuss some of their differences, but she refused to stay for even the rest of the session and abruptly ran out. As might be anticipated, it took the group some weeks to recover from this experience; but in response to the hostility they had experienced, the other members pulled closer together.

This disturbing situation could have been avoided had there been an initial interview—which is clearly a good idea regardless of the referral source, as a means of "protecting" groups, as well as prospective group members, from such negative experiences.

Depression is another area of assessment. Severe depression can be a contraindication to group participation, so the therapist assesses both the nature and level of the depression. A patient who would be completely helpless and unable to control tears would be more than the group could cope with and would negatively affect the group.

Cindy, who had requested group therapy, sat and cried throughout the entire initial interview and was unable to control herself. The intensity of the crying prevented her from answering many of the questions. She indicated that she had been in this state for some time. After the therapist described some of the interactions that would occur in group therapy, it was agreed that group was not appropriate at this time. She needed much nurturing, and although a group could offer some, she probably would not be able to get what she needed from the group; rather, she would be more likely to receive the support she needed in a one-to-one situation. A group might also tend to become impatient with her and frustrated by their own ineffectiveness in helping her. If Cindy had been able to talk about feeling sad, depressed, or unhappy and had been able to relate in other ways, she would be acceptable for group therapy.

Others who would be screened out in the initial interview are compulsive talkers, who would need too much attention and would be unable to share attention with other group members; psychopathic, suicidal, or homicidal individuals; and those seeking group as a way of making friends and developing a social life.

The prospective group member is informed that the first 12 weeks in a therapy group are considered a trial period. During this time, there are many "ups and downs"; the patient will sometimes like the group and at other times dislike it, will sometimes feel that it is helpful and of value and at other times feel it is useless. The new member may feel anxious because she is developing strong negative feelings (anger) toward another member, or anxious because she is developing strong positive feelings (tenderness) toward another member. Or the new member may begin to see new aspects of the self that evoke anxiety. If the new member tends to run away from difficult situations, it is during the first 12 weeks of group that this will most likely happen. Therefore, it is asked that a new member give an initial commitment to remain for a minimum of a 12-week trial period. We have found that it takes at least that length of time to have some basis on which to decide whether or not a new member can use group therapy and work with a particular group.

During her initial interview, Karen said she thought she would just "try" group for one or two sessions. The therapist explained that this was not possible; she, and everyone else, would be asked for an initial commitment of 12 weeks because it takes that long to have a basis for making a decision as to whether or not she could get something useful from the group. The therapist also explained that it would be too disruptive for the group to have people dropping in and out.

Karen then had to reconsider: If she decided to go into group, she would be promising to try it for 12 weeks. She realized that she did not have to continue her initial move toward group therapy, but that if she did choose to go in, it would be with the understanding that she would stay for at least 12 weeks. Karen thought about this, said she did not know how it would work out, but decided she would try it. For Karen, the preparation seemed to serve the purpose of enabling her to make a stronger commitment than she previously had.

GROUP RULES

In our groups, after both the therapist and the prospective group member have decided that group therapy is appropriate, the prospective member is told about our three group rules. The first rule is confidentiality—that what goes on within a therapy group is considered group property. It belongs to the group, and it is expected that it will be kept confidential within the group and not talked about "on the outside." Since group members are revealing personal information about themselves, they need to feel that they can trust group members not to gossip on the outside about what is said within the group.

As a way of ensuring this, group members initially introduce themselves by first names only. If someone should accidentally disclose information about a group member, that member will still remain anonymous. After members have been together in the group for a while, they may exchange last names. Some may even exchange telephone numbers, and if a group member is upset during the week, that person may sometimes call another group member to discuss the problem.

Group members may go out together for coffee after a group session. We do not forbid contact between group members out-

side the group sessions, although such contact may create difficulty in interpersonal relationships—which will then be dealt
with in the group session. It is understood, however, that *any*
outside contact between group members is considered a continuation of the group process and group property, because it
involves group members and will affect the group. The second
rule, then, is that outside contact is expected to be discussed with
the entire group. The nature of these contacts is usually typical of
other relationships in the members' social world. By discussing
this in the therapy group, members gain further understanding
of their relationships outside group as well.

We explain to group members that failing to disclose these
contacts and having secret conversations or meetings can sabotage therapy, both for the individuals and for the group. If a
patient keeps certain information secret, it is difficult to be open
about other aspects; the patient thus sabotages group participation. In addition, we emphasize that any *good* relationship can
stand up under the scrutiny of the group. If it does not, it usually
means that one member has been exploiting the other.

Peter, who had indicated a strong interest in group therapy throughout the initial interview, suddenly reacted to the
second rule. He thought it violated the members' privacy.
"What if one of the women in the group and I should begin to
go out after sessions? What if we like each other and have
intimate conversations and perhaps even become physically
intimate?" (Here we can see his fantasies developing.) The
interviewer explained that if the relationship was genuine,
looking at it in group would not diminish the relationship or
take anything from it. At the same time, though, the relationship might reflect something else that was going on in his
therapy or in the group, and by bringing this into the open he
could begin to understand what his behavior might mean.
Peter indicated that he could understand this. The interviewer noted that without the preparatory interview, Peter
would not have remained in the group very long.

The third rule, which we find is important to state explicitly and which is quite reassuring, is that we do not permit any physical violence in our therapy groups. Ours are "talking" groups, and group members must feel physically safe when they participate. Although someone may at times feel frustrated or angry enough to want to throw something or hit someone, these feelings cannot be acted out. Everyone must feel physically protected within the group. It is not only acceptable but also desirable and even therapeutic for a group member to say that he *feels* like throwing something or hitting someone. Once it has been said, it is in the open and other group members can try to understand what caused such intense feelings and what the feelings mean. But these feelings cannot be allowed to be acted upon. Mentioning this rule in the initial interview prevents such acting out. Should a person in a therapy group be on the verge of losing control, remembering or being reminded of this rule enables the person to exercise more control.

Although it is not–and cannot be–a rule, it is pointed out that an *ideal* in group therapy is to be as honest as possible. We recognize that this is not easy, and it is much more difficult in the beginning to be honest in a group setting than in an individual therapy session. Everyone comes into the group situation maintaining a certain public image–the "front" that is usually presented in social situations. It is only as members begin to trust one another that they can let down some of their facades and allow the group to see them as they see themselves. It is explained to the prospective group member that the more one is able to do this–to be oneself without maintaining a front, to communicate freely whatever thoughts and feelings one has–the more help one can derive from the therapy group.

The therapist also mentions the importance of attending *every* week, arriving on time, and paying fees regularly. These are responsibilities the person assumes when agreeing to become a member of the group. It is pointed out that a member who is irregular in attendance will lose the continuity of the group and will not be aware of what has happened. This, in turn, may make him feel like an outsider or an observer who must ask questions about what was missed. Frequent absences also affect the group, since each absence distrupts the group's cohesiveness and alters the relationships and interactions, thereby slowing the therapeutic process.

Similarly, but to a lesser extent, tardiness may result in the member's missing out on what has happened, so that part of the session must be spent catching up and figuring out what has been going on. Some members will resent the latecomer and be unwilling to repeat what was previously said. Late payment of fees may be taken as a sign that the patient is not committed to the therapy, is resistant to the therapy, wants to be "given to" without having to give payment in return, or is devaluing the therapy – showing by actions that it is not worth much. Thus, late payment, absences, and tardiness may be a way of either communicating to the therapist or sabotaging whatever help the patient could otherwise get from the therapy group.

ANSWERING QUESTIONS

Throughout the interview the prospective group member is encouraged to ask *any* questions, and an effort is made to answer questions the moment they arise. At the end of the interview, however, the prospective group member is told to feel free to call with any questions that come to mind after he leaves.

PREPARING FOR ENTRY INTO A GROUP

The therapist informs the incoming member of the time and location of the group sessions, as well as the date for entering the group. An effort is made to expedite entrance into the therapy group, so that the patient begins treatment within a few weeks from the initial interview. However, it is also important that the new member have time between the initial interview and the actual entrance into group to reconsider and reflect on this decision and to raise any further questions. Another consideration in allowing time between the preparatory interview and entrance into group is that the therapist must have time to prepare an ongoing group for the newcomer's entrance.

If the therapist has pressured the patient to enter a group, it puts added pressure on the therapist to perform. The patient feels, "You talked me into it, and you'd better make good." This may then make the patient more dependent on, and possibly more hostile toward, the "pressuring therapist."

Chapter 4
Selecting and Grouping Patients

The criteria for selection of patients for group therapy are complex and still rather vague. Although many group therapists have offered inclusion and exclusion criteria, our knowledge remains incomplete.

For any patient, the therapist must consider the group setting—for example, whether the group is a private-practice group, a clinic group, an inpatient group, or a group meeting in a settlement house or university. Patients who are acceptable for a hospital group might be unacceptable for a private-practice group. Participants in a university group (which meets from September to June) would not reach the depths that extended groups in clinics or private practice would. Settlement houses tend to set up groups with a more practical, theme-oriented purpose. The groups discussed here are primarily those that would be conducted in private practice or in a clinic, where therapy can continue for extended periods of time.

It is also important to consider the purposes and goals of the particular therapy group. Some groups are oriented more toward growth or education than toward remediation or more basic kinds of changes. As indicated in the previous chapter, some individuals are more likely than others to be able to use a group and to have the possibility of success in group therapy. We would like to examine some of the characteristics of these potentially successful group members.

Those who have already heard from friends or acquaintances about how valuable a group experience has been for *them* will be more positively oriented toward group therapy and consequently more motivated to enter a group to "get something" for themselves. Knowing second-hand about some of the functioning of a therapy group, they may look forward to having the support of other group members in trying to face and deal with their own life problems.

In addition, the potential for using the therapy group in a positive way is enhanced if group members have had some satisfying previous experiences in other kinds of groups, or if they have shown some capacity to relate to another person, whether a childhood buddy, a teenage "steady," or an adult friend. Knowing something about the patient's style of relating in past groups may provide some forecast of expectable interaction in a group situation and may help to determine the "fit" in a particular group. It may enliven a group in which several members are passive or compliant to bring in an active, provocative person; on the other hand, in a group that already has many active members, it may help to bring in someone more passive.

Some prospective group candidates may be acutely aware of their own interpersonal problems and may seek a therapy group to help them sort out their difficulties. They may feel incapable of working out these problems by themselves or in individual therapy and may thus seek group therapy. Along with this awareness, it is helpful if the individual is willing not only to look at herself within the group, but also to risk exposure to others. Everyone entering a therapy group has some anxiety about exposing his vulnerabilities, but in order to make use of the group, a member must be willing to take this risk. Besides talking to the group about his behavior, the patient must be willing to share feelings, thoughts, and fantasies, although in a modulated way.

Group candidates who are willing to examine their own actions instead of blaming others are more likely to be able to use group therapy in a beneficial way. If this is accompanied by a willingness to engage others and the capacity to tolerate a certain degree of criticism, confrontation, and hostility, the outlook for change is even more promising. It should be noted, however, that an individual who does not seem ready to enter a group at one time may be ready at a later time, after some individual therapy or after his life situation changes.

It was probably Slavson (1955) who provided the first basis for patient selection. However, he was unduly influenced by orthodox psychoanalysis and thought that there were specific therapies for particular illnesses. For example, he felt that psychoneurosis would be best treated by psychoanalysis, as would sexual problems and severe character disorders. On the other hand, he correctly suggested that a prospective group patient had to have had some satisfaction with adult figures in life and needed a certain amount of ego strength and superego development.

Neighbor and colleagues (1958) considered more specific criteria that might be seen as an elaboration of ego assessment. They excluded from groups persons who chronically experienced frustration in sharing the therapist, who exhibited intense anxiety, and in whom exploration would weaken defenses. Patients who are delusional or who display bizarre ideation are also excluded, as are those who have suicidal or homicidal tendencies. Then there are patients who, while they do not fall into the exclusion categories, might weaken the group process.

Neighbor and co-authors (1958) found it more productive to classify exclusionary criteria by *dysfunctions* than by diagnostic categories, since patients within a diagnostic category may differ in the extent of their dysfunction. Indeed, the new orientation of the *Diagnostic and Statistical Manual of Mental Disorders* (DSM-III) might make assessment according to diagnosis even more untenable. What must be assessed is the patient's ability to communicate and participate in a group. Thus, Stein (1963) stated: "The only point that might be mentioned is a general one: namely, that the patient's problems and personality be such that he can enter into the identifications with the other patients that form one of the major ties in the establishment of the psychotherapeutic group" (p. 154).

Although most clinicians have addressed themselves to pathology when reviewing criteria for exclusion and inclusion, Anthony (1965) mentions the factors of age and syndrome. It is quite possible that age, socioeconomic status, marital status, and sexual competence are some of the factors that will make a group attractive or unattractive to a prospective group member. We have had patients refuse to stay in one group "because I don't like the people; I have nothing in common with them," and yet settle down in a different group. One patient, a middle-aged woman, told us that she would enter only a group whose members had a variety of sexual experiences so she would not stand out as "promiscuous."

BASES FOR SELECTION

In selecting group members, we try to assess the patient's ego strength, including reality testing and the ability to observe, assess, or judge social situations. Someone with good reality testing and some powers of observation would be more likely to benefit from group therapy than someone with poor reality testing or poor assessment ability.

The individual's capacity to tolerate frustration is also relevant. In a group, there are often times when one member is frustrated by another's long monologue, or by the interaction between two members, or by not having an opportunity to bring in something that he considers important. How this is handled, and how this may affect the group, must be taken into account in deciding whether or not to accept a patient for a particular group.

The prospective member's needs and concerns will also enter into the decision. Many patients who come to us manifest profound difficulty establishing intimacy. Although they profess neediness and the wish to find a meaningful relationship, their relationships for some reason do not work out. On closer examination one may find various barriers to closeness. The patient may be unrealistically romantic and make faulty choices of partners. It is also possible that the motivating need for such a choice may override other considerations.

Sybil, a young woman, felt attracted to an ex-drug addict because he was able to provide sexual satisfaction, which she had not previously experienced. However, her other needs, including dependency and affection, could not be gratified by this man. Later in the course of therapy, she was consciously looking for a suitable marital partner. At this time, her wish to get married and to have a family predominated. Although her object choice represented a more mature judgment, fears on a different level caused the relationship to fluctuate. She became very concerned about the possibility of being abandoned for another woman and talked about her competitive feelings and jealousy. However, the libidinal aspects of the relationship were sufficiently gratifying that they served as a constant baseline from which the fluctuations could be analyzed. Real bonding could thus occur.

Connie, another young woman in the group, had many relationships with different men and was abandoned by them without fail. She engaged in a markedly masochistic pattern whereby she alternately made herself a doormat to these men and then became a scolding, nagging shrew. Whereas Sybil had a fairly healthy personality structure and libidinal ties could be interfered with in a neurotic fashion, Connie's deprivation had occurred at an early preoedipal level and suppressed rage had continued and infiltrated her character stucture.

Sybil was a good group therapy patient. She looked for approval, understanding, and love from the other group members; in so doing, all of her neurotic dynamics were projected with ease and could then be understood and analyzed. After she entered the group, her constant complaints about "the man in her life" were given short shrift by the group, and the focus was turned back on her own motivations. She was able to accept such interaction, reconstitute her defenses, and participate in a more mature manner.

Connie presented a more difficult problem. Being unconsciously gratified by her masochistic triumphs, she would tend
not to complain or talk about her problems. The ease of projection
necessary for group therapy was not available to her. Her libidinal needs were frozen behind a rigid, obsessional character
structure. Ideally she would have been able to express in a
therapy group some libidinal wishes toward nonthreatening
peers who did not represent an unconsciously hateful parental
image that she had to defeat.

Two factors should be stressed in selecting patients for group
therapy: (1) the ability to project and externalize, and (2) the
ability to tolerate intense affects projected by others. Group
therapy depends on interaction between members. If each group
member only introspected or kept feelings hidden, there would
be little interaction. The ability to externalize feelings is a facilitating factor in treatment since it increases interaction, which is
a sine qua non for group therapy. In selecting patients for a
group, then, the patient's ability to project feelings should be
taken into account.

The second factor is the patient's ability to tolerate projection
of intense feelings toward him. A group member may attach
special significance to another member who not only evokes
strong feelings in the present but also stimulates feelings that
have their roots in the past. At other times, a group member may
express such affect toward the therapist or toward the group-as-
a-whole. Because these highly intense affects are by nature quite
ambivalent, prospective group members need to be able to tolerate a variety of affective storms.

In evaluating patients for group inclusion and placement, we
also consider intensity of anxiety and the defenses erected
against it. Patients who evidence ego fragility in a therapy group
tend to be difficult to handle and can negatively affect other
group members or the group-as-a-whole. We would hesitate
about putting into a group individuals whose defenses show
hypochondriasis or addictions, although addicted patients may
do well in a homogeneous group. Such persons demand much
gratification from the therapist or other group members and are
less likely to be able to make use of a therapy group in which all
the members interact.

A somewhat different and milder case is the compulsive talker who seeks constant attention from the therapist and the group and who will often be set up for scapegoating by the group members. On the other hand, we might also question the advisability of placing someone who is an "isolate" into a therapy group; such persons utilize the group only for making social contact and "friends."

In the process of selecting patients for a therapy group, we also observe affect. Patients who are at either extreme—from severely depressed (possible suicidal) to very hostile (antisocial or homicidal)—are preferred for individual therapy only. Such patients put too much burden on a group. With the depressed or suicidal patient, the group members feel pressured to be concerned and giving, and may experience feelings of guilt for not living up to their own expectations for helping or even taking care of a fellow group member. The hostile or antisocial patient tends to disrupt a group by shouting, swearing, and verbally attacking others. Such a patient can have a negative effect on other group members, in some instances even causing another group member to want to leave the group. As one group member indignantly said, "I am not here to be the butt of Leon's fury. I am here to get help for myself."

The diagnostic categories that would be considered for group therapy in a clinic or private practice range from neuroses to character disorders and situational disturbances. Those with more marked pathologies, such as some of the severe character disorders, the narcissistic personalities, and certain schizoid personalities, may be able to make use of group therapy when it is combined with individual treatment. However, their anxieties, ego strengths, and frustration tolerance may be quite different from those of patients with neurotic disorders in that they will show less self-control, more anxiety, and more impatience, and be more demanding in the group situation. Borderline patients who are "sensitive" and have available a reservoir of unconscious material could also be accepted for group therapy.

Liff (1978) was of the opinion that group is the treatment of choice for borderline patients. The emotional interaction in a therapy group "shakes" the fixated channels and has an impact on the pathology from preverbal trauma. Though Slavson (1955) believed that severe character disorders should be referred for classical psychoanalysis, most of our groups today deal predominantly with characterological problems and narcissistic problems. Our decisions about treatment must be based on the nuclear conflicts and on the quality and intensity of defenses.

If the therapist is concerned about achieving group cohesiveness and in having patients relate to each other, then a patient whose characteristic neurotic defense is to avoid closeness would be difficult to treat in a therapy group. Such defensive structures are characteristic of a psychotic or prepsychotic process. On the other hand, schizoid characters may profit from groups, if one can accept them on their level. This type of person, strongly defended and resistant, is usually experienced by both group members and therapists as a "drag" to group process. However, we have found that if it is passively understood by the group that such a person is vulnerable and fearful, the members can usually accept the schizoid wish to stay separated and in isolation, and they will not scapegoat this individual. The group usually accepts these defenses as "the way it is for the time being" and takes and encourages whatever such an individual can contribute.

Much depends on the therapist and on the match of the therapist with the members of the group. Some therapists are more active, some more nurturing, some more controlling. A patient who might not work out with one group therapist could succeed with another.

It may be difficult to make an accurate assessment before the patient enters the group; the diagnostic evaluation can often be more precise after the patient has been placed in the group and his interactions observed. Patients who are inappropriate for group therapy tend to screen themselves out either in the initial interview or after being in the group for a while. They may decide on their own that they are not getting what they want from the group, or they may be scapegoated by others to such an extent that they leave.

Doug, a new member in a clinic group, lasted only through the first session. After introducing himself to the others, he proceeded to monopolize most of the session. He dramatically explained that he had entered group therapy only after his wife had been institutionalized with a nervous breakdown, which the doctors insisted he had caused. Then, using the members' comments as a jump-off point, he talked about his own crazy feelings and his negative views about therapy. He criticized other group members and questioned them in an aggressive, provocative manner. (None of this behavior had been apparent in the initial interview prior to group entrance.) The group atmosphere became increasingly tense, with the members offering each other support in opposing Doug. The next morning, Doug called the group therapist to say that it would be impossible for him to continue in the group because his "schedule had changed" and he would have to be working on that night every week henceforth.

CLINIC GROUPS

Selecting patients and fitting them into an appropriate group is probably a more complex task in a clinic than in a private practice. Various factors interplay in determining the placement of a patient in a group. One factor that may complicate the decision is the patient's own preferences for day and time of the meeting, as well as gender of the therapist. If the clinic requires that the patient meet first with the director of the group department and then with the group therapist for one or two sessions, the patient may be lost to treatment as a result of the delay. Another factor in a clinic is that the various group therapists may have conflicting needs for additional members in their groups; these needs may influence which group receives the referral of the new member.

Clinic patients may in some ways be considered more needy than private patients. They have turned to "institutionalized" therapy rather than to a private practitioner for any of a number of reasons. They may be unable or unwilling to pay prevalent private fees, or they may hesitate to put their lives "into the hands" of one individual and instead prefer a "team." They may not be knowledgeable about how to select a private therapist, or they may be anxious about making a choice themselves and prefer to trust "experts" to select a therapist and group for them.

GROUPING PATIENTS

There has been much discussion about homogeneous versus heterogeneous groups. But one might ask, "Homogeneous with regard to what criteria? Heterogeneous with regard to what criteria?" And we would tend to answer, "With regard to significant aspects of group members." Of course, we must then decide which aspects are significant. The following characteristics are usually considered:

1. Sex—Should the group comprise just one sex, or both?
2. Age—Should the members be of the same or similar ages, or is it all right to have a wider age span?
3. Marital status—Should all members be either single or married, or is there some advantage in having members with varied marital status?
4. Intellectual ability—Should all the members be within a narrow range of intellectual ability, or can there be a wide range?
5. Education—Should the group members be, say, all college graduates or high school graduates, or should there be a mixture?
6. Socioeconomic status—Should members all come from the same social class, or can there be a sprinkling from various social classes?
7. Ego strength—Should members have about the same vulnerability and about the same capacity to deal with problems, or is it preferable to have a range of competence and coping ability?
8. Problems—Need the real-life problems of the members be similar, or just the nuclear problems?

Slavson (1955) preferred homogeneous groups. He also preferred unisex groups, stating that groups comprising both sexes would encourage acting out, and that even putting homosexuals into a group would interfere with the therapeutic process. He advocated having members of the same generation so that the age spread was not too wide, and he also thought it best to have members with similar intellectual ability, education, socioeconomic status, ego strength, and nuclear problems. Yalom (1985) on the other hand, preferred groups comprising both sexes and believed that other differences between members were also therapeutically helpful.

Homogeneous Groups

Certainly there are instances in which homogeneous groupings seem more appropriate than heterogeneous groupings. However, the homogeneity is usually of a limited kind. Examples are therapy groups that have a special focus in order to deal with a special problem, such as groups for drug addicts, alcoholics, mothers, single parents, sexually abused members, or battered women. We would also expect homogeneity in terms of age in groups for children. In addition, there are some very disturbed patients who could not function in a heterogeneous group but would be able to use a homogeneous group (usually in a hospital setting). However, all these groups are heterogeneous with regard to other characteristics, such as sex, intellectual ability, or socioeconomic status.

Advantages. What are some of the advantages of homogeneous groupings? First, in a homogeneous group, the members can identify with one another more quickly. They feel more familiar with one another and more comfortable almost from the first session. The anxiety about being in a group may be overcome more quickly because of the sense of familiarity. Consequently, members may be able to begin to work together sooner than they could in a heterogeneous group. Relationships develop easily, and the work can proceed rapidly from the outset.

Hadden (1966), in discussing unisex groups, and Demarest and Teicher (1974), in discussing an all-women group, indicated that transference reactions were more intense in these groups than those they had observed in heterogeneous groups. According to Furst (1975), cliques (or subgroups) are less common in homogeneous groups, and recovery from symptoms is more rapid; treatment is therefore of shorter duration in homogeneous groups than in heterogeneous groups.

In addition, the mirroring that occurs in a homogeneous group may tend to circumvent some of the members' resistances and defenses. They do not feel like "outsiders," and being surrounded by persons with similar symptoms allows the members to confront their problems more quickly.

Disadvantages.   There has been some question about whether homogeneous groups will explore as "deeply" as heterogeneous groups. Since the members assume that they understand one another, they may not question or probe as much or seek explanations as members of a heterogeneous group might. The level of therapy may thus be more superficial than in a heterogeneous group.

Some doubt remains about whether basic conflicts that lead to symptomatic behavior can be resolved in a homogeneous group. In addition, because there is less diversity in a homogeneous group, the material eventually may not seem as interesting as that in a heterogeneous group. Further, there is not as much opportunity for reality testing in a homogeneous group as there is in a heterogeneous group, in which there are a variety of personalities.

Some of the homogeneous groups might be seen as "deviant" by the culture at large; groups for drug addicts are an example. Thus, while the members may admit their problems more readily within the group, they would need much more help to become comfortable with people outside the group.

Heterogeneous Groups

Neighbor and colleagues (1958) suggest balancing various types of patients in a therapy group: some with awareness of their own anxiety and the ability to express it, some with a high degree of perception and sensitivity. They also suggest including people with a variety of social experiences, defensive structures, and presenting problems, as well as different diagnostic categories. We would suggest a balance between assertive-active and more reticent members, and we would want to include one or two who might be catalysts for others.

Advantages. We believe that those who can use group therapy are best served by placement in a heterogeneous group. We include within our therapy groups people from a variety of social backgrounds and with different social experiences. These, together with the diverse personalities and character structures of the members, create a group in which there are a variety of perspectives and opinions. This diversity produces heterogeneous patterns of coping with new situations, which then leads to greater variety in the interaction.

In fact, even though similar symptoms may be experienced, they often have different contextual meanings because they occur in persons who are at different developmental levels, who experience different conflicts, who have had different histories, and who use different defenses. Glatzer (1956) has indicated that with such diversity of personalities, there is more rapid therapeutic movement as well as a greater sense of support and compassion.

The experiences that arise from the interaction of diverse personalities are rich, deep, and varied. Diverse points of view and critical observations stimulate and encourage members to examine their problems from various perspectives and encourage them to go further and not just "sit there" and be satisfied. The challenge of coping with different personalities and complex problems leads members to continually observe themselves and their interactions with others; they cannot just say "That's the way it is," or "I know you understand me." A heterogeneous group calls for more reality testing than a homogeneous group. Problems are explored first on one developmental level and then on another, leading to more self-understanding and working through.

Disadvantages. Members in a heterogeneous group may feel uncomfortable with one another, so it may take them longer to disclose their problems and to identify with one another. Such diversity may evoke more, and more lasting, anxiety than there might be in a homogeneous group. The members of a heterogeneous group are likely to be more defensive and more resistant in the beginning, and they may be more involved in trying to impress one another in order to evoke positive responses.

According to Anthony (1965), there may be more subgrouping in the heterogeneous group among those who identify with one another—such as those of similar social class, social background, or gender—and they may concentrate their interactions with one another, excluding the rest of the members. Finally, even though heterogeneous groups seem to achieve a deeper level of therapy, Furst (1975) believes that because of the diversity and inherent problems in the interactions, a heterogeneous group requires a therapist with more training and experience than would a homogeneous group.

REFERENCES

Anthony, E. (1965). Age and syndrome in group psychotherapy. *Topical Problems in Psychotherapy* 5:80–89. New York: Karger.

Demarest, E., and Teicher, A. (1974). Transference in group psychotherapy; its uses by cotherapists of opposite sexes. *Psychiatry* 17:187–202.

Furst, W. (1975). Homogeneous versus heterogeneous groups. In *Group Psychotherapy and Group Function*, ed. M. Rosenbaum and M. Berger, pp. 407–410. New York: Basic Books.

Glatzer, H. (1956). The relative effectiveness of clinically homogeneous and heterogeneous psychotherapy groups. *International Journal of Group Psychotherapy* 6:258–265.

Hadden, S. (1966). Treatment of male homosexuals in groups. *International Journal of Group Psychotherapy* 16:13–22.

Liff, Z. (1978). Group psychotherapy for the 1980s: psychoanalysis of pathological boundary structuring. *Group* 2:184–192.

Neighbor, J., Beach, M., Brown, D. T., Kevin, D., and Visher, J. S. (1958). An approach to the selection of patients for group psychotherapy. *Mental Hygiene* 42:243–254.

Slavson, S. R. (1955). Criteria for the selection of patients for various types of group psychotherapy. *International Journal of Group Psychotherapy* 5:3–30.

Stein, A. (1963). Indications for group psychotherapy and the selection of patients. *Journal of the Hillside Hospital* 12:145–155.

Yalom, I. (1985). *The Theory and Practice of Group Psychotherapy,* 3rd ed. New York: Basic Books.

Chapter 5
First Sessions

Therapists often have difficulty starting a group. First is the problem of finding a number of people who are ready for a therapy group at the same time and can meet on a particular day at a specific hour. Of necessity, the group is likely to be heterogeneous—drawn from the group therapist's own individual patients, referred by colleagues, or self-referred. Once a group of patients is available, the therapist should not wait too long before starting the group because of the likelihood of losing those who want to start soon.

We have found that it is feasible to begin a group with four or five "charter" members. If with this number there develops a solid core with continuity—everyone attending each session, being on time, participating in an interested way in his own style, relating to the therapist, and experiencing some feelings of belongingness and cohesiveness—the group can gradually be built up to a maximum of eight members. With more than eight members, some may feel competitive for the time available and for the attention of the therapist and the other members. Others may feel pressured by the presence of so many members and may not feel as free to express themselves as readily or as often as they might in a smaller group. There is also a tendency for

subgroups to develop. Groups tend to take on different characteristics once they go beyond eight members.

Before the First Session

Before the group is to have its first session, the members are
informed of the date, time, and place of the meetings and are told
how many will be present in the new group and, if they ask, how
many are males and how many females. No other information is
given before the first session. Members can thus introduce themselves as they wish and at their own pace. That is, they can reveal
at each session as much or as little as they feel comfortable with.
Some will open up immediately; others may take weeks or
months.

In the preliminary individual interviews, the therapist will
have explored some of the anxieties evoked by entering the
group, as well as some of the expectations. It is to be expected
that each patient will be seeking acceptance and approval from
the others, but there will also be some fear. The therapist may
want to elicit the patient's fantasies during the preliminary
interviews in order to assess these fears and to express sympathetic understanding. The therapist should acknowledge that it is
difficult to reveal one's thoughts and feelings to strangers. To
support the prospective member, the therapist stresses the rule
of confidentiality and the fact that such fantasies are common to
all persons who enter a therapy group.

The Patients' Fears

Patients who have had an individual relationship with the therapist before entering the group will worry that the group experience will interfere with or destroy the dyadic relationship.
They fear that just being in the group will create more distance
because they will now be relating to peers. The patient may also
unconsciously realize that the group will demand his allegiance,
resulting in a situation of conflicting loyalties—loyalty to the

group and loyalty to the individual therapist. The patient may have the unconscious idea that the group entity will be more powerful and therefore replace the dyadic relationship. Thus the patient is not only losing the safety of the dyadic relationship but also coming under the influence of a more powerful and uncontrollable entity which, it is feared, could result in the loss of the connection to the individual therapist.

On another level, the anticipation of the group experience may stimulate early memories and the unpleasant feelings associated with these memories—about entering kindergarten, first grade, or high school. Two subsidiary fears may be experienced. The fear of the unknown involves entering a new situation knowing neither what one will find there, nor what role one will have to play. Stranger anxiety is a reaction to meeting unfamiliar people and not being sure about how to interact with them.

Initial anxieties frequently focus on the fear of "exposure." Patients are concerned with *how much* and *what* is perceived by the other members. The fear of exposure usually reflects feelings of inadequacy and incompetence. The need to overcome rejection anxiety and to be accepted by the group leads to the strong wish that only favorable aspects of themselves will be visible to the others.

Fears of exposure are often linked to memories of going for a physical examination by a physician. Common are concerns that physical defects or evidence of incurable disease will be discovered. In the absence of a stable ego, such possibilities will affect the self-concept and self-feelings. Fears having to do with the body (the first ego was a body ego) have correlates on the psychic level. Those who feel inadequate are afraid to expose the weaknesses of which they are aware, anticipating a negative response from other group members. Incoming members are concerned with defending their "rotten core" (Lax 1980), and they fear that the group will find out how "diseased" they are, how incurably "crazy."

Fear of exposure is also linked to fears that hidden secrets will somehow be found out (Greenson 1967) and that shameful exposure will result, causing the other members to react with criticism, shock, or derision. The fear of exposure is related to the concern that what is said within the group will be talked about outside the group by other members. Some incoming members, whom we might consider counterphobic, seem to welcome the group experience as presenting both stage and audience for exhibitionistic and narcissistic displays.

The Therapist's Fears

Fear is not necessarily experienced only by the prospective group members. Also to be expected is some anxiety on the part of the therapist meeting with a new group. No matter how experienced or prepared the therapist, unpredictable elements and unexpected happenings cannot be avoided.

For a therapist who has been accustomed to individual treatment, the formation of a group is a unique challenge. Instead of feeling safely ensconced in the usual role with individual patients, the therapist is confronted by four or more people at the same time. The usual barriers of a desk or couch are eliminated, and everybody sits in a circle, in a more or less equal position, facing all the others. This radical change in the therapist's habitual position can stimulate fears about competence in the group situation. Therapeutic effectiveness will be influenced by some of the following anticipations and fantasies.

If group members are treated individually by other therapists, novice group therapists might wonder how they will come out in comparison. They may even be concerned about whether their own patients, who are now in the group, will still respect them when they are seen with greater transparency in group interaction. Now they will be seen "for what they really are." The question of social competence will arise.

Being accustomed to the accouterments and safeguards of the individual therapeutic situation, the beginning group therapist may become concerned with how much control can be exercised over the group. Concerns usually revolve around two areas: (1) being unable to control the impulses of group members and (2) the group's unresponsiveness and silence. In either case, there will be fantasies about the disintegration of the group and confrontation with one's inadequacies.

Therapists seem to have greater difficulty anticipating the group's silences than the discharge of impulses. If just silence were reflected in the group, the therapist would face a void, a nothingness, an unresponsiveness that would require concerted efforts to overcome. That is, the therapist would have to operate within the void, without any sign of where to go; this is likely to provoke feelings of impotence or helplessness.

Many therapists feel uncertain about the outcome of the first meeting and about how many members will continue. Group therapists may feel that their professional competence is at stake and that the patients will quickly deidealize them. If the therapist's own conflicts have deeper roots, the fantasies may be not unlike those of the patients. We emphasize the importance of a personal analysis and a good group experience for group therapists themselves before they try to conduct therapy groups.

External Factors

In starting a therapy group, the externals of the situation must be considered in terms of at least four factors that will affect the interaction between group members: privacy, intimacy, comfort, and concentration.

The location of the group therapy room is the first consideration. It is important that the patients have a sense of privacy. There should be no concern that other people will suddenly enter the room or use it as a passageway. It should be impossible for others outside the room to hear what is happening inside. Concentration and intimacy within the group are enhanced if there are no distracting noises or views. The room should be maintained at a comfortable temperature, since this can also be a distraction from the ongoing interaction.

The size of the room is a second consideration. It should be large enough to hold a group comfortably, but not so large that patients feel isolated or outside of the group. They should be able to sit close enough to see and hear one another, but not so close that there is no elbow room. The size of the room not only contributes to comfort but also facilitates confiding and intimacy.

The room's furnishings should be comfortable but not ostenta-
tious. It is important that group members concentrate on one
another and not be distracted by the furnishings. The arrangement of the furniture should be conducive to confiding without
being intrusive. Seating should be set up so that each member
can see all of the others, but should not be so close together that
it inhibits the expression of feelings.

We prefer that the seating allow members some choice of the
type of seat, since not everyone is comfortable in the same style
of chair. Thus, we have used a couch that is large enough for
three persons, but with the expectation that only two will sit on
it—one at each end, for those who cannot tolerate too much
closeness; a loveseat for two, for those who want to feel the
support of someone next to them; and separate chairs. Each can
choose the type of seat that "feels right," as well as a preferred
location.

Most members will choose the same seat each week. But when
a patient changes seats in the course of group therapy, it can be
taken as a sign of internal changes.

> Sue had always sat on the love seat next to Harriet (a
> somewhat older woman) and facing the therapist across the
> length of the room. After a long period of therapy, she moved
> to a chair next to the therapist, where she then assumed the
> more active role of assistant therapist, competing at times
> with the therapist.
>
> Wanda, who had always sat at the far end of the soft, low
> sofa, which put her next to the therapist and distanced her
> from all the other group members, suddenly decided one
> evening to sit on a chair that was at "a higher level" and more
> in the center of the group.
>
> George, who had been sitting on a chair for many months
> and passing judgment on what other members said, decided
> then to move to the sofa, "which is softer," and on which he
> could lean back and be somewhat more relaxed in his partic-
> ipation.

A member's changing seats affects the dynamics of the group,
pushing at least one other person into a new location, and at times

having a ripple effect, with several members deciding that they want a new perspective.

The lighting in the room should be variable, with lamps (with three-way bulbs) spaced around the room so that members can turn them off or on, brighter or dimmer. Here, too, it is of interest when someone prefers "not so much light" or at some other time wants "more light." In one group, Walter, who had said little since coming into the group many months before, turned off the lamp next to him a few minutes before he announced that he had something pressing that he wanted to bring up.

THE FIRST SESSIONS

The first meeting of a therapy group usually sets the stage for the subsequent therapeutic process and climate. The therapist introduces himself and asks the members to introduce themselves *by first name only*, to preserve anonymity. The therapist may then make an opening statement to the effect that the therapy group affords an opportunity to talk about feelings and to understand patterns of behavior. Emphasis is given to spontaneous and free communication, including dreams, fantasies, and physical sensations. It is fruitful also for the therapist to ask the group members how they feel about being in the group and to encourage them to share their anticipations and fantasies with one another.

If the therapist is friendly and concerned, this attitude will be communicated to the group members, who will then see the therapist as a "safe" figure. The therapist may stimulate discussion by saying, "Perhaps you can tell us a little more about that," or "Perhaps you could comment on the problem we were talking about." However, the therapist will be moderately passive and noninterpretive for many sessions in order to establish a safe group climate, avoiding areas that seem to be too sensitive.

In the early sessions of a therapy group, the members are more dependent on the therapist than they will be in subsequent sessions. Group members will tend to look toward the therapist for guidance and help. It may be necessary for the therapist to do more facilitating and questioning, as well as guiding, at first; it is expected that the therapist will take a more active role in the first sessions than in subsequent sessions. Long silences in the first few sessions may discourage or frighten some patients, who may then decide not to return again–leaving fewer members in the group, which can be demoralizing.

At some time during the first session, the therapist may wish to make a statement about the purpose of the group. Although it may have been discussed in the preliminary individual interviews, this is the first time all the group members are jointly hearing the statement. The therapist reviews the rules of the group, stressing confidentiality in order to facilitate self-disclosure.

The therapist can encourage group members who are having difficulty participating to interact with others. Once a member has said something, no matter how general or simple, it is easier to speak a second and third time. It is helpful if the therapist points out similarities between members or asks them to comment on one another's observations. If such comments are not forthcoming, the therapist can raise questions to elicit reactions to another member's contributions. During the first sessions, it is important that the therapist be flexible–neither sitting in rigid silence nor "taking over" as the director of the interaction.

We have found it useful at times to encourage group members to share their fears and fantasies with one another and to respond to one another's fantasies. Acknowledging the anxieties aroused by being in a new therapy group, the therapist may wish to ask the group members what could make them more comfortable in the situation. Since the members are likely to suggest different means of allaying their particular anxieties, the therapist can indicate that their individual modes of adaptation will be respected.

The group therapist must always keep in mind, however, that the more directive the leader is and the more structure she provides, the more the members' dependency will increase. The therapist's role during the group's first sessions is to facilitate communication and to refrain from interpretive remarks. With encouragement, the members will, hesitatingly, reveal what they expect to get from this new therapeutic modality. Some may stress that group participation will help them to grow and to mature. Others may express their fears of being disliked if they reveal themselves and of eventually *having* to leave the group. Both reactions are in defense against anxiety but are at opposite poles of ambivalence. It can be assumed that nobody is comfortable; everybody is anxious and no one knows what will happen.

Sometimes the group members will begin by themselves to explore one another and to look for similarities among them. Some may seek or give advice. Members may talk about why they are in the group and what they want from the group. Or they may talk about their feelings at the moment – anxiety, fear, self-consciousness, and so on. They will search for ways of reacting to one another and of feeling more comfortable. *Whenever* the members are talking to each other, it is best for the therapist to sit back and "stay out of it." It is in the interaction of the group members that feelings of familiarity develop, which is a first step toward belongingness, cohesiveness, and eventually becoming a working group. By sitting back and observing, the therapist will be in a better position to gain more understanding of each group member, observe the group process as it develops, and formulate general statements about the ongoing interaction.

Regardless of the ease or difficulty of the group members' verbal interactions, it is important for the therapist, in these early sessions, to convey to the members interest, curiosity, and quiet expertise – regardless of the anxiety or frustration that might be experienced in the group. The therapist should make some remarks, usually at the end of the early sessions, about the interrelationships among members, the common problems, and the fact that the group will continue to meet and to explore them.

In instances in which the group members have the same therapist for individual as for group therapy, the bond they have previously established will carry them through the first few months of the new group. They are already accustomed to the therapist's personality and style, and they can rely on these two constants to help them over some anxious sessions. Competitive feelings and jockeying for the favored position will gradually emerge.

In instances in which the members have an individual therapist who is not the group therapist, it is as if they are starting therapy from scratch again. It is a separate and often frightening experience. Such members may place more importance on their relationship with their individual therapist and participate peripherally in the group, or they may seek to establish another dyadic relationship with the group therapist. In time, depending on the dynamics, the therapeutic transference may be split, with one therapist assigned the benevolent aspects and the other the "hated" aspects of the early parental figures. It is essential that the two therapists have a good working relationship and be able to coordinate the therapeutic strategy for the patients.

The following is a statement by a group member, a social psychologist, after attending ten sessions of a group:

> When entering the group for the first meeting, I had a feeling of strangeness and some uneasiness. This was the first time, and there was no previous experience to fall back on. It was unpredictable what would happen. As one way of trying to become comfortable, I looked around the room, examining the faces of the others present, including the therapist, and tried to anticipate in imagination how the session would start and what would happen. There was an initial period of the group members' feeling one another out—taking tentative steps toward one another—giving their names and a *little* bit about where they were coming from and what they were looking for.
>
> During the first few sessions, the therapist and the group tried to pull in the silent members—questioning them, reassuring them directly and indirectly, and expressing sympathy for their discomfort and anxiety. By the third session, there was some pairing—one male group member giving more attention and responding more to another male who seemed in some way similar to someone else he already knew outside the group. Two women paired to give one

another mutual support in opening up and to exclude others who seemed more aloof. It seemed it was easier to relate to *one* other person in the beginning than to the whole group. But these pairings soon shifted and proved to be fleeting.

Group members were polite, on "good behavior," not stepping on anyone else's toes. It was many sessions before anyone disagreed with someone else or directly confronted or challenged someone. However, some members were willing to tell their perceptions of one another and to give some of their immediate thoughts and fantasies about other members.

At about the fourth session, I became the "junior therapist." In this role I was more distant and no longer felt like a member of the group. It was like taking myself out of the circle—not revealing any more about myself, but rather focusing on others. Thus it was possible to protect myself from exposure by placing myself temporarily "above" the others.

The group soon took on the character of a social microcosm. Each member seemed to be reacting in a characteristic way, taking on his habitual, comfortable role in a social group. The therapist was seen as a source of help; and members attributed superhuman powers to him. Norms began to evolve, and these incorporated the standards and values of the therapist. We shared feelings, both about being in the group and about outside and historical experiences. Each seemed to feel himself in an exposed situation. Feelings of cohesiveness developed and contributed to our being more productive than in the first several sessions. Some began to take risks in making disclosures about themselves. There was an expectation of honesty and some trust that one could be "real" in this situation. And masks began to be dropped. Members listened closely to what was being said, picked up on some of the nonverbal cues, and gave to one another—by questioning, acknowledging when a statement had touched them, expressing sympathy, and trying to offer explanations or interpretations. Much emotion was expressed from about the fifth or sixth session on, and it became clear that in a group there is more affect – and it develops more quickly – than in individual therapy.

REFERENCES

Greenson, R. (1967). *The Technique and Practice of Psychoanalysis*, pp. 128–133. New York: International Universities Press.

Lax, R. (1980). The rotten core: a defect in the formation of the self during the rapprochement subphase. In *Rapprochement: The Critical Subphase of Separation–Individuation*, ed. R. Lax, S. Bach, and J. Burland, pp. 439–456. New York: Jason Aronson.

Chapter 6
Engagement

In all forms of psychotherapy, the struggle with resistances, defenses, and transferences constitutes the major therapeutic work. Whereas in individual psychoanalysis a relationship is established between two persons (dyad), in analytic group psychotherapy the contract exists between the patient, the group therapist, and the therapy group (triad). All parties to the contract must be willing to engage with one another. *Engagement* refers to that quality of interaction in which the help-seeking persons believe that they can be helped by the "expert." This belief results from the therapist's interest and understanding, which the patient has experienced as empathic.

Engagement commences during the first interview, even if it is a pregroup interview. The prospective patient comes to the interview with one or more problems. The problem may be a physical symptom, anxiety, problems in living such as poor relationships with supervisors or inability to sustain a relationship, or maladjustment to life events such as separation, illness, or death. Patients usually know more than they are able to recognize or willing to reveal. Patients may have some vague notion of how they need to be helped with each type of problem (Stone 1983). Their expectations of therapy may not coincide with the therapist's recommendations; rather, they represent the patient's view and may contain an amalgam of transference wishes, need for greater self-esteem, strengthening of defenses, or urgency to bridge gaps due to alienation from others. The group therapist should be aware of these needs and should have tentative treatment goals in mind that do not run counter to the ones proposed by the patient. This helps to minimize initial resistance. While the group therapist need not be eclectic, the use of therapeutic techniques must be flexible as the patient changes and if the goals of therapy change. Slavson (1970) has called attention to what he labelled "sectarianism" in group psychotherapy:

> Eclecticism is more crucial to group therapy than to individual treatment. Because of the multiplicity of psychic factors in an assembly of persons, a unitary approach cannot but fail with a significant number of the participants. [p. 11]

ATTRACTIVE ASPECTS OF GROUPS

The therapist must first discover what the patient's resistances to therapy are and to what extent these resistances complicate engagement. The next step is to explore the patient's fears and wishes regarding entry into a group. Whereas some individuals may be shy in relating to strangers, others welcome a "stage" on which to gratify their exhibitionistic impulses. First and foremost, however, group therapy may appeal to some individuals because of the potential for catharsis and belongingness to a group that will understand and accept them. Other reasons for patients' seeking group therapy include avoidance of the individual therapist's scrutiny, support from peers, and the possibility to observe and to participate only when they feel ready.

Schwartz (1972) presented additional reasons for the attractiveness of group participation to potential members. The value of and belief in authority, so prevalent in the Judeo-Christian culture, are reexamined in a group setting, which allows for challenges of assumed authority and favors a distribution of power. Group therapy also encourages the individual to acquire new values regarding relationships with other groups, such as the nuclear family and social groups. New learning would involve such interpersonal skills as being able to allow for differences without oversensitivity, relating to authority without submission, and arguing without destroying friendships.

Last, but not least, the group experience neutralizes society's myths, such as the need to be rational, to keep one's feelings tightly controlled, to be quiet, and to obey authority. Instead, the group atmosphere stimulates individuals to think for themselves and to accommodate to external reality through their own efforts and through the understanding derived from their peers.

Individual psychoanalysis has been schematized and is predictable to some extent; this degree of certainty cannot be found in clinical analytic group psychotherapy. Both Schneider (1982) and Sandner (1982) observe that analytic group theory lacks a proven metapsychology. Scheidlinger writes, "An acceptable, global psychoanalytic group process theory or group psychotherapy theory is not in the cards, in the near future at least" (p. 21). Sandner comments, "Group analysis is a widely accepted therapeutic method, but the basic problems of theory and methodology are up to now not sufficiently worked out and investigated in a systematic manner" (p. 633). Of course, the reason for the lack of such theory and methodology is the fact that we have added a group to the basic dyadic process, making it a triadic one and one in which we are not able to predict the interactions of all the members. Slavson (1969) once computed that in a group of eight members there are 16,320 possible interactions!

It might seem to many therapists, particularly those engaged only in individual therapy, that the group modality is unproductive because variables cannot be controlled and predictions cannot be made with certainty. No therapist in any modality can exercise control over unpredictable life situations. However, the individual therapist has more control over the therapeutic situation because it contains only two people. The group therapist, having to deal with the interaction of many people, cannot exercise as much control over the therapeutic situation and the outcome of the interactions. As group therapists, therefore, we must be convinced from our own clinical experience that a group provides the patient with a therapeutic milieu and that the group itself will become a change agent (Kauff 1979, Wender 1963). The emotional reeducation occurring in the therapeutic milieu has been aptly described by Andrews (1964):

> The focus in therapy groups is largely on the ego level to produce alterations or additions to the current level of ego functioning, mainly in the area of object relations. The prime advantage of group is a corrective relearning of stable, positive object relations. [p. 491]

THE INITIAL PHASE

New patients disturb the status quo of an established group. By entering, they engage the group members and are engaged by them. The therapist observes what takes place and may intervene if a new member becomes too uncomfortable. If a new member is positively welcomed by the group and displays only positive feelings toward the group, it would be appropriate to explore the "hidden side" (i.e., any negative or ambivalent feelings).

Sophie was a young, single woman who had, with the help of counseling, detached herself from two sadomasochistic marriages. On the surface, Sophie would have been considered outgoing and friendly by the people with whom she interacted. Actually, she was a very private person who used her preference for being a "homebody" to wall out the external world and its demands.

Sophie had initially been reluctant to follow through on a recommendation for group therapy. She liked the idea but did not feel ready for it. After avoiding discussion of this topic for an extended period of time (during which the therapist was careful not to pressure her), she announced one day that she was ready to join a group immediately. Since it was characteristic of Sophie to be submissive to male

authority figures without voicing any resentment, her therapist became concerned about her sudden change of attitude. He predicted to her that repressed feelings would
reappear once she joined the group, and she and the therapist agreed that they would discuss these feelings in group
whenever they surfaced.

Sophie was friendly and outgoing in the group, giving the
impression of being sincere and wanting to be helpful to
others. While she volunteered information about her unsuccessful marriages, she made little attempt to reveal her
feelings. She was always ready to respond to other group
members and to be helpful to them. After a while, however,
when her inability to reveal her own feelings was pointed out
to her, she became much less participatory and stayed in the
background.

To engage her, the therapist focused on her many instances of blocking and helped her to identify the feelings
that were evoked during the group sessions and that had
been pushed out of her awareness. She said that while she
understood what was being asked of her, she felt unable to
respond to the request. Exploration of this revealed
transferential feelings toward the group and the therapist.

Sophie's transferential blocking in the group was
overdetermined and consisted of various character attitudes
and transferences. Sophie had been reluctant to join the
group because she felt it would be an invasion of her privacy,
but she was won over by her wish to please the therapist. In
the group she assumed the role she had played out in her
family—that of appointed caretaker and helper. Her relationship to female group members, in addition, was that of a
gossip partner, a role that her mother had foisted on her.
The family had no place for Sophie, or for her feelings and
wants. Resentments were to be kept under wraps and were
thus converted into fears and anxieties. Sophie was thus
unable to respond to the task of revealing personal feelings.

When the group therapist asked her to begin to relinquish
the familiar role and embark on an unknown journey (her
private world), she experienced him as critical and as setting

a task for her that made her feel inadequate. Once before she
had encountered such a situation in her own family. She had
admired her father for his scholarliness, but she knew that
intellectually she could not please him. Also, she resented
his emotional coldness and critical nature. Her compromise
solution was to identify with some of his traits—his private-
ness, his tendency to criticize and withhold. Thus, identification with the aggressor made it possible for her to maintain
him as an object.

Sophie exhibited these traits when the group wanted
more of her. If Sophie remained stuck in her previous
maladaptive solutions, no therapeutic gain would be possible. To prevent her from repeating her family history in the
group, it became necessary for the therapist to point out
repeatedly her evasiveness concerning her own opinions,
thoughts, feelings, unmet needs, and deep resentment for
having been put into such a role by her family.

When therapists start new groups, different forms of engagement are necessary. They cannot maintain a group climate before
they have helped the participants to become a group—to achieve
group cohesiveness. To do so, they must be more active initially
than at later stages. They must introduce the members to one
another or have them introduce themselves, and then lay down
the group standards, particularly the idea of confidentiality and
the interdiction of assaultive behavior.

In these initial sessions, the therapist can offer some sugges-
tions and interpretations of group process. For the most part,
however, the therapist tries to turn questions back to the group,
demonstrating a preference that the members talk to one another and indicating that more would be gained from such interaction. Group-as-a-whole interpretations are emphasized. At this
stage, the therapist attempts to establish a direct dyadic relationship between each patient and the group, for the moment
neutralizing what Foulkes (1972) has labelled "the oedipal triangle."

DeRosis and DeRosis (1971) noted that the early group phase
consists of stimulation, excitation, and mobilization; and Fried

(1976) observed that the idealized image of the therapist protects the group members from anxiety. When group therapists imply that they are unable to perform magic, it gives rise to the transfer of this magic to the collective group and arouses suspicion and antileader sentiments. Durkin (1964) elaborated that once the group has become disappointed in the therapist, the therapist is then cast into the role of "bad" preoedipal mother. These are trying times for group therapists, and according to Cooper (1978) they must do everything possible to help themselves feel worthwhile and maintain group homeostasis. Both Cooper and Bach (1957) maintained that the stage of disillusionment gives rise to regressive motivation on the part of the group members. According to Durkin (1964) and Saravay (1978), however, group development proceeds through several stages and recapitulates the psychosexual stages of infant development.

While Slavson (1966) was also in agreement that interaction between members and the establishment of object relations were paramount during the initial phase, he cautioned that interaction was the nexus of group therapy, although not its essence. Rather, the essence is the outcome of interaction and the promotion of insight.

ESTABLISHING A WORKING ALLIANCE

Having established group standards and modes of communication, treatment can move on to a different level. The therapist is now concerned with establishing a working alliance that will allow the group to deal with one another's resistances and transferences. Our goal is to have the group ally itself with the analytic attitude and to deepen the level of group and personal communication.

Konig's (1982) concept of a *working alliance* is based on the classical definition of the patient identifying with the work of the analyst. There exists no equality between group therapist and group patient; the therapist maintains his role at all times. Durkin (1964), presenting a somewhat different opinion, noted that once the transference toward the therapist as a "bad" mother has diminished and the group members see the therapist more realistically, the therapist is treated more like a peer.

According to Glatzer (1978), regressed patients identify more easily with their peers than with the therapist, leaving the latter in a somewhat neutral position, available for a working alliance. And both Konig and Glatzer stated that the presence of such an alliance is indicated when two conditions are fulfilled: (1) there is an emergence of aggressive material, and (2) patients use confrontations and interpretations meaningfully. This augurs well as an indication of the group members' ego development and adaptive processes. As Buirski (1980) so cogently observed, adaptation is an index of ego functioning, and the processes of adaptation and psychoanalytic change may be seen as synonomous.

THE MAGIC OF WORDS

The power and magic of words merit in-depth discussion. To some patients words have little emotional impact; they say one thing and mean another. Other patients experience words as an assault on the self. Words have developed very special meaning in our Judeo-Christian culture. The Book of John states, "In the beginning was the Word." Words have become associated with parental injunctions, religious and ethical considerations, unpleasant moments with teachers and physicians. There seems to be little emphasis on words as vehicles for neutral or joyful communication; thus the phrase "I am speechless" in the throes of powerful emotions.

Thus, words are usually associated with superego evaluations. Edwards (1984) did not believe that it was necessarily the superego alone that makes things intolerable. Based upon work by Bergler (1952), she postulated that the primitive ego-ideal provides the yardstick for the superego's indictment. The *ego-ideal* is an unconscious structure consisting of infantile grandiosity, omniscience, and introjections of parental images. This infantile omnipotence is projected onto authority figures in the form of idealizations. Comparing actual achievements to the ego-ideal evidences a discrepancy which results in an affective experience

of irritability, guilt, and depression. Patients will be encouraged
to come out of hiding and open themselves to interpretations only
if they can learn that "to err is human" and that one need not
endlessly atone for errors.

After many years of stasis in individual treatment with
another therapist, Louise expressed her wish to join a therapy group. Having grown up in a conservative family that
stressed accomplishment and moralistic values, she rebelled
and became involved with hippies and the drug culture.
Sensing her own alienation and isolation, she had undertak-
en, by herself, a complete withdrawal from drugs, and she
was proud of her accomplishment. She had held a responsible, well-paying position in the entertainment industry, but
she became disenchanted with these values, gave up her job,
took a menial position with low pay, and associated only with
people who had values similar to hers. Although she was able
to form heterosexual attachments, no relationship was sustained.
   When Louise entered the group, there was much discussion of relationships between men and women. Some of the
male group members referred in rather chauvinistic terms
to their female companions and to women in general. Although the women in the group resented this attitude, they
did not take the men very seriously. Louise was not specifically addressed, but just hearing the words bantered back
and forth was frustrating for her. She was reminded of her
family's values and could not tolerate the discussion. From
time to time, she had to leave the group sessions when her
emotions overwhelmed her. In a private session, she explained that the words were denigrating to her and voided
her accomplishments. Since she already felt inferior because
she was a woman and had planned her life accordingly, she
could not tolerate the impact of the words.

How can therapists deal with the impact of words? Primarily,
we must be careful to allow patients to have different values. To
diminish the severity of the superego, communications to group

members can be couched in neutral or humorous language, thus avoiding the severity that often characterizes authority-related statements. Group space must become play space, where members can try out new roles.

Anthony (1980) called attention to the similarity between therapy and play. He taught his patients to play spontaneously and to reverse roles in order to demonstrate that words are not engraved in stone. Similarly, Rossel (1979) recommended the use of jokes and humor in group therapy. It was his opinion that words could be treated like toys. Just as teddy bears can be pivotal in identity formation, so also are certain kinds of signs; and it is in fantasy, jokes, and humor that such objects and phenomena are involved. All verbal play suggests metaphorical use of language and allows people to negotiate claims and counterclaims, play with the definition of reality, and poke holes in pretensions and myths. Word magic permits us to go beyond the power of the senses and to question our confidence in the words we use daily. Humor plays on the boundary between thought and experience, with a sudden realization of the paradox that things are not what they seem. Real play always has serious intent—to establish a balance between external and internal material, between lightness and seriousness.

Kosseff, Epstein, and Tuttman (1982) agree that play in the therapy group effects personality changes. In fact, Kosseff believes that play is a precondition for change. The group therapist enables the patient who cannot play to learn to play. Healthy play offers the opportunity for trial relationships and for negotiating serious matters in a lighthearted way. Epstein stresses play as intrinsic to the development of the self, and Tuttman observes that play is never repetitious and permits for elements of surprise.

Karl was the newest group member and the youngest male in the group. Prior to his entrance, the group had been dominated by two middle-aged men. They saw Karl as an upstart who wanted to impress them with his knowledge and skills. When the two men rejected Karl's need for male friendship, he became unhappy. Although it seemed obvious that he was enraged, on the surface he became vague and dissociated. The group, aware of what was happening, invited Karl to make use of fantasy to express his feelings. Karl was able to reveal tentatively his wish to wrestle and fight with the two men. The group accepted his statement, and even the two men became interested and encouraging. Karl was thus able to relax and to handle the situation with some humor.

Transference Reactions

The third phase of group development deals with transference reactions. Having worked through their resistances, members are more prone to express their spontaneous feelings, as irrational as they seem. These affects may be directed toward the group-as-a-whole, specific group members, the therapist, or a combination of all of these.

As the group goes through its developmental phases, it must attend to several variables. For example, Sandner (1982) believed that the following five variables were interdependent: (1) the psychosocial competence of individual members in the service of mastery, (2) the specific situation into which the members of the group are brought together by the setting of the group leader, (3) the therapist's specific intervention technique and psychosocial competence, (4) the specific preoedipal, oedipal, or interactional constellation in the group-as-a-whole, and (5) the degree of regression and progression of all the members of the group as a collectivity, including the therapist, which leads to either very infantile or mature behavior. In other words, group phenomena must be processed analytically if their defensive meaning and the position of the transference is to be understood (Schneider 1982).

Yalom (1970), too, believed that the potency of the interpretation lies in the here-and-now, with recall of the past only helpful in understanding, not correcting, the behavior. Yalom assigns the greatest significance to the group process. It is an indispensable common denominator to all effective interactional groups: "The process focus is the power cell of these groups" (p. 127).

Yalom questions where else, except in therapy groups, it is permissible to examine in depth the here-and-now behavior or the nature of the immediately current relationships between people. Process commentary among adults is forbidden social behavior. When it surfaces in conflict situations, the battle is usually bitter and the chances for reconciliation slight.

During the period of transference expressions, the role of the therapist becomes more distinctive and active. It is necessary that the therapist make specific interpretations, and thus the situation corresponds to the triangular relationship to which Foulkes (1972) referred–patient, group, and therapist. The group has come out of its regressive phase and moves toward oedipal development, defined by Foulkes as the end stage of a maturational process.

From a structural point of view, Saravay (1975) wrote that the original regression induced by group formation has been reversed, with a gradual redifferentiation of the members' psychic systems. Nevertheless, this stage is a challenge to the group therapist.

We agree with Durkin (1964), who maintained that the therapist never knows all that goes on in a group. The highlights and individual histories of the patients help somewhat to orient the therapist. According to Durkin, the task is not made any easier by the fact that groups may not be interested in the transference of a particular member; they may be willing only to offer support. Also, transference constantly goes on in the outside world as an everyday event, unobserved by the group therapist. Only by attending to communication within the group does the therapist become curious. In our experience, transferences are not always subtle. More often than not, we are confronted with emotional outbursts that seem unreasonable and that seem to have come "from left field."

One evening Joan related to the group that a married man had fallen in love with her. She was anxious and sought the group's support.

Elizabeth, a single woman, refused to listen to or support Joan. This behavior was rather unusual for Elizabeth, who had been one of the more mature group members and was usually ready to listen to other members' stories. Contrary to her usual position, Elizabeth seemed quite put out and proceeded to lambaste Joan for her choice of partner. Enraged, she added that Joan should be a model for her and help her "win the race." But Joan's behavior, she said, was that of a loser, and as a result, both Joan and Elizabeth would "lose the race." In her rage, Elizabeth managed to turn the whole group against herself.

Analysis of this transferential reaction proceeded slowly and carefully. On the one hand, the therapist had to assure Joan that she had a right to her intuitive feelings and need not feel guilty. She had not done anything to Elizabeth. On the other hand, perhaps it was regrettable that Joan really could not be a model for Elizabeth, which left her in a lurch, dependent only on herself.

Only much later was the truth revealed. Elizabeth had wanted her mother to be a model for her. But her mother had been depressed, and her negative reaction to her daughter's birth had left Elizabeth's wish unfulfilled. In later life she looked to girl friends and bosses to be her models and was usually disappointed. Elizabeth blamed her mother for causing her difficulties in life. Joan had become her mother at that instant in group.

Peter, a long-term group member, suddenly announced that he had had enough of the group and of therapy in general. He had taken much of the group's time and had tried their patience by talking about his unsuccessful love affairs. The group had advised him that he seemed too perfectionistic when surveying his partners, and they questioned his need for inaccessible women. Peter had rejected many of the women he had dated; they were not pretty enough, not intelligent enough, or had other "flaws." Yet he professed love for a married woman who assured him that she loved him but had no intention of leaving her husband and children.

Peter had used incalculable amounts of group time talking

about his sufferings. Why did he now wish to reject the group as a reward for their patience? It was later revealed that Peter's mother had drummed into him that nobody would be good enough for him. On the other hand, his older brother had forced him to straighten out and do his chores. The successful brother had married a plain but motherly woman who had provided him with children of whom the couple were proud. Peter had resented his brother for his arrogance and for making him toe the line. At that moment in group, he had heard the members transferentially saying that he should straighten himself out and accept "second best."

Character problems are also manifested in transference aspects. For example, feelings of entitlement are highlighted in the group process.

Kate, a professional woman, had made productive use of therapy. She had individuated, become aware of her unconscious feelings, and made great strides both in therapy and in her outside life. Although things were generally going well for her, little everyday problems – unpaid bills, disagreements with her supervisors, physical discomfort – caused her to fly into temper tantrums. She would accuse the surprised group and therapist of not doing their jobs.

After a period of exploring Kate's tantrums, it was found that she considered the group a very special family, and the therapist a special parent. This made her a special person with a special place in life – no burdens and no responsibilities. After this interpretation was offered to her, Kate was able to handle her everyday problems better and more realistically.

As previously mentioned, a transference interpretation must be skillful and timely. The therapist cannot be too intrusive or interpret too early. The patient must tell his story with the accompanying affects. Regardless of the group's reaction, it behooves the therapist initially to accept the transference reaction as "real." These are genuine feelings being expressed, and there is the danger of narcissistic injury if the patient were to think that these feelings were not being given a hearing because they were "just" transference. On the other hand, the therapist must persist in curiosity and the need for exploration. Were the therapist not insistent on this therapeutic task, the expressions of transference would be only cathartic and would not result in personality change.

Change can come about only when the therapeutic process embraces both cognition and affective experience. As Konig (1982) remarked, the patient needs a certain distance between what he has just experienced and his observing ego in order to see what has been happening. The therapeutic process will oscillate between experiencing transference and thinking about it.

Saravay (1978) is of the opinion that change is brought about by identifications. In classical terms, the therapist, as the only common object of transference wishes, unites the total group. Phase-specific intermember transferences consolidate into a collective group transference toward the therapist when the common group identification is established. Through these internalized identifications with the therapist and with other members, therapeutic changes achieve internal stability.

We do not wish to imply that one-time or even two-time interpretations resolve resistances or transferences. The painstaking and laborious process has been illustrated by Glatzer (1969). This "working through" involves repeated clarifications over an extended period of time. Glatzer commented that removing the resistance of the unconscious ego enables the patient to accept the limitations of reality. We have often found that stressing that transference wishes are *wishes* helps the patient to become less afraid of them; their compelling character frequently frightens the patient, who believes them to be reality. Transforming insight into an affective experience leads to changes in character and behavior. Central to the working-through process is the suffering through and mastery of painful affects.

THE NARCISSISTIC AND BORDERLINE PATIENT

Group therapy practice today is almost devoid of the classically psychoneurotic patient. Instead we are confronted with characterological problems ranging from the neurotic and narcissistic character to borderline adjustments and ambulatory schizophrenia. The schizoid character may also be included in this diagnostic spectrum. Underlying these diagnostic categories are the narcissistic structures in varying degrees and the punitive superego, which hamper ego functions and the development of a coherent self-system. When such patients become members of a therapy group, special problems arise that call for parameters, or modifications, in technique.

Scheidlinger and Pyrke (1961), for example, describe a group in which the parameters had to be changed drastically to suit the population. In order to establish a supportive group climate, the therapist had to be more reality oriented and deal with the reality problems of the severely deprived women who composed the group. Scheidlinger and Holden (1966) relate that one therapist served refreshments and telephoned absent members to ensure continuous contact.

Earlier, Spotnitz (1957) had warned against analyzing and interpreting to borderline patients. Although not mentioning the term *masochism*, he clearly stated that any interpretations would be experienced by such patients as assaults on their fragile selves. He called on group treatment to help these patients outgrow their narcissism (and masochism) via identification processes in the group. Wolberg (1982) has taken a similar position, emphasizing the strong sadomasochistic elements in borderline patients.

While many practitioners seem to follow a trend in combining the treatment of narcissistic structures and the borderline syndrome, Fried (1971) preferred to address herself specifically to narcissism. She perceived the narcissistic patient as suffering from ego passivity and social isolation. Wanting the exclusive attention of the group leader and having little frustration tolerance, the patient seeks a powerful and magic helper, is preoccupied only with self, and looks for similar others. Corollary to this description is that the individual is able neither to have deep valid feelings about people nor to render objective judgments for his own good and interest.

Narcissistic patients have considerable resistance to developing transference (Rutan and Stone 1984). They do not trust the reliability of the other and resist acknowledging the importance of the soothing function of, as well as the merging with, the idealized object. Rutan and Stone recommended an empathic connectedness, allowing the narcissistic idealizing transference to take place, and concluded that empathic understanding allows the therapist to experience the ways in which these styles are attempts to shore up and protect a fragile sense of self.

It has been recommended by Wong (1983) that narcissistic patients be treated in combined individual and group therapy. Since such patients are easily scapegoated by the group because of their arrogance and exploitative behaviors, individual sessions provide a haven in which to vent aggression and to seek temporary relief from narcissistic injuries. Wong (1980) favored Kernberg's definition of the narcissistic transference: The patient denies the existence of the therapist as an independent human being.

The description of narcissistic pathology also seems to fit the borderline syndrome. Volatility is present in both narcissistic and borderline pathology, as is the reluctance to share the therapist with other group members. Some group therapists believe that the mechanism of projective identification poses severe problems when such patients are placed into groups, because they react to the group as if it represented an intrapsychic structure.

These patients repeatedly attempt to provoke the group and thus put themselves in danger of being scapegoated. Pines (1975) pointed out that such patients are full of strife and anger, and they attempt to destroy the "good breast" represented by the group. Whereas Masler (1969) preferred interventions on a group level, Pines described in detail how to treat such cases individually. He recognized that such patients need more time to become group integrated and therefore negotiated an agreement with them to stay in group until more benefits accumulated. He suggested the following guidelines for engagement:

1. Show the patient that he will always win.
2. Stress the similarities between the patient and other group members.
3. Initiate the working through of sadism and masochism.

Cooper (1978) concentrated on how to broaden the patient's perception beyond his narcissism. Foremost, the patient must be made to feel comfortable, with minimal threat to safety. She then appealed to the patient's narcissism to help him participate. Once this is accomplished, the patient must be taught to listen and to attend to the group process.

Agreeing with much that had previously been said, Roth (1979) commented that these patients suffer from an impairment in identity. Whereas the neurotic patient forms a relationship in which he wishes to be deeply understood, the narcissistic patient wants to be soothed. Roth recommended that the therapist be sensitive to these needs and give to this severely impaired patient what the group cannot give.

Roth's position is somewhat parallel to that of Kohut (1971), who permits an idealized transference to develop and does not interfere in that development by offering interpretations. Wong (1979) seemed in agreement with Roth when he suggested recognition and acceptance by the group of the patient's narcissistic needs. Instead of confrontational tactics, a more positive and supportive approach will help such patients to reveal more about themselves.

Our experience has shown the validity of the parameters just discussed. Engagement and integration in the group take much longer for narcissistic and borderline patients than for neurotic patients. The therapeutic approach for severely impaired patients must focus almost exclusively on their adjustment to the group rather than on intrapsychic conflicts. It is essential that the patient's fragile self be protected at all times and that sadomasochistic maneuvers not be responded to by either the group or the therapist. There are many pitfalls indeed, particularly when one misdiagnoses a patient as relatively functional and then sees unbounded narcissism make its appearance in the group.

Claire, a young woman, was focusing in individual therapy on her career problems. Here and there were indications that she was troubled about her marriage, her friendships, and living up to her ego ideal. She maintained a smiling facade, and it seemed impossible to connect with her deeper feelings. Group therapy was proposed. Since this woman was competent in her professional life and seemed to have sufficient ego resources to manage whatever she undertook, it seemed that her group entry would be no more difficult than the usual.

Initially, Claire maintained her pleasant face in the group. But soon the group became aware that she would not participate on an affective level. Words were used defensively and without connection to feelings. When the group asked her to talk about herself, they heard unlimited ambition and wishes for unrealistic self-aggrandizement, tinged with obsessional defenses and a chronically depressed affect. She managed to make the group her battleground and evoked negative responses from group members. This became a justification for her thinking that the group members were of "inferior" status, just "not good enough" for her.

The focus of the battle turned to whether she would continue group sessions because they were interfering with other appointments and responsibilities she had recently taken on, knowing full well that they would conflict with the group meetings. A compromise was worked out whereby she was permitted to arrive late to sessions. Even this proved to be only temporary, however. She complained that she felt harried and unable to benefit sufficiently from group treatment. In the end, she rejected the group and returned to individual treatment, leaving behind a very angry group.

Even with hindsight, it is impossible to say whether any other approach would have maintained Claire in the group. She had always been able to manipulate reality in such a way as to cause treatment interruptions and difficulties. Because she returned to the group therapist for individual treatment, it seems plausible that she preferred to maintain an idealization of the therapist and to bask in its glow.

The course of group therapy proceeded differently for Tom, who was an extremely schizoid person, afraid of any group interpretations or comments. He would come late to sessions and make himself comfortable in a corner, taking off his shoes and leaning back with his eyes closed. One should not come to the conclusion, though, that he was unaware of what was going on in the group. He had an uncanny ability to pick up the group theme as he was entering the room and would offer a few homilies on that theme. Even when interrupted while dozing, he was able to enter the discussion and make relevant comments. His strange manner was his way of making himself comfortable – of filtering out affect and entering the discussion when he felt in control.

We find that it is not helpful to confront styles of behavior that are designed to minimize anxiety and make the patient comfortable. The group therapist must be concerned with the members' comfort or discomfort and must instill hope in them. Every forward movement they make must be praised, while regressions must be accepted and patiently waited out, with the expressed hope that things might change in the future. Empathy with the members' suffering is of great help to them, as is being allowed to belong to a group in their own idiosyncratic fashion.

The therapeutic goal cannot be the same for all patients. Insight and interpretations help the healthier ones; maintenance of relationships, the less healthy. In most instances, the acceptance of the less healthy by the other group members, as well as their identification with common problems shared in the group, maintains these patients and makes them feel important.

REFERENCES

Andrews, E. (1964). The struggle for identity in mothers undergoing group therapy. *International Journal of Group Psychotherapy*

13:346–353.

Anthony, E. (1980). Reflections on 25 years of group psychotherapy. *International Journal of Group Psychotherapy* 30:23–49.

Bach, G. (1957). Observations on transference and object relations in the light of group dynamics. *International Journal of Group Psychotherapy* 7:64–76.

Bergler, E. (1952). *The Super Ego*. New York: Grune & Stratton.

Buirski, P. (1980). Toward a theory of adaptation of analytic group psychotherapy. *International Journal of Group Psychotherapy* 30:447–459.

Cooper, E. (1978). The pre-group: the narcissistic phase of group development with the severely disturbed patient. In *Group Therapy 1978: An Overview*, ed. L. Wolberg and M. Aronson, pp. 60–71. New York: Stratton Intercontinental.

DeRosis, H., and DeRosis, L. (1971). Concurrent psychoanalysis. *International Journal of Group Psychotherapy* 21:294–300.

Durkin, H. (1964). *The Group in Depth*. New York: International Universities Press.

Edwards, N. (1984). The preoedipal development of the critical superego and its manifestations in psychoanalytic group psychotherapy. *International Journal of Group Psychotherapy* 34:47–66.

Foulkes, S. (1972). Oedipus conflict and regression. *International Journal of Group Psychotherapy* 22:3–15.

Fried, E. (1971). The narcissistic cocoon: how it curbs and can be curbed. *Group Process* 4:87–95.

———(1976). The narcissistic beginning of a therapy group. In *Group Therapy 1976: An Overview*, ed. L. Wolberg and M. Aronson, pp. 155–166. New York: Stratton Intercontinental.

Glatzer, H. (1969). Working through in analytic group psychotherapy. *International Journal of Group Psychotherapy* 19:292–306.

———(1978). The working alliance in analytic group psychotherapy. *International Journal of Group Psychotherapy* 28:147–161.

Kauff, P. (1979). Diversity in analytic group psychotherapy: the relationship between clinical concepts and technique. *International Journal of Group Psychotherapy* 29:51–65.

Kohut, H. (1971). *The Analysis of the Self*. New York: International Universities Press.

Konig, K. (1982). Working relationships in analytic group psychotherapy. In *The Individual and the Group: Boundaries and Interrelations*, ed. M. Pines and L. Rafaelson, pp. 107–112. New York: Plenum.

Kosseff, J., Epstein, L., and Tuttman, S. (1982). Anchoring the self through group: aspects of change. Symposium of the Eastern Group

Psychotherapy Society, May 7.

Masler, E. (1969). The interpretation of projective identification in group psychotherapy. *International Journal of Group Psychotherapy* 19:441–447.

Pines, M. (1975). Group therapy with "difficult" patients. In *Group Therapy 1975: An Overview*, ed. L. Wolberg and M. Aronson, pp. 102–119. New York: Stratton Intercontinental.

Rossel, R. (1979). Humor and word play in group therapy. *International Journal of Group Psychotherapy* 29:407–414.

Roth, B. (1979). Problems of early maintenance and entry into group psychotherapy with persons suffering from borderline and narcissistic states. *Group* 3:3–22.

Rutan, S., and Stone, W. (1984). *Psychodynamic Group Psychotherapy*. Lexington, Mass.: Heath.

Sandner, D. (1982). Considerations regarding the state of theory in group analysis. In *The Individual and the Group: Boundaries and Interrelations*, ed. M. Pines and L. Rafaelson, pp. 631–637. New York: Plenum.

Saravay, S. (1975). Group psychology and the structural theory: a revised psychoanalytic model of group psychology. *Journal of the American Psychoanalytic Association* 23:69–89.

_____(1978). A psychoanalytic theory of group development. *International Journal of Group Psychotherapy* 28:481–507.

Scheidlinger, S., and Holden, M. (1966). Group therapy of women with severe character disorders: the middle and final phases. *International Journal of Group Psychotherapy* 16:174–189.

Scheidlinger, S., and Pyrke, M. (1961). Group therapy of women with severe dependency problems. *American Journal of Orthopsychiatry* 31:776–785.

Schneider, P. (1982). Interpreting analytical group psychotherapy, more specifically the individual interpretation and the group interpretation. In *The Individual and the Group: Boundaries and Interrelations*, ed. M. Pines and L. Rafaelson, pp. 487–498. New York: Plenum.

Schwartz, E. (1972). Why group now? *Psychiatric Annals*, vol. 2, no. 3.

Slavson, S. R. (1966). Interaction and reconstruction in group psychotherapy. *International Journal of Group Psychotherapy* 16:3–12.

_____(1969). The anatomy and clinical applications of group interaction. *International Journal of Group Psychotherapy* 19:3–15.

_____(1970). Eclecticism versus sectarianism in group psychotherapy. *International Journal of Group Psychotherapy* 20:3–13.

Spotnitz, H. (1957). The borderline schizophrenic in group psychotherapy. *International Journal of Group Psychotherapy* 7:155–174.

Stone, W. (1983). The curative fantasy in group psychotherapy. In *Group Therapy Monograph #10*, pp. 10–35. New York: Washington Square Institute.

Wender, L. (1963). The psychodynamics of group psychotherapy. *Journal of the Hillside Hospital* 12:134–139.

Wolberg, A. (1982). *Psychoanalytic Psychotherapy of the Borderline Patient.* New York: Thieme-Stratton.

Wong, N. (1979). Clinical considerations in group treatment of narcissistic disorders. *International Journal of Group Psychotherapy* 29:325–345.

_____(1980). Combined group and individual treatment of borderline and narcissistic patients: heterogeneous versus homogeneous groups. *International Journal of Group Psychotherapy* 30:389–404.

_____(1983). Fundamental psychoanalytic concepts: past and present understanding of their applicability to group psychotherapy. *International Journal of Group Psychotherapy* 33:171–191.

Yalom, I. (1970). *The Theory and Practice of Group Psychotherapy.* New York: Basic Books.

Chapter 7
Group Dynamics

There have been many questions and discussions in the literature about whether groups subvert the individuality of their members, and about whether, in so doing, they superimpose a "group mentality." Particularly in the field of group therapy, opinions have been sharply divided between those who believe that the dynamics of groups are antitherapeutic and those who believe that it is possible to utilize these dynamics to clarify therapeutic issues.

Group dynamics has been defined as a field of inquiry about the nature of groups, the laws of their development, and the interrelationships of individuals, groups, and larger institutions. Through group dynamics, adjustive changes occur in the group-as-a-whole, brought about by changes in any part of the group. Temporary instabilities arise out of conflict between individuals in the group, as well as between subgroups.

Interest in the field of group dynamics has been long standing on the part of sociologists, anthropologists, educational psychologists, and social psychologists. But it remained for Kurt Lewin (1951) to conduct experiments, scientifically organize data, and establish the first research center explicitly devoted to research on group dynamics, a term popularized by Lewin. Group dynam-

ics and its applications were initially studied by the National
Training Laboratories at Bethel, Maine, but the research was
eventually moved to a Center at the University of Michigan in
Ann Arbor.

The argument about individualism versus group dynamics has
been well summarized and reviewed by Cartwright and Lippitt
(1957). They saw the group as mobilizing powerful forces that
could produce both good and bad consequences for the individual.
Ideally, however, with an understanding of group dynamics, the
good effects would be maximized. The dilemma was clearly
stated:

> We seem, then, to face a dilemma: The individual needs
> social support for his values and social beliefs; he needs to
> be accepted as a valued member of some group which *he*
> values; failure to maintain such group membership produces
> anxiety and personal disorganization. But, on the other
> hand, group membership and group participation tend to
> cost the individual his individuality. [p. 91]

Cartwright and Lippitt observed that, indeed, aspects of individual values were subverted by group norms. They saw the solution, however, in the makeup of the group. If the group was
heterogeneous and allowed members the freedom to deviate, the
group-as-a-whole could then bring about creative solutions to
conflicts. Because each group is made up of members who are
also loyal members of other groups and have unique individual
interests, each group must continuously cope with the deviancy
of its individual members. Resolving these conflicting interests
does not weaken the individual or the group, but rather demonstrates how members can be interdependent as well as independent, thereby strengthening both the individuals and the group.

Durkin (1964) attempted to reconcile the views of group
dynamicists with those of the psychoanalysts:

> Group dynamicists continued to define the group as a struc-
> ture that emerges from individuals in constant dynamic
> interaction with one another. The individuals are considered

to be interdependent parts of a larger whole which is different from the sum of its parts. [p. 24]

Two group therapists who used a group-dynamic orientation were Bion (1955) and Foulkes (1965). Bion distinguished between the work climate and the emotional climate of a group. He observed that the work activity of a group is influenced by certain emotional states that are nonpurposive and not under conscious control, indicating that the emotional climate of a group is maximized if the leader assumes a nondirective stance. Foulkes saw the group as a network that is different from the individual members who participate in it. To understand the individual, it is necessary to understand the whole network. It is also important, however, to understand how the individual affects the network. Foulkes addressed not the individual members, but rather the group themes.

In using the term *group dynamics*, we are recognizing the fact that there are group-determined phenomena in every group. Certain processes occur within a group due to the simple fact of its just being *a group*. These processes are then conceptualized in group-dynamic terms. What we *see* are interactions between individuals who are members of the group. But the results of these interactions are abstracted at the group level, and understanding these abstractions offers us a greater likelihood of achieving desired consequences in working with groups.

Thus, *group dynamics* are the context within which psychotherapy takes place. If we can see the *individual* dynamics within the context of the *group* dynamics, we may be better able to use the group for therapeutic purposes, as opposed to just doing consecutive individual therapy while other members observe.

Group dynamics includes such concepts as group structure, status and roles, traditions, mood, theme, pressures, and norms.

STRUCTURE

Within any group there is a regularity in communication among group members. Each member of the group tends to be fairly consistent in the number of interactions he has during a therapy session, and some members are more active than others. Each group tends to develop its own equilibrium in terms of the overall rate of interaction, as well as in terms of who interacts with whom and the types of interactions that take place.

Each group member tends to interact more frequently with certain members than with others, and to interact in certain predictable ways. In some groups, two or three people may dominate while others take a back seat; in other groups, everyone interacts and there is more equality of participation. For example, Sally, the most active woman in one therapy group, usually talked to Phil and Fred, the two most active men, and looked to them for approval, support, and understanding. She seldom looked at Nora but obviously competed with her for the attention of these two men. In another group, the four males as a subgroup tended to dominate each session, talking to one another and looking to one another for support, while the four females as a subgroup provided an interested, though sometimes critical, audience.

Spectators watching either group through a one-way mirror or seeing a videotape of a group session could report who tended to interact with whom and whether the interaction tended to be positive or negative, whether it was protective or nurturant, attacking or rebuffing, defensive or competitive. And after a series of such group sessions were observed, there would be a consistency reported in the interaction of the members. Thus, we can refer to *patterns of relating* and even draw diagrams of these patterns for a given session.

When these patterns of relating persist over a period of time, we refer to the *stability* in the relationships between group members. Such stability lends *structure*, which members as well as observers are aware of and can describe. Thus, the structure of the group emerges from the interactions of the members, and the structure changes as the members change. The relationships may gradually shift over a more extended period of time, and we may see some minor shifts in the structure, such as changes in pairings, alliances, oppositions, and subgroupings, as in the following example:

One evening in group, Helen complained that Phil and Fred seemed always to talk only to Sally and that Sally directed most of her remarks to Phil. Nora joined in, saying that she had been noticing this for a long time and was annoyed by it because there had been sessions during which she felt she had supported Phil and Fred when each was going through difficult times. Lester agreed with this view, but added that he himself did not expect much attention from anyone because he usually did not say much in group anyway. Phil accepted these remarks, admitting to Helen that he had not been aware of this pattern, although he was aware that he had some special feelings for Sally. Fred defensively said that there had been a period when he and Nora had talked more to each other, but then she had rejected his advice to her once, and he had decided to "mark her off."

In the next session, Phil seemed to make a special effort to talk to both Helen and Nora, and they responded to his questions and comments. In fact, Helen, in this session and subsequent ones, spoke only to Phil, as the most significant person for her, and he responded, forming a new pair in the group. Lester began to make an obvious effort to become more active and to make at least one or two comments in each session. On the other hand, Sally became less active for several sessions, seeming to observe the others more.

The equilibrium of a group is disrupted whenever a member leaves or a new member enters; such changes produce differences in the number and kinds of interactions each member engages in, and there may be a shift in who interacts with whom. Thus, the exit or entrance of a member will affect the structure of the group.

STATUS AND ROLE

It is obvious to the group members and the group leader within any group that certain members have a higher status than others. The members themselves can identify—and sometimes do—who is a "central person" and who is a "fringe person." Such status may come from having been a member of the group for a longer time or from being physically attractive or verbally facile or from having any other characteristics the group admires and values. Low status, on the other hand, may result from being quiet in the group or appearing ill-at-ease or from unattractive behaviors or disabling physical characteristics. Position in the group affects not only the way others behave toward a member, but also the member's own self-esteem.

High-status members have more influence in the group. What they say is considered more significant and more worthwhile than the same statement made by another member. Their opinions are solicited and valued, while low-status members may be ignored or their statements devalued or disregarded. As a member becomes more "attractive" or "impressive," his opinion is more valued and his ability to influence the group increases.

> When Phil spoke in group, members did not contradict or disagree with him, even when they knew he was wrong; they might simply refrain from comment. But when Lester spoke, members often did not take him seriously or even criticized him for what he had said, regardless of its accuracy. And he would then back down.

Group members are also aware that each member has certain predictable behaviors or statements under specific predictable circumstances; at times the group may even become a "chorus," with a high-status member joining the person in simultaneously saying the words.

Certain group roles accompany high status, while other roles are associated with low status. For example, a high-status member may more often be seen in a parental or courageous or worldly role, while a low-status member may more often be seen in a child-like or foolish or stupid role.

The central dynamics of each member seem to be portrayed in the role the member takes in the group over an extended period of time; this could be referred to as his "characteristic trait." For example, Sam is seen by his therapy group as always inviting others to "chase" him. He will suggest something about himself, such as an early experience or a current attitude, but will then "tease" the group by not elaborating or explaining and then playing hide-and-seek with other members who pursue him with questions, coaxing, bullying, or other efforts to get him to say more.

In a specific session, however, a member may take on certain roles appropriate to that session, becoming, for example, the compromiser, the assistant therapist, the bully, or the helpless child. Roles may be reciprocal within a given session. For example, if one member plays a child, another may play her parent; if one member acts shy and withdrawn, another may be more solicitous and encouraging. These roles and interactions may shift from one session to another.

TRADITIONS

Each group tends to develop its own traditions, customs, and expectations of members. One group may have built a tradition of observing birthdays in a special way or celebrating certain holidays. Some groups have a custom of gathering together before group in the waiting room and chatting together as a warm-up before therapy. Other groups may hang around outside the therapy building for a short time after the session ends.

In many groups it is customary for members to take the same seats from one week to the next, while in other groups the seating shifts each week.

In one group, Toni always sat at the far end of the couch, nearest to the therapist and far from the other members. Other group participants changed their seats from week to week, although the leader preferred one general location. One evening, when Toni arrived a few minutes late, Steve, a newcomer, was sitting in her seat. As soon as she entered the room, she walked directly to the couch, stood in front of him,

and said "Move!" – and he did. No one else in the group would
have considered sitting in *her* place since they knew the
strong feelings she had about it. It had become traditional to
leave the space open for Toni, even though the other members varied their seating from one session to the next.

MOOD

The *group mood* refers to the predominant feeling tone during a therapy session. Some sessions may have a serious tone,
with much activity and participation by everyone. Some sessions are "heavy" and slow, with little interaction and many
periods of silence. Other sessions may seem playful, with members joking about their defenses, laughing, and even at times
becoming giddy. The group mood refers to the atmosphere or
"climate" within the room, which in some sessions can be protective, warm, and helpful, and in other sessions, challenging and
combative.

One evening in group, Ruth began talking the moment
everyone was seated. She said she had been miserable all
week and was still mourning the death of her sister, although
more than a year had passed. First Ruth expressed to the
group, as she had a year before, her anger toward her
brother-in-law for his actions during the last few days of her
sister's life; but then she also expressed anger against herself for not yet forgiving her brother-in-law. Group members
tried in various ways to be helpful, pointing out that no one
could have prevented the death, and trying to understand
why Ruth was "so hard on herself." She warded off and
pushed away all help and became more and more unhappy,
moving from anger to tears. As the group continued to
experience their powerlessness to change the situation, they
withdrew into themselves, experiencing the frustration,
hopelessness, and despair that Ruth had felt about her
sister's death and about her continued mourning. A heavy,
dark cloud seemed to hang over the room.

Another session of the same group started with Carl's describing his wedding five days earlier. The members enjoyed his happiness and joked a little about his new roles as husband and stepfather. Nancy then informed the group that she had been invited to a Halloween party which was to be given the next weekend by a male co-worker in whom she had expressed some interest. She was a bit self-conscious and giddy as she described how he had invited her, and she went on to describe her costume for the party. In a good-humored way, the group teased her about her hopes and expectations for the developing relationship. She laughingly confessed that she had not planned to tell the group about the party, but had gotten caught up in the atmosphere surrounding Carl's marriage. Although the ensuing interaction focused on her relationships with men, and especially with men in the group, and then moved on to discussions of the men's relationships with women in the group, there was a lightness and camaraderie in the group mood.

THEME

The *theme* refers to the issues the group is working on in a given session, the group's current concerns. The theme, as might be anticipated, tends to change from one week to the next, although at times the group will continue on one theme for several sessions.

It would be expected that during its early sessions, the group would be concerned about dependency on the therapist and the need for support and nurturing by the therapist, as well as about their desire for guidance about what should be discussed and how it should be discussed. After many sessions, the group's concern will shift to issues of control or to expressions of anger and aggression, but with many sessions still focused on what the members "want" from the therapist and on whether the therapist is "giving" enough. Further along in the life of the group, we can anticipate issues of competitiveness, sexuality, identity, and intimacy, with more focus on the relationships among the group members. They might express concern about one another, as well as sympathy and affection. However, sessions will occasionally center on the "ungiving parent" or on the desire for support, and some sessions will be filled with aggression.

POWER

The group provides support for its individual members. For example, the group may help a member mobilize to a significant action outside the group. A therapy group member may commit himself to an action and "report back" to the group, whereas individually he might not have felt compelled to follow through with it.

> Harriet, a woman in her late 30s, had been complaining for some time about her mother's mistreatment and rejection of her, along with mother's intrusiveness in her life. After offering some sympathy about the difficult situation, the group questioned Harriet about why her mother's opinion was still so important to her and why she could not confront her mother. They urged Harriet to assert herself and to tell her mother that she, Harriet, knew how she wanted to dress and how she wanted to furnish her own apartment, and that she would welcome her mother's visits but did not want to hear her criticisms and denigration. Hesitatingly, Harriet said she might *try* to talk to her mother. The following week, Harriet told the group that for the first time in her life she had been able to handle her mother in a way she previously never even could have conceived of.

This type of "reporting back" to the group is common. Having disclosed a plan or intention to the group, the member tends to follow through on the "commitment" to the group.

> Henry, who had been dissatisfied for some time with his very small studio apartment, told the group that he was going to look for something more comfortable. Group members explored his feeling that he did not deserve anything

better than what he had. Nothing happened for several weeks. Then one evening he announced that he had found a lovely one-bedroom apartment in the same complex and had arranged to sign the lease during the coming week.

As Cartwright and Lippitt (1957) have pointed out, "groups mobilize powerful forces which produce effects of the utmost importance to individuals." A group member may alter his opinion or attitude either because he cannot withstand group pressure or because he begins, through group discussion, to see the situation differently.

In one group, Ben had taken a temporary leave to go to England on business. While he was away, he wrote a letter to the group stating that he thought that Lara, who was in only group therapy, should also go into individual therapy. Freda spoke up first, saying how nice it was of Ben to take time during his business trip to write and to show such concern for Lara. However, after the other members strongly criticized him for expressing his hostility toward Lara in this way— from a distance rather than when he was in the room, where he would have to interact with her and with the other group members—Freda said she had changed her mind and that she agreed with the other members.

More pressure is felt when the members have a strong sense of belongingness, and members show a greater readiness to be influenced by one another in a more cohesive group that they see as meeting their needs. In fact, some group members may modify their out-of-group behavior in anticipation of other members' comments.

It is usually uncomfortable for a group member to maintain a position in opposition to the group, especially when the group is communicating its opinion of the member as unreasonable, irrational, illogical, or foolish. Under these circumstances, the person may rethink his decision or modify his plans and accept the influence of the group.

Louis reported to the group one evening that he and his wife were considering having another baby. The group questioned the wisdom of this. He already had two children, he had taken on a large mortgage in buying a house, and he was working at two jobs in order to earn enough money to support his family. It was suggested that he talk to his wife about postponing the pregnancy for a while. Giving some thought to their comments, he agreed that it might be better not to rush into having a third child. He was apparently able to influence his wife also, at least for a while. She took on a part-time job in order to contribute to the family income. About ten months later, however, he announced that she was pregnant.

At the extreme, a group may "push out" a member who is too deviant from the other members if they find they cannot influence such a member.

VALUES

As the individual members become closer and form a group, they begin to share common values and beliefs. For one thing, they share the idea that therapy can be helpful. Related to this, they value "honesty"—being oneself in the group rather than pretending to be something else. Also, they value active participation. Concomitantly, they value empathy and trying to understand "where the other person is coming from."

The group values indirectly influence the individual members who have internalized these values, and these values affect their behavior. There is a commitment to "work" on problems and to strive for open examination of thoughts, feelings, and actions, although at times there may be unconscious resistance or regression.

In trying to understand or make predictions for any specific group, the important values and standards of that particular group must be taken into account.

Norms

Norms are the shared ideas of group members about what should and what should not be done in a group; how members should feel as well as act; and perhaps even what should be accomplished in the group and how it should be accomplished. The norms provide standards for behavior accepted as legitimate. In every group, there are certain expected and prohibited behaviors. They may be stated or assumed, but the norms provide guidelines for the individual member.

The norms usually are not specifically stated as "rules," but rather are vague ideas in the minds of group members about behaviors that are appropriate or inappropriate under various circumstances, although some norms may initially be presented by the group leader to members before they enter the group; such norms include those of confidentiality, violence, payment of fees, absences, and latenesses. In addition to direct statements, the group leader may also "teach" by supporting certain actions or by the kind of interpretations made in the group. A newcomer to a group does not know the unspecified norms and only through experience learns the meaning given by the group to various behaviors and interactions—what the group approves and what it disapproves, what it regards as "acceptable" and what is not acceptable. In fact, a newcomer may even learn that the significance of a certain behavior varies according to *who* does it or according to the *circumstances* under which it is done.

Norms may prescribe how one should or should not behave toward the other members; for example, norms may dictate how interpersonal issues are to be managed. Or they may indicate how one should or should not express feelings. Such norms will vary from one group to another in the specifics and the nuances of interacting and expressing feelings.

Some norms may be verbalized by members, either before or after the act. Members may encourage "do more of that" or may scold "don't do that again." Members evaluate what is wrong and what is acceptable. For instance, in a late evening group, Richard always reminded latecomers that "we start at 8:00 P.M." Whenever anyone arrived late, they glanced directly at him as they entered and sat down. And sure enough, each time, he pointedly looked at the clock and commented on the exact time.

The norms may also make clear the privileges and obligations of group members – the rights and duties. These would be expected to change as a member's position changes in the group from, for example, "newcomer" to "veteran."

Norms may prescribe – "You *should* have done it this way" – or proscribe – "You should *not* have done it that way." They may be implied if a member encourages another, "Do more of what you just did with him," or when a member discourages another, "Don't ever again do what you just did to her." Or they may be overtly stated: "That is inappropriate; this is appropriate."

William had been discussing his interpersonal relationships in an objective, detached way. Ron finally interrupted and said, "You sound just like a textbook, William." Sally then pointed out that William was being formal and distant rather than personal, and she stated that this was not appropriate.

In another session, Helen, a recent member, said she felt that people were attacking her, and she wanted group members to be nice to her. Frank answered that the purpose of group is *not* to be nice but to be honest – so you can see and hear your effect on other people and, in the subsequent interactions, see more about yourself. He then went on to say that he did not think that the group members were attacking her, but rather that when people expressed their own feelings about, or observations of, her behaviors, Helen was taking it as an attack or criticism. This was her own problem.

Some norms become apparent only when they are violated. Thus the actions of a new member, or a deviant member, often cause the norms to be made more explicit.

One evening, Tammy brought a brown paper bag into the group room and put it beside her feet on the floor. As the session began, Don started sniffing, looked around the room, and finally spotted the bag. He asked Tammy what she had in the bag, adding that he was disturbed by the smell. She said it was chicken; and he suggested that she put it outside the room so that it would not distract the group. She complied, and as she reentered the room she said that she had not realized it would have this effect. She then went on to explain that she had not eaten dinner and planned to eat the chicken after group. She then offered to share some of it with Don. In response, Don simply said, "It is better not to bring food into the therapy room." But at the beginning of the next session, Don spontaneously reported to the group that after the last session he and Tammy had eaten the chicken together in the waiting room.

In stating what should *not* be done in a group session, the members often clarify their own ideas about what *should* be done. They may then try to get the deviant members to conform to their norms—to look at themselves more closely, for example, or to explore feelings more deeply. On the other hand, a veteran group member may use the innocence of a new member as an excuse to violate a group norm.

One night, Roger said he was going to Hong Kong the following week on business and would have to miss the group session. Gloria, the newest member, began to question him about Hong Kong. Had he ever been there before? Yes. What was it like? What did he do there? Did he have time to do other things besides business? What sights did he see? Roger responded cordially to each question, which then led to another question.

Finally Susan exclaimed, "What's going on here? I can't stand it anymore. This is *not* therapy." The other two women and two men, who had been silently observing Roger and Gloria, immediately echoed Susan's feelings. Oscar stated emphatically, "It is certainly *not* therapy, and it is something that could be discussed *after* the group session." Roger admitted that he had realized that it was not therapy and not appropriate to talk about, but he was going along with Gloria because he did not want to get into "deep stuff" tonight. Walter said he had been considering whether to break in and do what Susan had done and was glad she did it. And Shirley said she had something important to talk about tonight, and she was glad that Susan had stopped the "small talk."

Conflict sometimes leads to a specified norm. In one group, for example, there was a confrontation between the smokers and the nonsmokers, and a compromise solution evolved. There was to be *no* smoking during the therapy sessions, but smoking was permissible in the after-sessions.

Most new members will conform to the group norms in order to be accepted by the group. If a new member persists in not conforming to the group norms, however, the group may criticize or reject such a person and precipitate his leaving.

Theresa had been talking about how difficult it had been to be with her mother on their last visit. Her mother had been critical, as usual, and demanding, self-involved, and petty. After being in the same room for a while with her mother, Theresa would have to leave because her frustration would build to the point of exploding. Through this adjustment, however, she had been able to spend an entire weekend with her mother. The group members questioned her about some of the feelings that the weekend had evoked and about how she had controlled herself so as to avoid the old, familiar arguments and the usual sudden departure. Theresa talked about having seen her mother from a different perspective this time and realizing that she didn't *have* to get caught up in defending herself or attacking back. Leonard said that he could not do this yet. On his visit to his mother, as soon as she would begin making emotional demands on him, he would go "wild." His visits had thus been few and far between in recent months.

Then Sol, the newest member, said he would like to help Theresa. He said there were many things about his father that he just could not stand. But this past Sunday, he had visited his parents and decided just to "surrender" to the situation and to make himself *enjoy* all the things about his father that he could not stand—and it had worked! He got through the day without becoming angry. Theresa bristled, asking, "Are *you* giving *me* advice about how *I* should feel around my mother?" When Sol said yes, Theresa became angrier. She saw what he had done as submitting to a parent and denying his own reactions. She said she was proud that she had been able to maintain her integrity by acknowledging her own feelings to herself and not acting on them, and in that way had gotten through the weekend, for the first time, without any scenes. Some members tried to question Sol about the feelings he had had when his father was acting dictatorial or disregarding others' wishes while making arbitrary decisions. Other members tried to point out the inconsistency of "enjoying" what one cannot stand. But Sol refused to admit that he had any feelings other than pleasure during the day with his father or that even in retrospect he felt angry or resentful.

This interaction continued for some time, with the entire group trying to get Sol to look at the incongruity of what he was saying. He would not budge from his position. Then, suddenly, George became angry at Sol and said that Sol reminded him of his father; there was no getting through to him either. Cindy said that she felt irritated but realized it was because she could see some of herself in Sol. Cathy sympathized with Sol, seeing his advice-giving to Theresa and his subsequent behavior as defensive—to protect himself from opening up in the group. Stan tried to toss it off lightly by saying that that was "just the way Sol was" and no one was going to persuade him to be different. But the others tried to encourage Sol to look at himself in relationship to both his father and the group members. Finally, sensing the futility of their interaction with Sol, several raised the question of whether he really belonged in the group.

Cohesive groups are less tolerant of deviance than are noncohesive groups, in which such deviance takes on less significance. On the other hand, in cohesive groups, members are more willing to accept the influence of other members and to conform to the group norms. Members who feel very attached to the

group, who value their membership in the group, will conform to
the norms more than will members who place low value on the
group or who remain on the fringes of the group. In any group,
however, some norms will be more strongly adhered to, while
other norms will be less strictly enforced.

Different groups will have different concerns and different
ways (direct and indirect) of maintaining their norms—that is, of
exercising social control and pressuring members to conform. A
member may be positively affected in a session by recognition,
praise, or affection from others, and negatively affected by
others' criticism, ridicule, or teasing. In fact, even in anticipating
certain responses, especially from certain "central figures" in the
group, a member may modify what he is saying, adapt his
behavior, or even change his attitude.

Members' attitudes about the norms become apparent in their
attempts to maintain or change them. The norms in some groups
may be quite flexible, whereas the norms in other groups may be
rather rigid.

One evening in group, Frank asked Nancy, "Why do you
dislike me so much? I see you looking annoyed and irritated
with me when I'm talking." Nancy answered, "Sometimes
you start talking about your self-image and your insecurity
in here, and you will be making a good point, but then you go
on and on, and it becomes a boring monologue, and I get fed
up."

Tom responded, "I think *each* of us should take responsibility for stopping anyone who is going on in a monologue.
Otherwise it's a disservice to the group as well as to the one
who is talking. *We* don't get anything from what he is saying,
and he is provoking negative feelings in the rest of us, so we
reject him, and then he thinks less of himself." This idea had
not been enunciated in the group before, and it implied
certain norms: (1) It is desirable that members other than
the speaker also benefit from what the speaker is saying,
and (2) It is not "good" to invite rejection, which then affects
one's own self-esteem.

Group members internalize the norms that have arisen from
the ongoing interaction in the group. Each individual will, to

some extent, direct his own behavior in terms of the anticipated response of specific others, as well as of the group-as-a-whole.

Norms may thus evolve about being personal and looking at oneself, exploring feelings, managing interpersonal issues, and the privileges and obligations of members, as well as the rights, duties, and responsibilities of members. There may be more specific norms about "taking over," bringing food into the therapy room, indulging in monologues, usurping "reserved seats," and so on. In any group, some norms will be strongly adhered to, while other norms will be understood but not so strongly enforced. Members will conform to the group norms in order to be accepted by the group. For those who are not concerned about being accepted by the group, however, or who may seek to be rejected as a way of leaving the group, the norms do not have the same power.

REFERENCES

Bion, W. (1955). Group dynamics: a review. In *New Directions in Psychoanalysis*, ed. M. Klein et al., pp. 440–447. New York: Basic Books.

Cartwright, D., and Lippitt, R. (1957). Group dynamics and the individual. *International Journal of Group Psychotherapy* 7:86–102.

Durkin, H. (1964). *The Group in Depth*. New York: International Universities Press.

Foulkes, S. H. (1965). *Therapeutic Group Analysis*. New York: International Universities Press.

Lewin, K. (1951). *Field Theory in Social Science*. New York: Harper.

Part III
Working with Groups

Chapter 8
Interventions of the Therapist

Group therapy is a modality different from individual therapy, with its own techniques and goals (Anthony 1971). Individual therapy focuses primarily on intrapsychic dynamics; group therapy focuses more on interpersonal relationships, social adaptations, and ego functioning. The group becomes an integral part of the therapeutic process and provides what individual therapy cannot (Freud 1959): opportunities for reality testing, for validation of one's own observations and interpretations, and for immediate affective experiences in relationships with others.

Feedback from the other members helps patients become more aware of their effect on others and therefore more familiar with themselves. At the same time, group members experience their own immediate reactions to one another, learn to identify and discuss their feelings, and practice comparing their own reactions to those of other members. They may see aspects of themselves in other group members and observe how these aspects are responded to—by others in the group and *by themselves*. A group can help one discover that one is not unique or strange in one's problems or reactions; others have similar problems, character traits, and attitudes. Each member may notice that there are various ways of coping with the same problem and

145

may find in another group member a model for new ways of responding or behaving. At the same time, the group may allow the individuals to differentiate themselves from other members and consequently to develop increased awareness, and perhaps increased appreciation, of themselves. Helping someone else in the group may also improve the member's self-esteem.

If group therapy is to be effective, the therapist must fulfill several functions, perhaps the most important of which is to set up and maintain conditions that contribute to the stability and cohesiveness of the group (Yalom 1975). Only if group members continue in the group can they gain something from the experience; and only if they are willing to trust one another will they participate openly and reveal hidden parts of themselves.

It is crucial that the therapist facilitate meaningful interaction between the group members. It is not just that the members talk; the talk is for the purpose of understanding oneself and others, one's impact on others, and their impact on oneself. In addition, the therapist's interventions can contribute to the stability and cohesiveness of the group, can encourage the participation and involvement of the members, and can facilitate meaningful interaction. An *intervention* is any comment, question, gesture, or other action of the therapist that affects interaction within the group, raises questions as to what is going on, works toward an interpretation, or is otherwise therapeutic.

As long as the group is interacting in a meaningful way, the therapist generally will not interrupt the flow. A too-active therapist discourages contact among the group members and encourages the members to remain passive and dependent. On the other hand, the therapist often does not have to say anything; someone in the group will often say what the therapist had in mind, and it is usually preferable for a statement to come from a group member rather than from the therapist.

When a group is in its beginning phase, however, or if the group is composed of more disturbed or more dependent members, the therapist may have to be more active and intervene more often—to structure the situation, to provide controls and guidance, to stimulate participation, and to be a model.

Before intervening, the therapist should consider the following questions (Foulkes 1960): What is the purpose of this intervention? Is it to stabilize the group, develop group norms, contribute to the involvement of the members and the cohesiveness of the group, or facilitate meaningful interaction that will result in therapeutic change? And at any particular moment, the therapist must also question, "In what way will this intervention accomplish my purpose?"

This chapter will present a summary of some interventions at each of three levels: that of the individual group member, that of the dyad or subgroup, and that of the group-as-a-whole.

INTERVENTIONS AT THE INDIVIDUAL LEVEL

A new therapy group is not yet "a group," but rather is a collection of separate individuals who are dependent upon the therapist for guidance, support, encouragement, and understanding. It takes time, effort, motivation, and intimate shared experiences for these diverse individuals to become a functioning therapy group. In the early phases, it is usually necessary for the therapist to help members reveal themselves to the group in order to become acquainted with, identify with, and help one another. The therapist may help individuals become active in various ways. Once group members begin to participate, they find it less frightening than they had anticipated and are then more inclined to participate again.

In one group, Dick, a new member, kept trying to enter the conversation. He would say a word or two, but was not assertive enough to push ahead. When others talked "over him," he backed down and was quiet. He repeatedly allowed himself to be "streamrolled" and finally gave up. When there was an opening in the discussion, the therapist turned to him and said, "Dick, you had something you wanted to say a little while ago. Can you tell us what it was?" This invited his participation but did not force it. It showed an interest in what Dick had to offer and thereby implied that what he had to say was worthwhile. He could have said, "No, it isn't relevant now; I don't want to say it," or "I forgot what I was going to say." Or, as happened in this instance, he could have taken the opportunity to make his comment.

Similarly, the therapist may intervene to *include a silent or nonparticipating member.*

Georgia, who had previously spoken of her mother's constant criticism, was silently listening to another group member, Jean, talk about *her* mother's criticism. After Jean finished, the therapist asked, "Georgia, how did you feel about what Jean was telling the group about her mother's criticism of her?" This gave Georgia an opportunity to share a common reaction with another member. She was free to say, "I don't have any feelings," or "I don't want to talk about it now," or "It reminds me of the way my mother used to criticize me."

Because she did not want to comment at that time, the therapist did not pressure her; it was important that she feel free to refuse. Having the option to make a choice could contribute to Georgia's sense of self and eventual self-worth. At the same time, Georgia became aware that she was not alone in her reactions against a critical mother.

Often the therapist observes a member nonverbally reacting while someone else is talking. The therapist can ask the member to put the reaction into words so that the group can deal with it openly. By asking group members to *translate the nonverbal to the verbal*, the therapist helps them to identify feelings and thoughts so that they can understand and control themselves better. At the same time, it allows the other members to get to know one another better.

During one session, the therapist said, "Oscar, I noticed you frowning while Peter was talking. Can you tell the group what you were frowning about?" First, Oscar became aware that he *was* frowning. He responded, "Oh! Was I frowning? I didn't know it." He then said that he had been puzzled by what Peter was saying, which led other members to admit that they, too, had been puzzled. Peter then clarified what he had said.

At times the therapist intervenes through questions to *obtain essential information* that a member has not shared with the group.

Sy had been in the group for a short time. Each week he mentioned how anxious he was at work and talked about how this anxiety carried over into other situations. After a few weeks, the therapist asked Sy if he could talk in more detail about what happened at work. Sy replied that his father owned the store where he worked and was always there, always criticizing what Sy did. Sy became angry but could not express the anger; he felt anxious instead. Another member pointed out that the previous week Sy had become annoyed with another group member and soon afterward had mentioned feeling anxious.

In another group, Sally sat, noticeably upset, but saying nothing. Finally she blurted out that she had just been fired from her job. The group members expressed surprise because she had indicated that everything was going well. The therapist suggested that she fill the group in on what had preceded the firing, which she did. Fred's comment that the incident she was describing reminded him of some of the incidents she had reported with her husband gave Sally and the group more material to consider.

Another type of intervention at the individual level is to *clarify what is happening at that moment.* If the group members are confused by what a member is saying or by why he is saying it, they may react negatively, rejecting the member or ridiculing him for not making sense.

The members of one group had been talking about their relationships with their fathers. Max began to talk about a vacation trip to Israel that he was planning. Fran, in a hostile, challenging way, asked Max why he was changing the subject. Max became upset and flustered and could not reply. At that point, the therapist stepped in to clarify what Max was saying. His going on vacation related to the topic of fathers because, as the group might recall, his father lived in Israel, and his vacation would include visiting his father. The members then turned to Max and asked him to repeat what he had said.

A member who is confused by what is going on in the group may withdraw into her own daydreams and thoughts. The therapist, aware of the withdrawal, may intervene to *reintegrate the patient*. At times the therapist may also be confused; if so, it is usually safe to assume that some of the members are, too. Here, the therapist might turn to the group for clarification, saying, "I don't understand what Joe means. Can someone else explain it to me?" Often another member *will* explain, understanding a cryptic reference better than the therapist does. This may happen for a number of reasons. The member may have participated in "rehearsals" before the group (in the waiting room), making it possible for those members present at that time to guess the whole story from the few signal words; or other members may be more "in tune" with the person speaking. Group members often become "adjunct therapists," thereby enhancing their own self-esteem. When the therapist looks to someone else for assistance, it communicates that it is all right to ask others for help and that the therapist is not omniscient.

Sometimes the therapist intervenes to *protect members from their own actions*. A member may be antagonizing the group or monopolizing its attention and time. In these instances, the member may look to the therapist to "set limits."

Sara shouted at the group one evening, "None of you care about me. You don't want to help me." But when group members asked how they could help, she could not think of anything they could do. She said she felt abandoned by the therapist and did not think the group members could offer her anything anyway. The group members pointed out that she continually rejected and criticized them, to which she shouted, "You just want to get rid of me." She continued in this way until the other group members became annoyed with her. The therapist then stepped in, saying that it was important for Sara to be able to bring out her fear of being rejected, but the rest of it could be left for some other time. (The timing was not appropriate for interpreting the transferential feelings either toward the therapist or toward the group as mother.) This enabled the group to move on, and Sara, being satisfied that she had been given something, sat back and let the group go on to other business.

Helping a member gain control over himself or over the situation is a similar type of intervention. Sometimes it is obvious to the group and to the therapist that a member is acting out in some way, unaware of what he is doing. The therapist may choose to inquire about the behavior.

Terri, a newcomer to the group, had asked the members if they would minimize the cigarette smoking by having only one person smoke at a time. Buck appeared at the next session with a cigar, which he smoked through the entire session, while the cigarette smokers took turns one at a time. Nothing was said. This continued for several sessions. Finally, Terri said that she thought the cigar smoking was a hostile act. Buck denied this. The therapist pointed out that Buck had not smoked *any* cigars in his year and a half of being in group, until Terri said the cigarette smoke bothered her; he had then smoked throughout each session, even though she had asked him not to. The therapist asked, "Do the cigars show some of your resentment about Terri's being here and making such a demand on you?" Buck denied it and made a big show of putting out the cigar right that minute.

At the following session, Buck reported he had been thinking about it all week and thought that he *had* felt resentful. He proceeded to give some of his reasons for resenting Terri, the least of which was that she did not like cigarette smoking. The most important was that she had talked about lesbian behavior, which upset Buck, and he reacted by smoking cigars. Since that discussion he has not smoked another cigar in group. He has, however, talked at times about his negative feelings regarding homosexuality.

In another instance of acting out, Shirley always cried if any of the *men* in group challenged or questioned her. Finally the therapist asked, "Is this your way of telling them to stop questioning you? Or a way of not answering the question?" She thought for a minute and then, with tears streaming down her cheeks, nodded yes. She could not tell them to stop, and she could not answer their questions. So she would just cry. She subsequently tried both to control the crying and to stop the men verbally by stating, "I cannot answer you" or "I can't talk."

With Buck, the therapist tried to connect the acting-out behavior to the feeling. Because Buck could not confront Terri with his indignation that she might have engaged in homosexual acts, he showed his resentment by smoking a cigar. The clue to the acting-out behavior was Buck's *sudden deviation* from his usual behavior in the group. Shirley's crying, on the other hand, was *typical behavior*. The therapist did not question Shirley's behavior until Shirley was strong enough to deal with it. To have pointed out the purpose of her crying earlier on, when she felt helpless and overwhelmed, would not have changed Shirley's behavior. With both Buck and Shirley, then, it was necessary for the therapist to explore, at the appropriate time, the defensive behavior that was interfering with group cohesiveness.

A member's overreacting or inappropriately reacting to another (suggestive of a transference reaction) will also interfere with group interaction. The therapist should *relate the present behavior in group to the member's earlier experience (interpret the transference)*, pointing out that, although stimulated by the current group situation, the current behavior has more to do with the past than with the present.

Mabel, who had recently come into the group, was quite

responsive to Henry. One night when he was talking, Bess began asking him questions. Mabel immediately jumped in, in a way uncharacteristic of her, and angrily asked, "Why are you attacking him? Why are you picking on him?" She wanted to protect Henry from Bess. The inappropriate reaction signaled that there was something to look at. The therapist asked, "Who does Henry remind you of?" Mabel paused for only a minute and began to cry. It turned out that she had a younger brother who was retarded, and she had been responsible for taking care of him as a child. Their mother often rejected him, and Mabel frequently had to protect him from her. There were two transferences operating—to the retarded brother and to the attacking mother. The group had set off feelings in her of what it was like when she was a little girl taking care of her retarded brother. Until that session, no one had even known that Mabel had a brother.

In another group, after Dan had spoken, Adam became furious, shouting, pounding on the couch, and reacting in a manner completely out of proportion to what Dan had said. The therapist asked, "Adam, does Dan remind you of someone else who talked to you in this way and aroused strong feelings?" Adam immediately answered, "Yes, my father." He added that he always went into a blind rage whenever his father spoke to him in that tone of voice. So it was not the content of what Dan had said, but the tone of voice that had set off the fury. Feelings from the past were precipitated by what was happening in the present. By recognizing that he was reacting to something from the past, Adam gradually gained control of his rage.

In group, many transferences go on concurrently. Disruptive transference reactions may be directed toward any member of the group, toward the therapist, or toward the group-as-a-whole. The therapist cannot see or deal with all the transferences simultaneously. The group members often see what the therapist does not, however, and will generally point out overreactions.

This happens more frequently as members become experienced in the therapy group.

Resistances may prevent interaction or disrupt the group. The therapist should *point out resistance* so the group can continue its meaningful interaction. Resistance serves a defensive purpose: avoidance of change. Even a person who wishes to change his behavior may feel more secure remaining the way he is, since change brings the unexpected.

George, having worked through much hate and anger toward his sadistic mother, was beginning to relate to women and to progress in his career. One night in group he sat silent, not participating. When questioned, he said that Wendy's wanting only to talk about herself, not caring about anyone else, reminded him of his father. He said that Sam was critical of everybody, always sticking pins in other group members, and that this was also just like his father. It turned out that every group member resembled George's father in some respect. Surrounded on all sides by his father, he could not talk. In this instance, the transference had become a resistance. As he recognized this and expressed some of his fantasies about killing members of the group and his father, he was more able to interact with others.

Wilma showed her resistance to group by coming late to sessions—usually about twenty minutes late—so that the group members were already engrossed with one another by the time she arrived. She would make a grand entrance, sweeping across the room to the most distant seat, taking off her cape and fluttering about while deciding where to put it, smiling at everyone, and finally sitting down with a loud sigh. This, of course, was disruptive to the conversation and focused attention on her. It was essential that the therapist point out the behavior and bring it into the open for group discussion.

By *recognizing a member's accomplishment or risk taking* during group, the therapist contributes to the member's feelings of self-worth.

Helen, a group member for about a year, had never revealed that she was diabetic. She was ashamed and did not
want the group to know about it, although she had talked
about it extensively in individual therapy. Her diabetes
made her very anxious and affected every aspect of her life.
The fact that her diabetes was a secret limited what she
could say about her problems in social relationships.

Finally, Helen announced that she was diabetic, wincing
as she spoke, and fearing the worst. The group was quite
nonchalant about the whole thing. For them, it was not the
terrible issue she had always felt it to be. Instead, they
asked about some of the problems diabetes caused her.
Helen's bringing her diabetes into the open began to clarify
some of her other behaviors. The therapist's commenting
that it took a lot of courage for Helen to talk about her
diabetes gave Helen recognition and helped the group to
realize how difficult this topic was for her. It also served as
a model for members' giving recognition to one another for
risk taking in the group.

INTERVENTIONS AT THE DYAD AND SUBGROUP LEVEL

Dyads and subgroups can be divisive; in such cases, when two or
more members are arguing and cannot stop themselves, the
therapist should intervene to *reintegrate the members.*

In one group session, Morris said to Ken, "You are just like
my mother; you don't listen to me, and you don't try to
understand what I'm saying."

Ken responded, "You're only concerned with your own
feelings, and no one else's feelings matter."

Morris returned, "You are just like my mother. She tells
me I'm not listening, and I'm not concerned with her feelings."

After this had continued for a while, the therapist turned
to the other members of the group, who had been listening
attentively, and asked, "What do you see going on here?"

Several members began to offer interpretations. The shift in focus to the listeners helped the two original antagonists to get out of the cycle they had been caught in.

In another group, Tess talked about her concerns over confidentiality and her feeling that she could not trust Sam. He replied by making fun of her and exaggerating her concern. Frustrated, she offered more evidence for her distrust. He mocked her for not trusting anyone. No one spoke as the interchange continued.

Finally, the therapist noted that Sam was not taking Tess's feelings seriously and suggested that that might be why Tess didn't trust him. Other members then joined in with comments about similar episodes between Sam and other group members.

The therapist's intervention provided the opportunity for more interaction and cohesiveness; and it helped Sam look at his characteristic way of relating to others, which kept them at a "safe" distance from him.

Although pairing in a group can sometimes be beneficial to each member of the pair, the therapist should intervene when the pairing interferes with meaningful interaction.

Jim and Dan defended one another whenever other members raised questions or made negative comments about either of them. During one session, Jim discussed his social difficulties with women. He asked several women in the group for their perceptions of and feelings about him. Several said they felt threatened by him, were afraid to confront him, and saw him as arrogant and angry. Dan interrupted, insisting that Jim wasn't that way at all. The therapist asked Dan why he felt it necessary to defend Jim, since Jim himself had asked for the women's opinions. Dan replied that the women misunderstood Jim; but Jim himself picked up the therapist's point and assured Dan that he really wanted to know how the women felt because it might help him in other relationships. Jim felt that they were not attacking him, but were simply answering what he had asked. Dan then sat back quietly while a lively interaction proceeded between the women and Jim.

At times a pairing excludes other members of the group, such as when two members have had private conversations outside the group session. Here the therapist may need to intervene to *make public what was private.*

In one group, Jean and Beverly referred tangentially to an affair Jean was having with a married man. The therapist said, "Jean, none of us were there when you and Beverly talked about this. Can you bring us up to date?" This gave Jean the opportunity to report what had been happening, and it gave the group the opportunity to participate in the discussion of the affair. If the therapist had not intervened, the private conversation between Jean and Beverly could have led to subgrouping, which would have sabotaged the group's cohesiveness.

A different type of intervention occurs when the therapist *points out similarities between two or more members.*

Fran had been talking one evening about how her mother disregarded what she said and felt. Debbie chimed in with similar reactions to her mother, though the specifics were different. The therapist asked Louise, "Does any of this sound familiar to you?" Louise said it sounded as if Fran and Debbie were talking about Louise's mother. The therapist summarized that the three of them had experienced similar mothering and shared similar expectations of older women.

If the therapist observes two or more members competing for the group's time and attention for an extended period, thereby preventing other members from participating, the therapist should intervene in order to *diminish the competition.*

Wendy and Freda had been competing with each other for most of the evening. Freda would start to talk about a recent experience, and Wendy would interrupt with a long story of her own. Freda would criticize and continue with another experience. Neither responded to the other; and no other group member commented. At last the therapist asked the general question, "What is going on?" Wendy and Freda both realized that they had felt resentful and deprived while the other was talking, each feeling that the other was getting special attention from the rest of the group.

Another intervention at the subgroup level may occur when *several members are "ganging up" on one member*, to pressure him in some way.

Albert usually presented a helpless, lost image. This particular night he had two problems: He had to find another job because he had just been fired; and he had to interview prospective roommates because his current roommate was getting married. Three women in group gave him specific, step-by-step advice. Albert told them twice that he did not want their advice; he knew how to do what he had to do. The women ignored what he was saying, and told him he would be better off if he followed their advice. Albert withdrew into silence. The women began to talk to one another *about* Albert, until they had agreed on what he should do. The therapist asked the women why they had ignored Albert's request to stop giving him advice. What had been set off in them, and how did they feel about him? What benefits were there for them in reaching consensus on what he should do?

In this instance, the focus had moved from Albert to the three women, who formed a united subgroup for the evening. The therapist asked the group for observations on the women's interaction. Albert, having had as much as he could take for the time being, had already "left" the group. At a subsequent session, when he appeared strong enough to deal with it, the therapist asked whether he elicited this response from other women, and what it was about his actions that brought out this type of response. Albert said the women he met were "always trying to mother me," always telling him what to do and trying to solve his problems. Later, Albert was able to think about the traits in himself that evoked this response in women.

At times, two or more members may engage in an *intellectual discussion* about what group therapy is, what it does, and whether it is effective. This can be a resistance to affective interaction. When the therapist points it out, other members may express their feelings about the intellectualizing, which immediately changes the atmosphere and the focus.

Intervention is also appropriate if it appears that two or more members are *subgrouping to scapegoat another member*.

INTERVENTIONS AT THE GROUP-AS-A-WHOLE LEVEL

Sometimes the therapist should intervene at the level of the group-as-a-whole. It may be a general statement about the atmosphere of the group, the group theme, or the action at a given moment. The therapist may point out barriers to meaningful interaction or guide the interaction in one direction rather than another.

In the early stages of a group, group members will look to the therapist as an expert guide; they will depend on the therapist to raise the "right" questions and to make connections for them, and they will use the therapist's behavior in the group as a model for their own. After a group has passed through the beginning phase and has developed some cohesiveness, the members take on more responsibility. If, however, the group reverts to focusing its attention on the therapist and looking to the therapist for answers, the therapist should point out that the group members are acting as if the therapist were omnipotent and omniscient, and as if they were helpless without the therapist leading them and telling them what to do (Bion 1959); such an intervention helps to *reestablish the group's reliance on itself*.

The therapist might have to intervene at the level of the group-as-a-whole in order to *ease the entrance of a new member into the group*. The group may ignore the new member. Group members may talk about past members, or about how good the group *used* to be; or they may continue a discussion from the previous week, which completely excludes the new member. If this continues for an extended period, the therapist may raise the question, "Does this focusing on the past have to do with our having a new member?" The group will then begin to acknowledge that there is a person in the room who was not present in previous sessions. On the other hand, the group may focus on the new member in a way that suggests that they want to shock the person or influence the new member to leave.

Wilma, a very attractive, buxom young woman, joined one group. After a warming-up period in which the group members introduced themselves to the new member, Henry began describing a recent sexual experience, giving explicit details. This reminded some other members of their experiences; and they began elaborating on their sexual exploits in a "can you top this?" manner. Wilma began squirming in her seat and looking somewhat embarrassed. The therapist asked, "Are you trying to shock Wilma so that she will question whether this is the right group for her?" The first response was that nothing unusual was being discussed; there had been other discussions of sex. But one of the women said, "Yes, we have talked about sex before, but never in this way." Other members then began to explore what they had been doing and recognized that Wilma's physical appearance had stimulated the direction the interaction took.

If one person presents a problem or a feeling reaction, the therapist may decide to broaden the focus, to *generalize from one person to the whole group.*

Sam had described visiting a friend and being left alone in the living room while the friend went into the kitchen for coffee. As he sat there alone, Sam suddenly saw himself in a full-length mirror. He felt disgust at what he saw reflected in the mirror. The therapist asked, "How do other members feel when you see yourself in a mirror? What are your reactions?" In the ensuing discussion—during which *every* member of the group spoke—a common feeling of not liking oneself and of avoiding full-length mirrors came out. These negative self-feelings became the topic of discussion.

In another group, Warren said he was thinking of leaving the group because he felt so angry at some of the members that he did not think he could control himself. Warren felt he must control himself completely, not giving *any* indication that he was angry, or he would kill the other person. Since he did not want to kill all the group members, he felt he had to leave.

Rather than focusing on Warren, the therapist asked if anyone else in the group had problems with anger. Oscar said that he was exactly like Warren. He always kept his anger under control—except when he engaged in sports; then he became a "wild man." Richard admitted that he could never express his anger; he held it in until he exploded. Then the women spoke of their problems coping with anger. The therapist summarized that every member had some difficulty dealing with anger. In this respect, then, Warren was not unique. Once the discussion of handling anger had broadened to the entire group, Warren could feel a bond between himself and the others. The idea of leaving group was dropped; he no longer had to make himself an outcast.

Questions may be raised at the group level about a significant *universal event* or experience, such as a birthday or a holiday.

Ralph mentioned that he had just had a birthday and spoke of the sad feelings associated with birthdays when he was young. The therapist asked if anyone else in the group had had similar feelings about birthdays, suggesting that birthdays often stimulate sad feelings.

Often, an episode outside the group can be brought in to *provide a shared group experience*.

John told a long story about being criticized at work, becoming angry, and, subsequently, anxious. The therapist asked if John ever went through this sequence of feelings in the group. John said he was experiencing anxiety at that moment. He thought it was because earlier in the session Nancy had interrupted him. He had wanted to answer her back but held it in because he did not think he could handle her reaction. He then had begun to experience palpitations, shortness of breath, and a headache. Group members, who had observed the interaction between John and Nancy, commented on their own perceptions of what had happened and offered their reactions and interpretations to John.

Had the therapist focused on John's work situation, the other members could have offered opinions based only on John's report rather than on their own observations of what had occurred a short time before.

Sometimes a group will be giddy and playful after a previous "heavy" session. They may joke with one another, talk about recent political events or sports, or admire one another's clothes. In this way, they avoid dealing with one another in a deeper, more serious way. The therapist may *point out this avoidance* or ask whether the group is behaving this way because of the previous session and whether they feel the need to rest a while before plunging into more serious matters again. Such avoidances are resistances to the task of the group (Kauff 1979).

Silence is another type of resistance. Usually the therapist waits until a member breaks the silence. If there have been *many silences* in one session, however, the therapist might consider it significant to explore.

In a clinic group one evening, there had been many periods of silence. Eventually the therapist commented, "There have been more silences tonight than at previous sessions. Why do you suppose this is happening?" It took a few minutes before the members admitted that they thought they were avoiding dealing with some of the angry feelings they had toward the therapist because he had just taken a two-week vacation at an unexpected time. Instead of expressing the anger verbally, the group acted out the anger by being silent. Once that had come out into the open, group members could begin to discuss their feelings more extensively and to interact with one another in mutual support of their resentment of the therapist.

The group therapist will find it necessary at times to intervene to *limit the group's attacking, excluding, or scapegoating of one member*. Otherwise, the member may be driven from the group, leaving the group in need of coming to terms with the loss and their role in it.

The members of one group were frustrated because Bruce refused to expose any of his feelings. When questioned about his reactions to events in the group, Bruce replied that it was debasing to talk about feelings or show feelings. He preferred to keep the group "on a high, intellectual level." The other members tried to persuade him, seduce him, force him, but he would have none of it. The therapist finally asked why the group was reacting so strongly to Bruce's refusal to discuss his feelings. What did his refusal mean to them? As they spoke, it became obvious to them that they wanted him to become like them. It was threatening to them that he was not participating in the same way they were, but instead was observing them, occasionally making an intellectual comment. This shifted the focus from Bruce to the rest of the group and encouraged a different type of interaction, permitting Bruce to enter the discussion as he felt ready.

Intervening at the level of the group-as-a-whole is also appropriate in order to *interpret a group dream*. A group dream is any dream brought into the group session. If the dream is being presented to the group, it usually has something to do with the group. The dream may have group members or the group therapist in it; but even if it doesn't, there may be symbolic references to group members or group events. After a member has told a dream, the therapist may invite comments about it. Sooner or later, every member of the group will disclose associations, interpretations, fantasies, or feelings aroused by the dream. Some members may relate the dream to an incident from the previous session. Others may be reminded of a dream of their own, which they will then tell the group.

Whenever a member or a therapist decides to terminate from group, the therapist should intervene to *assess the termination's effects both on individual members and on the group-as-a-whole.*

Jack was a verbal, good-looking, masculine-appearing, active member of the group. At the time he terminated, some group members voiced their regret that he was leaving and said they would miss him, but there was not extensive discussion.

A few weeks later, Chip said he was going to leave the group, which led Dick to say, "You just want to be as good as Jack and show that you can leave therapy just because Jack left." This indicated to the therapist that not enough time had been spent talking about Jack's leaving and what it meant to the others. The therapist suggested that the group explore their current feelings about Jack.

Frances said she felt the group had lost the only man it had; not one of the three males left in the group was a man. She openly expressed her contempt for them because they could not measure up to Jack. Tom had been silent for three weeks; but now that the question of Jack's leaving was raised, he said that he felt that Jack's leaving was a tremendous loss, because Jack was the kind of man he wished his father had been. Jack had become for him the supportive "good father." When Jack left, Tom felt he had lost everything. Dick said that Jack had helped him to focus on his desire for a career as a writer, had encouraged him to register for a college course, and had taken an interest in his progress in the course. Eventually, each member of the group talked about Jack and what his leaving had meant. They shared their sense of loss, thereby solidifying their intimacy and cohesiveness. No one terminated from group.

Determining the Level of Interventions

It is the responsibility of the therapist to decide whether to intervene at the level of the individual, the dyad or subgroup, or the entire group, depending on what the therapist thinks will facilitate meaningful interaction between group members.

Group therapy is not a substitute for individual therapy, and the therapist must guard against doing individual therapy with one patient while the rest of the group passively observes. A group member who needs individual attention should get it in individual therapy and continue to make use of what the group alone can provide.

In intervening, the therapist has to consider group processes and dynamics in addition to individual psychodynamics and conflicts (Scheidlinger 1980). What is appropriate at one time in one group may not be appropriate at another time or in another group. Consequently, no definite rules can be laid down to specify exactly when the group therapist should intervene and at what level.

At any specific moment, the therapist may have to consider any of the following questions: Is it more important to bring in a member who had been silent for some time or to point out a commonality between two members who have been distant from each other? Is it more important to get group reactions to a member's recent termination or to encourage an agitated, anxious member to explore his current feelings? These decisions have to be based on the therapist's previous experiences with therapy groups and knowledge of that particular group's history, as well as knowledge of the individual group members and an intuitive assessment of the situation at that moment.

References

Anthony, E. (1971). Comparison between individual and group psychotherapy. In *Comprehensive Group Psychotherapy*, ed. H. I. Kaplan and B. J. Sadock. Baltimore: Williams & Wilkins.

Bion, W. R. (1959). *Experiences in Groups*. New York: Basic Books.

Foulkes, S. H. (1960). The application of group concepts to the treatment of the individual in the group. *Topical Problems in Psychotherapy* 2:1-15.

Freud, S. (1959). *Group Psychology and the Analysis of the Ego.* New York: W. W. Norton.

Kauff, P. (1979). Diversity in analytic group psychotherapy: the relationship between theoretical concepts and technique. *International Journal of Group Psychotherapy* 29:51-65.

Scheidlinger, S. (1980). The psychology of leadership revisited: an overview. *Group* 4:5-18.

Yalom, I. (1975). *The Theory and Practice of Group Psychotherapy,* 2nd ed. New York: Basic Books.

Chapter 9
Resistance

The word *resistance* often has a pejorative connotation among therapists. Resistance causes therapists to feel frustrated in their therapeutic work and stymied by the inability of patients to accept clarifying interpretations. Although the classical position has been that every resistance must be confronted and interpreted, all resistances are not the same. Some forms of resistance cannot be resolved in this manner. It is often not recognized that resistance may be a deeply ingrained coping method which has an adaptive value to the person and which provides self-continuity. In group therapy particularly, where the individual is exposed to more pressures than in individual therapy, it is neither possible nor advisable for the therapist always to interpret such behaviors. More often than not, character resistances in particular serve to anchor the individual's identity, and an attack on them by an interpretation only increases opposition.

Although the literature has been replete with suggested interventions concerning transferences and defenses, few recent papers specifically focus on resistance. Much of the current group therapy literature, still resonating Kohut's writings, has concerned itself with the concepts of self and selfobjects in therapy groups. Attention has been given to the therapist's maintaining an empathic stance vis-à-vis group patients, which implies that therapists are dealing not with neurotic patients in group therapy, but rather with disorders of the self. These group therapists further suggest in their writings that an empathic listening stance might facilitate the therapy more than confrontations and interpretations would. It seems to us that certain resistances, such as character resistances, are intimately related to the self-concept. They contain values, attitudes, and identifications that serve to protect the continuity of the self. While one may not have to accept Kohut's theory in its entirety, it is quite likely that if therapists were more empathic to resistance manifestations, treatment would be facilitated. It is from this point of view that this chapter proceeds.

HISTORICAL OVERVIEW

Resistance in Psychoanalysis

Freud (1923) stated that resistance occurred when a patient's free associations became blocked. Exploring this, he surmised that the analysand was unwilling to talk about hostile or erotic thoughts and affects concerning the analyst. Freud subsequently classified five types of resistance (1926): ego resistance, superego resistance, id resistance, secondary gain, and transference resistance.

Greenson, in 1967, presented an overview of recognition of resistance and interpretation to the analysand, and the process of working through. While Freud viewed resistance mostly as a fear of analytic interpretations, Greenson stated that resistance was not an artifact of psychoanalysis, but rather a repetition of past events.

Present-day theorists emphasize the intimate relationship between resistance, transference, and object relationships. They state that the patient "resists" experiencing the painful affect that is accompanied by the wish for some kind of human relationship. Indeed, Loewald (1980) says that the phenomena of transference and resistance make clear the inextricable relationship between subject and object. In a similar vein, Dorpat (1981) states that affects are central to the development of human relationships and that resistance is a self-imposed barrier against experiencing such affects toward the self and others.

Classical analysts (Abraham 1919, Fenichel 1954, Freud 1908) became aware of what might be called *character resistances* — that is, deeply ingrained traits automatically (unconsciously) used by the person in dealing with the world. Reich (1933) held that no neurosis can be cured without character analysis. Schafer (1983) expressed the opinion that such character traits are self-maintained limitations on how life is to be lived. These resistances represent a "closed world" and interfere with the empathic attitude of the analyst. Such barriers are set up for (1) the maintenance of masochistic object ties and (2) the maintenance of the integrity of the self.

Although defense and resistance are intimately related, for the purpose of this discussion we define *defenses* as those mechanisms that ward off internal psychic embarrassment, while *resistances* are expressed in the external world within the context of object relationships.

Individual Resistance in Group Therapy

Because group psychotherapy is an interactive modality, it offers a rich laboratory in which to study and explore resistances, especially character resistances. Slavson (1964) believed that the function of resistance is to oppose any change that would disturb the psychic equilibrium. Resistance on the part of one group member, he believed, would reinforce the resistance of other group members. However, the processes of identification, mutual support, and universalization have the effect of overcoming defensive resistances.

Ackerman (1961) and Fried (1961) viewed resistance as a special form of defense which protects the patient's continuity of the self in the process of treatment. Transferences and resistances are to be understood as failures of social learning which must be promptly checked against reality so as to provide an opportunity for new social learning.

Many group therapists address themselves to descriptions of character resistances. Kadis (1956) elaborated on the patient's fear that he might repeat an unacceptable (masochistic) role in the group that would duplicate his role in the family of origin. Special manifestations of aspects of a masochistic character structure are discussed by Beukenkamp (1955), Livingston (1971), and Rosenthal (1963). The shoring up of self-esteem in masochistic characters before in-depth interventions are attempted is advocated by Durkin (1954), Scheidlinger and Holden (1966), and Scheidlinger and Pyrke (1961) for those patients who are in treatment for ancillary reasons.

In general, however, clinicians believe that group members are often able to deal with one another's resistances more effectively than the group therapist can (Bry 1953, Durkin 1964, Foulkes 1975, Rosenbaum 1952, Spotnitz 1968), since they feel less defensive with one another. A therapist's intervention frequently produces a negative effect. According to Bry, group therapists must be aware of the type of questions they ask and the manner in which their comments are made in order to prevent an increase in the intensity of the resistance.

Spotnitz (1968) defines resistance as an "immature method of functioning" and sees its origin in defenses charged with transference. He deals with character traits as though they were resistances to communication; in fact, he conceives of them as primitive communications disclosing early object relationships. While group members have a right to resist, they must look at what interferes with positive feelings. However, warns Spotnitz, resistances should not be destroyed or even removed unless the therapist understands their nature, their useful function, and the consequences of their removal. In addition, he points out that there are patient behaviors that make treatment difficult, if not impossible, and that if continued, would lead to termination. These behaviors cannot be interpreted; rather, the therapist must repeatedly state this consequence of such behaviors.

Yalom (1975) has described eight types of patients with narcissistic character resistances that interfere with group treatment: the monopolizer, the help-rejecting complainer, the moralist, the assistant therapist, the schizoid patient, the silent one, the psychotic, and the homosexual. Each of these patients may become a "deviant" group member, and each, representing a unique problem, can be treated in a group only when he is no longer considered a "special" case.

Group Resistance in Group Therapy

Group resistance is a phenomenon peculiar to the group modality. When a group became silent or unresponsive, Kadis and colleagues (1974) considered this a group developmental issue and called it a "G response." They considered such group behavior as fulfilling the function of homeostasis, its goal being the maintenance of group equilibrium and of whatever level of anxiety the group can sustain.

Other group therapists (Bry 1953, Durkin 1964, Fried 1965, Slavson 1964, Spotnitz 1968) have a somewhat different view. While they agree that G responses do occur from time to time, there are other group responses that may be viewed as resulting from converging individual resistances.

Durkin calls attention to resistance operating when pairing and subgrouping are manifested. If the therapist addresses such behaviors, resistance may be understood and overcome fairly smoothly. If, however, the therapist lets them go, they may develop into a group resistance and an atmosphere charged with tension. In Durkin's opinion, it is preferable to tailor-make interpretations for each person rather than having a group resistance develop. Bry observes that when a group approaches basic conflicts, silences or acting-out or other attempts will be made to block therapeutic progress.

Fried pointed out that when most members of a group identify similarly with one or more group members, a serious phase of resistance results. This is usually due to identification conflicts when patients feel they will be deprived of making identifications at the point of crucial encounter because of their differences.

When group members' individual resistances unite to become a group resistance, Spotnitz's plan of treatment is to deal with the group as a unit. After the total picture has been resolved, the individual components are then worked through, since the group

will then be in a more cooperative mood. Spotnitz would call
attention to a group of behaviors that he regarded as resistant by
repeatedly exploring its pros and cons until the patients consciously accept it as an obstacle to therapy. He asked questions of
the group members to encourage them to verbalize thoughts and
feelings bound up in the group resistance. It is Spotnitz's opinion
(1968) that when addressing a group resistance, the therapist
must clarify the psychodynamics of the pattern; then the specific
role played by each member is explained. "The analysis and
resolution of group resistance is a more powerful therapeutic
mechanism than the analysis and resolution of individual resistance" (p. 19).

WHAT IS RESISTANCE?

Although the word *resistance* has certain pejorative connota-
tions in our culture, we maintain that the presence of such
behaviors is more salutary than the absence of them. Manifestations of resistance evidence the ego's capacity to defend itself
when discomfort is experienced.

We shall define resistance in the treatment situation as *any*
behaviors that oppose the process of explorative therapy. Typical and somewhat mundane resistances such as forgetting an
appointment, arriving at the wrong time, or forgetting to pay,
are encountered in any therapy. Since the early days of psychoanalysis, therapists have been taught that there are two important
parameters without which treatment cannot occur: physical
presence of the patient and payment of fees. Without these,
treatment must cease.

FACTORS CONTRIBUTING TO RESISTANCE

Some people are ashamed because they have to seek treatment;
they experience it as a failure. Others fear that therapy will
reveal an irreparable flaw in their personality. These kinds of
painful affects will cause resistance. Even individuals who have

already undergone individual therapy may resist a referral to group therapy because they feel abandoned by their individual therapist – whether or not he is the group therapist.

At times a referred patient may have a negative reaction to the group therapist due to perceived differences in social status, age, gender, race, or religion; and this can contribute to resistance. Or, if a patient is not self-motivated and feels forced to come to therapy (by a spouse, boss, or agency), resistance may occur. A patient's insistence on dealing with a specific problem rather than engaging in personal exploration is also considered resistance.

Fear of Strangers

Another frequently encountered factor that may cause resistance is the fear of strangers experienced by new members entering the group. They do not know what the others will think of them when they reveal themselves, and they anticipate the worst.

It is important that patients feel that they are in a suitable milieu with which they can identify and in which they can ask others to identify with them.

> John, a middle-aged European man with an extremely moralistic upbringing, could not tolerate the more casual and relaxed interaction between group members. He was resentful, sarcastic, and critical of their "manners," insisting that they could not understand where he came from, and that he did not want to include them in his life.

> Caren was a middle-aged, single woman who insisted that she not be put into a group of young people or older people. She feared that with either group she would be censured and rejected for her promiscuity.

Fear of Regression

As has been noted (Durkin 1964, Foulkes 1975, Glatzer 1978, Scheidlinger 1968), the group, while communicating on an ego level, possesses qualities that stimulate a regression in the service of the ego (Hartmann 1958) and elicit charged transference affects. Although most people can allow themselves to project their transferences, others manifest a resistance to transference regression. They insist on talking about trivia, everyday details, and present problems, and refuse to acknowledge the group's or the therapist's guidance to become self-disclosing. They frequently accuse the therapist of having too much power over the group and cannot understand why both the group and the therapist see their behavior as resistant. They behave as if they have been falsely accused and deny that their behavior is motivated. They complain that the group does not understand them, and they feel like failures if the way they communicate is questioned.

Michael, a young professional man, divorced and remarried, entered a group. He presented himself to the group as friendly, unobtrusive, and noncompetitive. He soon developed genuine interest in the other group members. He was forever helpful and pleasant. One could discern his competitive tendencies with men and women over control issues; yet he was completely oblivious to these.

One evening, he presented a dream in which he was shooting off the head of the Statue of Liberty. Although most group members pointed out that he must entertain resentful feelings and thoughts about women in authority, he steadfastly denied it. When questioned about why he would want to do in the dream what he had described, he professed deep and profound ignorance.

INDIVIDUAL RESISTANCES IN GROUP

People enter group with their own style, characteristic of the way they relate to others. The style in itself represents a resistance. Anxious members will sit next to or near the group therapist. During the session, they will watch the therapist's face for approbation and comfort.

John took a seat to the right of the group therapist and sat quietly during the first session. He felt comfortable in the role of observer. When group members questioned his reasons for being there, he offered appropriate, rational answers. He told them that it would take him time to get to know them and trust them before he could speak about more intimate details of his life. During succeeding sessions, he interacted by becoming the questioner and explorer of others. Some basic trust was established when John offered the group a dream—an intimate part of himself. John's case is an example of appropriate resistance in a healthy ego when anxiety was stimulated by group entry.

When Joanne entered the group, she took a seat across from the group therapist. She was an attractive, lively young woman who exhibited an urgency to become intimate quickly. She was immediately self-revealing and bombarded other group members with questions. She could not sit back and observe; she had to be where the action was. From the first moment on, she maintained a highly emotional and charged presence in the group.

Group members reacted with some reserve to her emotionality, and she was quick to accuse them of being unfeeling and ungiving. When her attempts to form friendships outside the group were questioned, she portrayed herself as the only loving person in the group. Joanne's method of coping with anxiety was to be intrusively friendly and helpful. When this was unsuccessful with the group, underlying feelings of resentment became evident.

The Assistant Therapist

In any group, there are certain individuals who will assume the role of "assistant therapist." While most group members may assume this role at one time or another, some seem to be role-fixated, which prevents them from interacting openly with other members. On the surface it appears as if they had internalized the analytic work and, because of their enlightenment, are imitating the group therapist. However, their position, though positive on the surface, reflects the strong desire to be in control and to prevent others from invading their psyche. More often than not, they are ashamed of and fearful of expressing dependency needs. They derive secondary gain by acting self-sufficient.

Interventions addressed to this resistance must consider whether such behavior is transient and reflects a period of needed consolidation for this person, or whether it is persistent. Should it be a temporary rest-stop in personal development, no interventions are necessary. Indeed, the therapist must acknowledge the helpful contributions from the "assistant therapist." In so doing, the therapist accepts the fact that a period of consolidation is necessary and prepares the way for further development.

Sharon had entered the group confused about both her career and her heterosexual relationships. She presented a labile picture and reached out to the group in the hope of finding a more loving family than her family of origin. Her initial suppliant position was responded to with warmth and concern by the group members. While her ability to reveal herself vacillated, she was generally seen as sincere and struggling, and as one of the more mature members of the group. Once her career choice had been made, she had to deal with her choice of mate. At this point, she fell into the role of assistant therapist. She still participated actively in the group but was reluctant to discuss her relationships with men. Recognizing her need to consolidate her insights, the group and the therapist praised her for her contributions to others. After a time, she was able to continue and openly face her remaining problems in the group.

Should such role fixation become permanent in a group member, interventions are called for. It is sometimes helpful to point out how much the individual is giving to others and how little he asks for himself.

Transference Resistance

Transference resistance is a frequently encountered phenomenon in groups. Patients will project feelings that originated in their families of origin onto other group members and the therapist. These are characterized by exaggerated affect and wishes concerning other persons, and represent temporary resistance to the therapeutic process.

Tom developed a strong sexual attraction to Shelley, who rejected his advances. He wanted Shelley, who seemed warm and understanding, to be his best and only friend. He wanted to talk with her about his feelings and his life. Tom was jealous when Shelley talked about other men she met. No exploration or interpretation by group members or the therapist appeared helpful to Tom.

When Sharon entered the group, she made a play for Tom, who seemed uninterested in her. Then came a time when Tom made another advance to Shelley and was rebuffed. He turned to Sharon for a quick, "in-between" sexual encounter, devoid of meaning for both of them. In the group, Tom expressed his disappointment with Shelley and stated that he felt she was seductive and betrayed him when he fell for her.

To understand Tom's transference, we must return to his early life. Tom, the only boy in his family, was doted on by his mother, who made him her confidante. However, she also made him feel inadequate and unmanly. His mother's possessiveness gratified Tom narcissistically and made him feel powerful and superior to his father. However, he felt betrayed that his mother did not substitute him for his father. Tom tried to get from Shelley what he felt his mother had denied him and felt betrayed by Shelley/Mother for not preferring him over other men.

Character Resistances

Some of the resistances illustrated by the previous clinical vignettes are also character resistances—that is, deeply entrenched characterological patterns. Unlike a neurotic treatment resistance, which appears only in a small part of the person's interaction, character resistances result in the individual's total behavior becoming an impediment to growth. We are confronted with an amalgam of many defensive systems that have congealed into an entrenched behavior pattern that has become fused with the patient's identity. Since threat of loss of identity can be a most basic and intense fear, little behavioral change can be expected. Indeed, we may gauge by the rigidity of the personality whether such a person is a suitable group patient at all (Slavson 1955).

Although we cannot hope to transform an obsessive-compulsive character into someone free of such behaviors, we may be able to help enhance such a person's self-esteem. This in turn may lessen the rigidity of defenses. With a hysterical character, we may not be able to transform the flamboyance or the craving for admiration, but we may be able to help with problems of ego passivity and lack of self-assertion. Similarly, with so-called narcissistic characters, an achievable therapeutic objective may be the bolstering of *true* self-esteem, as well as the possibility of working toward engagement in a meaningful relationship.

Nonpsychologically Minded Group Members

There are people of action who do not feel the need to question their behaviors. Such people usually exercise tight control and show a certain concreteness in their expression and behavior. They are helpful to other group members. Because of their helpfulness, they become important group figures. They come faithfully to group sessions; when their attitudes are questioned, they smile sheepishly but continue in their own way. It is difficult to pierce such a resistance. Such group patients usually feel inferior to others and believe that they held inferior positions in their families. They stay in the group because it is the only place they feel accepted and important. They can be helped, with nonanalytic techniques, with some of their acknowledged problems and still partake of the higher level of group functioning, almost by osmosis.

GROUP RESISTANCES

Group resistances are more difficult to resolve. In these instances, the group responds with uniformity. Members talk about trivia and social events. Or, they can all be angry and withdraw from communicating and exploring their feelings. Other forms of group resistance are subgroupings, pairings, scapegoating, and acting-out behavior. Individual members may frequently come late to sessions; payment of fees may become irregular; group communication may be maintained only in the alternate sessions.

The underlying dynamics vary with each instance. Usually there are unspoken feelings of resentment against the therapist for one reason or another. At other times, the leaving or entering of members or cotherapists may produce such reactions. Kadis and colleagues (1974) believe that some group resistances serve to maintain group equilibrium in order to manage that amount of anxiety which the group can tolerate at that time. Other explanations focus on resistance to change. The group members need to consolidate on their particular level of development before struggling with a new developmental step.

Group resistances occur when there is a change in the status of a group member, such as marriage, divorce, childbirth, change of job, and the like. Such changes in the external life of group members usually signify that such members have taken active steps while others have not. They are important because they usually herald a change in the group; but they are delicate because they may impel some members to give up and leave the group.

An example of a group resistance occurred when a man and a woman entered the group as new members. The woman smiled, was pleasant, and assumed an expectant stance. The man was a "wise guy" and dissipated his anxiety by being jocular and provocative. For many sessions, the group ignored both new members. No matter how hard the young man tried, he was rejected by the other men in the group, while the women ignored him. What was unknown to both new group members was that they had entered after two of the most resistant members had left the group. Both departed members had been given much attention by the group, which was angry at the departures, felt they had been "had," and possibly thought that they and the therapist had failed. Only when the group was made aware that they did not want to risk embracing new members for fear that they would also leave did the resistance give way.

In another group, the female cotherapist neared the end of her group training and was ready to leave. The group had many mixed feelings about her, ranging from admiring her cool sophistication to dismissing her as a distant and uninvolved person. When the therapist and cotherapist announced that the latter would be leaving the group soon, and that another cotherapist would enter, the group's response was deep silence, which finally broke up into so many fragmented responses that their inability to deal with the situation was striking. When the group members were asked specifically whether talking about it might be helpful, their response was that it did not mean anything and nobody thought it was necessary to discuss it.

It was remarkable that an old, well-established group did not function at all when they were unable to face their guilt about welcoming the cotherapist's leaving. Here again, however, it must be stressed that the therapist can deal with the material only to the extent that the group will allow. Further probing and pressure are of no avail.

The beginning of a group session usually manifests obvious, temporary resistance, which often can be easily resolved, unlike some of the other instances of group resistance.

One group of eight members had just entered the room and settled in comfortably when Oscar announced that he would not be at the next session because he had to go to a trade show in Germany, which he was supposed to write about for a magazine article. Roger, an architect, was immediately interested in what kind of trade show, since he frequently attended them. There was an animated exchange between the two, with the other six group members sitting and observing or just looking around the room. After several minutes, the therapist asked, "What's going on in here?" With a smile, Roger said, "We're avoiding getting into therapy." Several members nodded, and with that, talk about the trade show ended, and Gertrude started talking about her reactions to the previous week's group session, which had been quite emotional.

Pairing

Pairing can be observed at various times in the group's life (Bion 1959). The pairs will differ in composition and motivation. Pairs with various functions may form for the sake of feeling identified with a particular problem, for protection from other members, because of sexual attraction, or because of the need to have a particular close friend of the same sex (reminiscent of adolescent development).

Pairs constitute small subgroups, and at times the group may divide itself into various small subgroups. While such subgrouping must be classified as resistance to the group process, it may also have beneficial effects. Identification with others, a feeling of being understood, sharing similar problems intimately – all may lead to increased self-esteem and strengthening of the ego. When these effects have been assimilated, the need for subgrouping will disappear.

Scapegoating

Scapegoating is a rather pernicious form of group acting-out behavior. At times the therapist is guilty of promoting such behavior toward a difficult patient. Toker (1972) sees the function of the scapegoat as an object that can channel and focus aggression. Some patients behave provocatively and frustrate any attempts to help them; nevertheless, scapegoating cannot be condoned. The group therapist's intervention may well tip the balance toward such a member's being integrated into the group rather than succeeding in being forced to leave the group.

GENERAL GUIDELINES

Group therapists must expect patients to display resistance. When not persistent and rigidly entrenched, they are manifestations of an ego's coping with anxiety brought about by change. It must be remembered that such manifestations may also be viewed as communications that when deciphered, add much grist to the therapeutic mill. We agree with Spotnitz (1968) and Glatzer (1978) that resistances evidence hidden transferences that must be explored. Helping patients to express feelings associated with the resistance provides the best avenue for its resolution.

As a general rule, we find that it is better if the group therapist leaves the confrontation of such behaviors to the members of the group. That is not to say that we believe in a democratic or egalitarian therapy group. The responsibility for treatment lies with the therapists, who must continuously make decisions based upon their knowledge of the patient and the group. For example, the therapist must decide whether certain forms of behavior should be tolerated because they also serve an adaptive function, or whether they need to be confronted because they may develop into a treatment-destructive resistance. Group members have a great impact on each other, and patients will often accept interpretations from their peers more readily than from the therapist.

There are, however, instances when the group or individual group members need contact with the group therapist. This need can be likened to "demand feeding," which should not be withheld. The interventions are made in the form of clarifications, interpretations, or encouragement to talk more about a particular problem.

Interventions can be made more palatable to group patients. Winnicott (1971) suggests the therapist provide "play space." The therapist should express a willingness to engage in game-playing without insisting that only one kind of game be played.

The emphasis should be on the patient's becoming engaged and signalling a willingness to play. We are reminded here of the fact that children are engaged therapeutically through play therapy; therapy can take place only through play. The activity of playing is an essential developmental aspect that continues throughout the whole of one's life.

The Therapist's Own Resistances

Not only group patients but also group therapists manifest resistances to therapy. This may be especially evident in the less experienced therapist, but it is also apparent in even the most experienced therapist. And the therapist's resistances often contribute to the patient's resistances. Or at the very least, as a result of their own resistances, therapists may not recognize or deal with group members' resistances.

Causes of Therapist Resistance

There are many bases for, or causes of, resistance in group therapists. They may be overwhelmed by their own feelings of anxiety or insecurity, often, although not always, due to lack of experience. Whether or not they have had experience, they may feel inadequate. Resistance is sometimes a result of their fears or concerns about the group members' intense emotions, especially anger. Alternatively, their fear of being criticized or disliked by group members may result in resistance. Also, feelings of shame or embarrassment (for instance, about having aggressive or sexual feelings toward a group member) may cause therapist resistance. If the therapist is feeling depressed and/or unable to cope with what is happening in the group, resistance can result.

The therapist's own needs to be admired or loved can interfere with therapy if the therapist is then hesitant to provoke negative reactions in patients. And if the therapist feels guilty about mishandling previous interactions or exposures by group members, there may be resistance to act.

Communication of Resistance

Whether or not they intend to, therapists communicate their own resistances to the group – through their actions, comments, questions, silences, and even posture. Also, the therapists' resistances will come out in specific behaviors, such as focusing on a patient's reality situation, resorting to advice-giving, or avoiding dealing with members' resistances. Or, therapists may evidence resistance by assuming a fixed role, such as that of the group's superego or taskmaster. At the opposite extreme, the resistance may come out in the therapist's being a passive observer of the group, not questioning group members or confronting them, leaving the group to handle everything on its own, maintaining a laissez-faire approach.

Alternatively, the therapist may resist by being the "good guy" – by helping group members too much, trying to please them or placating them, or at other times "showing off" with interpretations to impress the group.

Becoming Aware of Therapist Resistance

Therapists can become aware of their own resistances by observing the effect on the group members. For example, group members may become less active and less interactive, increasingly focusing on the therapist, waiting for the therapist to "lead," and being dependent on the therapist, which may result in long silences.

Or, anger displaced from the therapist may come out in members' moralizing and "preaching," becoming critical of one another or of the group, or scapegoating one another. At other times, members may react to the therapist's resistance by intellectualizing and giving advice to one another, avoiding feelings, or avoiding reacting to one another. Also, members may focus "out of the group," talk about external or innocuous material, or just "joke around." More serious "signs," such as absenteeism, lateness, nonpayment of fees, and terminations, may communicate a message to the therapist about his resistance.

Handling Therapist Resistances

When group sessions become static and do not "flow," when spontaneity is absent or prolonged affective states hinder the therapeutic work of the group, group therapists will become cognizant that something is amiss. If the therapist is unable to understand the nature of the problem by introspection, it may be a good idea to turn to the group members. The observable problem should be clearly stated and the group encouraged to explore whether they are reacting to the therapist's behavior or reactions. If repeated attempts to resolve the issue fail, the therapist might reveal to the group her own emotional responses to the impasse. Should such an intervention still produce no results, the therapist may wish to consult peers or senior therapists.

References

Abraham, K. (1919). A particular form of neurotic resistance against the psycho-analytic method. In *Selected Papers*, pp. 303–311. New York: Basic Books, 1953.

Ackerman, N. (1961). Symptom, defense, and growth in group process. *International Journal of Group Psychotherapy* 11:131–142.

Beukenkamp, C. (1955). The nature of orality as revealed in group psychotherapy. *International Journal of Group Psychotherapy* 5:339–345.

Bion, W. (1959). *Experiences in Groups*. New York: Basic Books.

Bry, T. (1953). Acting out in group psychotherapy. *International Journal of Group Psychotherapy* 3:42–48.

Dorpat, T. (1981). Basic concepts and terms in object relations theory. In *Object and Self*, ed. S. Tuttman, C. Kaye, and M. Zimmerman, pp. 149–178. New York: International Universities Press.

Durkin, H. (1954). *Group Therapy for Mothers of Disturbed Children*. Springfield, Ill.: Charles C Thomas.

_____(1964). *The Group in Depth*. New York: International Universities Press.

Fenichel, O. (1954). Psychoanalysis of character. In *Collected Papers*, 2nd series, pp. 198–214. New York: W. W. Norton.

Foulkes, S. (1957). Group-analytic dynamics with specific reference to psychoanalytic concepts. *International Journal of Group Psychotherapy* 7:40–52.

———(1975). *Group-analytic Psychotherapy*. London: Gordon & Breach.

Freud, S. (1908). Character and anal eroticism. *Standard Edition* 9:167–178.

———(1923). The ego and the id. *Standard Edition* 19:3–66.

———(1926). Inhibitions, symptoms and anxiety. *Standard Edition* 20:77–174.

Fried, E. (1961). Techniques of psychotherapy going beyond insight. *International Journal of Group Psychotherapy* 11:297–304.

———(1965). Some aspects of group dynamics and the analysis of transference and defense. *International Journal of Group Psychotherapy* 15:44–56.

Glatzer, H. (1978). The working alliance in analytic group psychotherapy. *International Journal of Group Psychotherapy* 28:147–161.

Greenson, R. (1967). *The Technique and Practice of Psychoanalysis*. New York: International Universities Press.

Hartmann, H. (1958). *Ego Psychology and the Problem of Adaptation*. New York: International Universities Press.

Kadis, A. L. (1956). Re-experiencing the family constellation in group psychotherapy. *American Journal of Individual Psychology* 12:63–68.

Kadis, A. L., Krasner, J., Weiner, M., Winick, C., and Foulkes, S. H. (1974). *Practicum of Group Psychotherapy*, 2nd ed. New York: Harper & Row.

Livingston, M. (1971). Working through in analytic group psychotherapy in relation to masochism as a refusal to mourn. *International Journal of Group Psychotherapy* 21:339–344.

Loewald, H. (1980). *Papers on Psycho-analysis*. New Haven: Yale University Press.

Reich, W. (1933). *Character Analysis*. New York: Orgone Institute Press.

Rosenbaum, M. (1952). The challenge of group psychoanalysis. *Psychoanalysis* 1:42–58.

Rosenthal, L. (1963). A study of resistances in a member of a therapy group. *International Journal of Group Psychotherapy* 13:315–327.

Schafer, R. (1983). *The Analytic Attitude*. New York: International Universities Press.

Scheidlinger, S. (1968). The concept of regression in group psychotherapy. *International Journal of Group Psychotherapy* 18:3–20.

Scheidlinger, S., and Holden M. (1966). Group therapy of women with severe character disorders: the middle and final phase. *International Journal of Group Psychotherapy* 16:174–189.

Scheidlinger, S., and Pyrke, M. (1961). Group therapy of women with severe dependency problems. *American Journal of Orthopsychiatry* 31:776–785.

Slavson, S. R. (1955). Criteria for selection and rejection of patients for various types of group psychotherapy. *International Journal of Group Psychotherapy* 5:3–20.

———(1964). *A Textbook in Analytic Group Psychotherapy.* New York: International Universities Press.

Spotnitz, H. (1968). The management and mastery of resistance in group psychotherapy. *Journal of Group Psychoanalysis and Process* 1:5–22.

Toker, E. (1972). The scapegoat as an essential group phenomenon. *International Journal of Group Psychotherapy* 22:320–332.

Winnicott, D. W. (1971). *Playing and Reality.* New York: Basic Books.

Yalom, I. (1975). *The Theory and Practice of Group Psychotherapy,* 2nd ed. New York: Basic Books.

Chapter 10
Countertransference

Beginning with Freud (1910), countertransference has been recognized as an important concept in terms of the interaction between therapist and patient. The concept of *transference* has been understood in terms of the patient's "transferring" feelings from earlier imagos to the therapist in the present situation, while *countertransference* has been associated with therapists' temporarily losing their objectivity and stepping out of their therapeutic role. Countertransference is those feelings in a therapist that interfere with the maintenance of a neutral stance and with objective listening.

Both transference and countertransference refer to feelings or affects that are evoked in the present situation but which contain "transferred" elements of historical origin. Both transference and countertransference are unconscious, although they can be brought into conscious awareness. And both transference and countertransference can result in behaviors based mainly on the evoked feelings rather than on "reason."

Like everyone else, group therapists have been influenced by their upbringing and culture. They are affected by their own prejudices, likes and dislikes, and values, learned early in life

189

when they were most vulnerable and receptive. Thus, during a group therapy session, the therapist may experience toward various members feelings of sympathy, attraction, resentment, anger, irritation, pity, and so on, which may result in his being inattentive or restless, becoming drowsy, fantasizing, responding excessively, or ignoring patients' negative feelings and emphasizing only the positive feelings. Countertransferential feelings may cause the therapist to inappropriately fulfill a patient's needs or wishes or to become defensive and anxious when experiencing the patient's needs and demands.

THE PSYCHOANALYTIC LITERATURE

A review by Fenchel (1982) observed that studies of countertransference frequently begin with two statements made by Freud (1910, 1912). The first statement is that countertransference is an impediment to the flow of analysis and must be analyzed; this is referred to as the "classical position." The second statement maintains that it is necessary to foster an affiliative relationship that remains unanalyzed and is part of the working alliance.

Sharpe (1947), a classical analyst, defined the functions of the analyst that must be preserved throughout treatment as (1) empathic listening and (2) the ability to make interpretations. According to Sharpe, whenever these functions are interfered with, countertransference is at work.

Those who consider themselves classical analysts generally agree with Freud that the analyst must maintain a neutral position, a stance that permits evenly hovering attention. When this listening stance is interfered with, it is assumed that unresolved neurotic feelings in the analyst form a resistance to empathic listening. Freud's position regarding the affiliative relationship focused more on the interpersonal aspects, including the working relationship. Here the psychotherapist was concerned with exploring in the here-and-now the feelings that the analysand was attempting to induce in the therapist. This position was elaborated upon by Langs (1976) when he discussed his concepts of the bipersonal field and the therapeutic frame.

The Classical Approach

Kernberg (1965) distinguished between the classical approach and the totalistic approach to countertransference. The classical approach conceives of countertransference feelings as arising from unresolved neurotic conflicts, and it is recommended that the therapist try to overcome them. According to Kernberg, "analytic concern" is a force that helps to neutralize the effect of aggression and self-aggression in the countertransference. It involves the respectful recognition of destructive tendencies in most people, but also the wish to help these people in spite of the destructive tendencies. Furthermore, analytic concern implies ongoing self-criticism, willingness to accept impossible situations passively, and a continuous search for ways to handle prolonged crises.

Glover (1955), a proponent of the classical view, stressed the humanness of the psychoanalyst, who is a person (as is the patient), and stated that one cannot expect the analyst to enjoy the negative aspects of the patient or the negative feelings that the patient directs toward the analyst. Because of the analyst's desire "to help and heal," a patient who does not make the expected progress may evoke the analyst's anger and sadistic tendencies. As Glover put it, "practically all day and every day the analyst must listen; his desire for achievement must be indefinitely postponed" (p. 96). A therapist who is disappointed with a patient's verbal flow may respond by withdrawing, implying that he will not "give" any more until the patient has fulfilled his requirements. When the patient's silence meets the therapist's silence, however, the silent combat confirms the patient's view that analysis is a pugilistic encounter: Who scores the most points? On the other hand, Glover also made clear that excessive interventions and technical interpretations often spring from the therapist's view that the patient must reexperience painful trauma in their original intensity. With tongue in cheek, Glover commented that while the adaptive value is undeniable, "there is no inherent virtue in psychic pain" (p. 96).

The Totalistic Approach

The "totalistic approach," according to Kernberg (1965), views countertransference as "the total emotional reaction of the psychoanalyst to the patient in the treatment situation." Adherents of this view state that the analyst's conscious *and* unconscious reactions to the patient in the treatment situation are reactions to the patient's reality, as well as the patient's transferences, and to the analyst's own reality needs, as well as neurotic needs. This definition implies that the therapist may have transferential reactions to real aspects of the patient, as well as to real people in the patient's extra-group life. For example, the therapist might react to the patient's method of earning money, or to the type of persons with whom the patient associates, or to the patient's family's behavior.

The totalistic approach, as represented by Little (1951) and Racker (1957), followers of the Kleinian school, has based much of its theory on the treatment of very disturbed patients. Little believes that with psychotic patients, countertransference becomes an important diagnostic tool, providing information on the patient's predominant emotional position vis-à-vis the therapist, as well as changes in that position. In many instances, countertransference may have to do "all the work."

Recent Approaches

Schafer (1983) addresses what the admonition of analytic neutrality has done to some analysts. It is entirely possible, according to Schafer, that some therapists are so overly concerned with their therapeutic stance that they substitute their own reaction formations for empathic listening. Such analysts often prefer an atmosphere of strained distance and veiled antagonism to the stimulating atmosphere of a positive transference. For the sake of representing a reparative figure, Schafer states, they keep the peace by resisting the analysis of resistance.

Epstein and Feiner's (1979) collection of papers on countertransference leans more toward the totalistic position. However, Epstein agrees with Schafer that analysts historically suffer from a shared self-idealization, which includes such values as a high degree of rationality, control over impulses, and detachment from personal feelings and needs. Both Epstein and Feiner recommend that therapists view themselves as genuine participants in an ongoing process. Such a therapeutic stance becomes less elitist and allows for greater spontaneity.

Whereas Schafer believes that the analyst's fantasies and countertransferences can be useful, he cautions that they are not infallible. Epstein points out that such countertransferential feelings must be communicated to the patient with caution. Awareness by itself reduces their intensity, and exploring their source may indicate the kind of intervention the patient needs. The effects of such interventions must also be carefully observed. Epstein states that recognizing with patients the feelings that they induce may make the patient more comfortable and trusting. "The patient comes to rely on the analyst as a good-enough mother, as the best person with whom to work through hate-ridden internalized intrapersonal relationships" (p. 232).

THE GROUP THERAPY LITERATURE

Groups, by their very nature, will evoke dormant countertransference feelings. The intensity of such reciprocal interactions between group and leader has been well described by Liff (1975) in his discussion of the charismatic group leader. He described people in our present-day culture as feeling "dead" inside, avoiding responsibility for themselves and society. They want to be "turned on" by a leader; the leader, "turning them on," enjoys being their savior, performing miracles and leading them out of distress into joy and safety.

Flescher (1953) accepted a broad definition of countertransference as "all emotions and attitudes in the therapist that, whether or not they are linked with his personality, influence his therapy." Eleven years later, however, Schwartz and Wolf (1964) still preferred the more classical definition, presenting countertransference as "behavior induced in the therapist which is responsive to transference and provides the patient 'transference satisfaction' when the therapist satisfies the patient's transference demands." They pointed out that countertransference may be to the patient, to subgroups, or to the group-as-a-whole. Therapists may experience the group as their family or as the "good" mother or the "bad" mother. When there is fear of the "bad" mother" group, the therapist may become controlling of the group or may try to placate the group and win its love or admiration.

Countertransference reactions, according to Goodman, Marks, and Rockberger (1964), not only distort the therapist's perceptions, but also can adversely impact the therapeutic movement within a group. The authors made the point that countertransference can at times lead to seemingly impenetrable resistance phenomena in a group. They conceived of countertransference as an attempt by therapists to repeat and resolve their own family situation within the therapy group. But the authors stated that whenever a therapist proceeds from personal distortions, the impact on the group has a boomerang effect, further compounding the resistance within the group. Moreover, when the therapist "becomes bound up in affects related to his personal past, which are inappropriate to his current situation," he cannot act constructively in the group situation.

Along similar lines, Mullan and Rosenbaum (1962) believed that if the countertransference dynamic is not recognized, or if it is denied, it retards therapy indefinitely. In fact, Mullan (1970) made the point that group therapy failures are often the result of countertransference.

According to Mullan (1970), the group situation brings forth and sharply delineates dormant countertransference reactions in much greater number and intensity than does individual therapy. It is a means whereby the therapist's defenses and countertransferences can be experienced, visualized, and lessened because of the openness of the group sessions and the absence of certain ritualistic requirements that are often imposed in individual therapy. Further, he advised heeding patients' observations, interpretations, and intuitions about the group therapist.

Glatzer (1975) reported that even well-trained group therapists are often impeded by their countertransferences. And Foulkes (1975), noting that unanalyzed countertransferences set up resistances and impede the flow and progress of a group, advised "the conductor" (meaning the therapist) to analyze his countertransference openly within the group process.

A broader definition of countertransference also includes the "induction of feelings." This implies that patients are sensitized to therapists' vulnerable points and behave in such a way as to stimulate these weaknesses. Proponents of the "induction theory," such as Spotnitz (1976), Ormont (1980), and Goldberg (1980), believe that the group therapist should reflect back to patients the feelings that they have induced. Less emphasis is placed on cognitive interpretations, the focus being on an affective interplay in the here-and-now. This procedure, according to Goldberg (1980), both results in the patient's feeling understood and reestablishes the therapeutic framework. He presents several possible approaches:

1. Dominant magical, unrealistic expectations frequently lead to therapeutic impasse. The blockage is due to the patient's having given up his curiosity about his feelings and behavior. If the therapist becomes curious about the affect engendered in him by the impasse, it stimulates the patient to seek its causes and get back to the therapeutic work.

2. Impasses may be due to the therapist's unconscious disavowal of her identification with the patient. The resultant distancing gives rise to the patient's suspicion that the analyst resists the relationship.

3. The therapist must be careful to separate induced feelings from personal genetic countertransference reactions. He will be successful if he mirrors only the induced feelings.

4. The therapist needs to recognize and use the metaphor implied in the patient's communications and interpersonal behavior. The metaphor is indicative of the level and type of experience the patient is receptive to at her stage of development.

5. The therapist must dare to express and to enact emotionally what his patient dares not imagine.

As group therapists, we also favor an enlarged definition of countertransference (akin to the totalistic position previously discussed) and lean toward utilization of recognized counter-transference to resolve blocks in group functioning. We base this orientation on the belief that group therapy climates are more "open" and less ritualistic than is individual psychoanalysis, and that interventions are made within such a context.

UNDERSTANDING COUNTERTRANSFERENCE REACTIONS

Group therapy, probably more than any other type of therapy, makes severe, critical demands on therapists. They are asked to be experts on group process and to maintain a positive group climate while separating themselves out of this process in the role of an observer. They are required to promote interaction between the group members and to help individuals "become part of the group." At the same time, they must individuate patients and deal with each member's particular reactions against the backdrop of the group. There is no doubt that they are constantly exposed to large doses of affect, from the group-as-a-whole, as well as from individual members, and often become the target of aggression. Both the group-as-a-whole and individuals in the group may attempt to "set the therapist up." Then, frustrated by the therapist's ability to remain at some distance from "the charmed circle," they vent their hostilities, seeking to undermine the therapist's position.

Because group therapists are human and would prefer to be liked and admired, they are vulnerable in many ways. Drawn by the group process, with the temptation to "become one of the group," they have to fight their own regressive tendencies to free themselves from superego burdens. When confronted with in-transigent group or individual resistances, they must counteract their own sadistic impulses and refrain from punitive action. When confronted with the perversity of human nature and impossible environmental frustrations, they are asked to empathize, yet to remain sufficiently separate to fulfill their therapeutic role. In this way, the therapist has at all times to maintain a nonjudgmental, noncritical, nonpunitive role, which allows group members to reveal their feelings of shame, embarrassment, guilt, and so on.

Most clinicians would agree that first and foremost among the therapist's functions is the need to maintain an objective observational listening stance so as to be able to gauge what kind of intervention, if any, is needed at a given time. Yet such a stance cannot become detachment, but rather must be coupled with an attitude of concern and must be conveyed to patients within a hopeful context.

We would like to differentiate between the group therapist's countertransference *feelings* and *actions* within the therapy group. There may be times when therapists become aware of their feelings only *after* they have observed their own actions and group members' responses to the actions and have reflected on these actions and their meanings. At other times, group therapists may previously have become aware of their countertransference feelings and then may, in the ongoing group session, self-consciously try to monitor and control their actions so as not to show these feelings to the group members. There may also be times when they become aware of their countertransference feelings as they are being experienced during the session and must decide "on the spot" how to handle the situation.

Stereotyped Roles

Analytic group therapy requires continuous oscillation between group interventions and individual interpretations. Thus any stereotyped role—focusing *only* on the group or *only* on the individual—is suspect.

Those who focus on the group and neglect the individual in the group may be afraid that by focusing on the individual they will encounter group anger, or the anger of the "mother group." Others may feel insecure and ill equipped to give to both the individuals and the group at the same time, and so choose to concentrate on the group. These therapists may cling to the fantasy that the group will do the therapeutic work and that in this way they can avoid exposing their own shortcomings as group therapists. The therapist may then promote a narcissistic overvaluation of "the group" and its "curative" elements at the expense of individual members.

A more serious problem at the group level is the possibility of the group therapist's allying with the group against a member, thereby scapegoating that member. Or, if a therapist is competitive with a cotherapist, allying with the group against the cotherapist.

On the other hand, a predominant tendency to conduct "individual" analysis in the group may be due to therapists' fears they will lose control over the group if they foster group process and group cohesiveness. Therapists who do *not* turn to the group and encourage the group to analyze what is happening often rely on "firing off" interpretations to individual members. In this situation, there is not only a control issue operating, but there is also, when an abrupt interpretation is experienced by the patient as an assault, the possibility of sadism in the therapist.

Similar interpretations of stereotypy can hold true with regard to the group therapist's silences and the withholding of interventions. Some silences can be beneficial. Silence may be used to allow group members to integrate previously achieved insights. Or the silence may be for the purpose of encouraging the members to seek their own solutions to problems arising in the group. At other times, however, a therapist's silence may be a punitive reaction because the group has ignored or refused to accept the therapist's comments or interpretations. The silence may be due to the therapist's fear of the group's power. If silence is the preferred and stereotyped mode of behavior for the group therapist, it should be scrutinized for its countertransferential meaning.

By contrast, a constant, friendly, "protective parent" role on the part of the therapist may serve the purpose of making it difficult for patients to express their angry thoughts and feelings. Since therapy cannot be achieved without the expression, at times, of unmodulated affect, the effect of a constant, stereo-typed, friendly role can be untherapeutic. Therefore, therapists who are *always* friendly and protective should look for countertransference bases.

Reacting to Externals

A group therapist may react countertransferentially to a patient's external characteristics – physical appearance, for example, or reputation, or life situation.

At the simplest level, the therapist may respond to the physical characteristics of a patient.

> A young man, newly a patient in group, reminded the female therapist of an older male cousin whom she had been very close to and had admired when she was a child. It took some time for the therapist to become aware of the fact that she was seeing and responding to the patient as if he were her cousin – seeing him as a more competent and warmer person than he actually was. When the therapist did become aware of the physical similarity, she realized that she had been reacting to the patient countertransferentially. Becoming more objective, she recognized that the patient felt inadequate and unable to relate to other members of the group and was full of resentment and anger. At this point, the therapist was able to become more helpful to the patient, seeing and reacting to him more realistically.

> In another therapy group, the therapist quickly became aware of being too impressed by the fact that one of the group members had a national reputation for being witty and creative. Being impressed had interfered with her stepping in at times to question why he was using his creativity and wit to denigrate, hurt, or make fun of other male group members with whom he felt competitive.

Therapists may at times respond countertransferentially to a patient's life situation, perhaps personally identifying. For exam ple, therapists may feel "understanding" because they have been in a position or situation similar to that which the patient is currently in and may assume that the patient is experiencing the same feelings they had. Or, therapists may see a group member as a "son" or a "daughter" and therefore become too helpful, too sympathetic, too nurturing and giving, too free with advice. Therapists may even be propelled by their "rescue fantasies," or feelings of their own omnipotent power to become the patient's savior. Thus, countertransference feelings may result in the therapist's trying to provide patients with *real* fulfillment of their needs. Should the sympathetic stance become too intense, overshadowing the therapist's function of scrutiny, then indeed countertransference has occurred.

At times, a group therapist may show favoritism, being more active and more responsive with one group member than with the others.

Because Ginny was small and dainty and appeared vulnerable and fragile, the therapist for a time was protective of her and "shielded" her from challenges by other members, whereas the therapist sat back and let Phyllis, who was large-boned and somewhat masculine, fend for herself in dealing with challenges and criticism. Then, in a crisis situation, the therapist became aware that she was being supportive of Ginny, while in a previous similar situation with Phyllis, the therapist had been confronting.

When the therapist does not become aware of such "special treatment" of a group member, envy or rivalry can be created in other group members, thereby complicating the therapeutic process.

In one group, the therapist was especially pleased when Margaret, who had recently experienced a death in her family, began telling the group about her grief. As the newest member, she had not yet been integrated into the group, and the therapist saw this as a way for Margaret to receive the group's support and sympathy. Instead of occasioning a "sharing" type of experience, however, her revelations became an extended monologue, with Margaret going deeper and deeper into herself and brushing aside questions and comments from other members. Because the therapist felt protective of Margaret, and perhaps identified with her grief over such a loss, she let Margaret go on much too long in exploring her own inner feelings without responding to other members' comments. Later in the session, the anger and resentment of the group came out, initiated by Terri's saying, "Here is Mama's little girl making her itty-bitty baby steps," and followed by others saying that they felt they had been used and manipulated by Margaret, *with the therapist's indulgence.*

On the other hand, therapists may see the patient as similar to someone they dislike and/or have rejected in their own family and may act on the basis of these feelings.

In one clinic group, the senior group therapist found it necessary, after several group sessions, to point out in supervision that the student cotherapist was overreacting in a negative, attacking way to one of the older men in the group. In the ensuing dialogue, the cotherapist became aware, for the first time, of the fact that this man reminded her of her own critical, abusive father.

In some instances the group therapist may identify with the patient's transference object. For example, a group member may respond to the therapist as his tyrannical father, and the therapist may in turn unconsciously "become" this father and relate as the father would. Or, the therapist might have an adverse reaction to the patient's transference feelings and reject the patient for having such feelings. In either case, countertransference elements are affecting the therapist's behavior.

Some patients who have had deprived childhoods tend to eroticize their feelings and demand erotic gratification from the therapist. They may develop a sexualized and romantic transference to the therapist. If the therapist were to respond in the same mode, countertransferential "acting out" would occur. Or, the therapist might feel anxious and threatened by such erotic demands and react in the opposite manner, becoming overly harsh and punitive, which is another countertransferential reaction.

Therapists' Insecurities

Even supposing that group therapists can achieve an adequate balance between the group-as-a-whole and the individual members, keeping some perspective on the figure–ground relationships, and recognizing their own tendencies to react to certain external features of group members, therapists' interventions may still betray some of their own insecurities and countertransference feelings.

For example, some therapists will not allow any group member to assume the role of group leader, even temporarily, since this would threaten their position. Other therapists have difficulty in letting anyone terminate from the group, even when there has been obvious improvement, because they experience the leaving as an abandonment or as a personal rejection.

When a group member idealizes the group therapist as magnificent and all-wise or all-powerful, the insecure therapist may unreflectively accept and enjoy this idealization and respond in this mode rather than maintaining a neutral role. At other times, therapists, out of their own insecurity and lack of confidence, may need love and admiration and may use the group to gratify their unresolved needs to "show off" and impress others. Or, they may become helpless and look to the group-as-a-whole to be the "good mother" and to feed and take care of them.

In contrast, group therapists may at times experience the group as depriving them of the satisfaction of whatever contributions they could make. They may then react to the group with expressed resentment or by withdrawing into a completely passive stance; or they may go to the opposite extreme and become over-controlling and dominating. Due to their own insecurity, therapists may for a time discourage the expression of aggressive feelings and permit only supportive, sympathetic feelings; then, swinging to the opposite extreme, they may go through a period of encouraging aggressive feelings at the expense of libidinal feelings.

Therapists may become angry in response to counter-transference. For example, they may take a group member's lack of participation as a personal insult and become angry. Or they may become angry at the group for "not working hard enough." In either instance, because of their own insecurity, there may be an implicit threat of punishment.

On the other hand, therapists may take umbrage at the nega-tive feelings patients project on them and seek defensively to make themselves more "real" or more acceptable to the patients. Or, they may retaliate by scapegoating the patient within the group setting.

Therapists may at other times have countertransference feel-ings toward a subgrouping that they feel is interfering with their work in the group.

George, Lester, and Sam sometimes wisecracked and joked with one another during the session. The therapist's initial reaction to this subgrouping was to feel frustrated and annoyed that they were interfering with the group's work. At those times when she could pause and question herself about what was going on, however, she was able to recognize that there was resistance on their part to the emotional topic with which the group was dealing. She could then ask, "What are you trying to avoid looking at?"

HANDLING COUNTERTRANSFERENCE

Countertransference reactions may be analyzed intrapsychically or may be dealt with openly on an interpersonal level. A good example from a cotherapy situation was given in a paper by Kadis and Markowitz (1973). In a group they shared as thera-pists, it became evident to Markowitz, a male psychiatrist, that Kadis, a female psychologist, was overly sympathetic to a female group member and thereby prevented a bonding between the member and the male therapist. After this problem was dis-

cussed, without resolution, between the two therapists, Markowitz decided to expose it in the group. Instead of pursuing an
introspective, analytic intervention, he dealt with it by saying
that "Mama" was overprotective with the patient-daughter and
prevented her from getting anything from "Papa."

Therapists can use their own reactions to "tune in" to what is
happening with the group members.

> In one group, for example, the therapist said, "I am feeling
> impotent and wonder if you might be trying to make me feel
> that way. What is gained by your exclusion of me?" The
> therapist had become aware of his own feelings and decided
> to confront the issue by questioning what the group was
> trying to set up. Instead of expressing frustration and anger,
> the therapist relieved himself from the pressure of
> countertransference by asking the group about their possi-
> ble motivation in inducing negative feelings in him.

The question of whether group therapists should spontaneously reveal their own anger toward patients is open to debate.
Although, generally speaking, it does not seem advisable, it is
possible that there are some circumstances in which it might
have a positive effect. One circumstance would be when the
group has maintained strong resistance for an extended period of
time and is obviously angry at some action the therapist has
taken. Therapists aware of these dynamics may utilize the angry
feelings "induced" in them as a basis for exploration of angry
feelings in the group.

> In one situation, the group had lost a member with bor-
> derline personality traits who had consistently refused to
> accept the group's observations and who finally separated
> from the group in anger. The group spent a long time
> vacillating between self-doubt and trying to "kill off" any
> existing affective ties with the departed member. After
> some weeks, the group therapist announced that two new
> members would be entering the group. For a few weeks, the
> group acted out their anger at the therapist by refusing to

interact, which made the group therapist feel uncomfortable and angry. Obviously, the group had not been able to mourn the last member's "death," felt guilty about their hostile feelings, and were using the therapist as a "whipping boy."

The therapist had to deal with several issues that could have been countertransferential. He questioned himself. Was he the cause of the previous member's having left the group? Was it now poor timing on his part, due to his own feelings toward the group, to introduce two new members? Perhaps the therapist wanted to replace the old member because he felt *he* had failed in some way and wanted the group to forget about that member by being given two new members. After becoming aware of his own feelings of frustration and annoyance, and understanding why he was reacting to the group as he was, the therapist said to the group that he thought they wanted to "kill" him for what had happened with the last member and for now wanting to add two new members. However, since he could not be killed off, it would be more helpful for the group to talk about the problem. This acknowledgment of the group's "induced feelings," with the reassurance that nothing dreadful was about to happen, resolved the group resistance.

SENSITIZATION TO COUNTERTRANSFERENCE

It is important that therapists learn to recognize when they are reacting countertransferentially to a group member, to a subgroup, or to the group-as-a-whole, and that they deal with their reactions, whether positive or negative, erotic or aggressive. If they are in touch with their own induced feelings and attitudes, they can *choose* whether or not to deal with the group member(s) at that moment and can decide how best to respond in order not to be counterproductive. First, however, they must become aware of their own countertransference. We would like to suggest some ways in which therapists can become more sensitive to their countertransferences.

If a cotherapist is present, that person may pick up on the therapist's countertransference and comment on it either in the session or afterward in conference. Or, if therapists record or videotape a session, they may become aware of their own countertransferences in replaying the tape.

At times, soliciting group members' perceptions of an ongoing episode may help therapists become aware of their counter-transference. For example, the therapist might ask, "How do some of the rest of you see this situation?" or "How do you feel about what just happened?" The therapist may even say, "I am puzzled" or "I am confused," and then ask, "Can someone else tell me what they see happening here?" There are times when a group member may see the countertransference more clearly than the therapist does. In fact, even without being questioned, group members will often volunteer their observations and inter-pretations of group therapists' actions and thereby help them recognize their countertransference.

Group therapists attempt to maintain a somewhat non-gratifying stance, similar to that of the psychoanalyst. Therefore, if therapists find themselves often intervening to give encourage-ment, reassurance, and sympathy to certain group members, they may reflect on whether and why countertransference is operating. Or if therapists find themselves often making critical or negative comments to one person, they may begin to question whether this is countertransferential.

When therapists become aware of their own feelings of help-lessness, anger, guilt, or protectiveness, they should also search for the cause of their countertransference. Or if they recognize a strong need to control or direct, or a strong desire to impress or "show off," they can explore the countertransference.

It helps in some instances to consult with a colleague, to meet periodically with an informal group of peers, to participate in an ongoing workshop on countertransference, or to seek supervi-sion to aid in the recognition and handling of countertransference reactions.

Glatzer (1975) remarked that one source of communication blocks is ignorance of individual and group dynamics. Previous discussion has raised the possibility of the therapist's own unre-solved neurotic complexes. It seems advisable, therefore, for the group therapist to have experienced personal analysis and group therapy, as well as training in individual psychotherapy, group therapy, and group dynamics.

Sharpe (1947) accepted the inevitability of countertransference as a by-product of a profession that allows for minimal personal gratification during the working day. She recommended that analysts have rewarding gratifications outside of professional life and that they achieve a certain maturity and wisdom before entering the profession.

As we have noted, group work itself produces countertransferential pitfalls. Therapists are often surrounded by a nimbus of potency and grandiosity; they may feel they possess the right theory, the magic. We believe that strong safeguards against such feelings are the personal experiences and struggles that lead the therapist to understand and accept the vicissitudes of life. In addition, it is important that group therapists continue throughout their careers to acquire knowledge of themselves and of their assets and limitations, in order to develop a stable self-image that cannot be easily influenced by a specific success or failure. Finally, in addition to accepting their own limitations, group therapists must come to terms with the limitations of their patients, and accept the fact that people are unique and that their ways of working out their life problems vary greatly indeed.

References

Epstein, L. (1979). The therapeutic function of hate in the countertransference. In *Countertransference*, ed. L. Epstein and A. Feiner, pp. 213–234. New York: Jason Aronson.

Epstein, L., and Feiner, A, eds. (1979). *Countertransference*. New York: Jason Aronson.

Fenchel, G. (1982). Countertransference: its pitfalls and utilization. *Issues in Ego Psychology* 5:4–10.

Flescher, J. (1953). The different types of countertransference. *International Journal of Group Psychotherapy* 3:357–372.

Foulkes, S. H. (1975). *Group-analytic Psychotherapy*. London: Gordon & Breach.

Freud, S. (1910). The future prospects of psychoanalytic psychotherapy. *Standard Edition* 11:139–152.

_____(1912). Recommendations for physicians practicing psychoanalysis. *Standard Edition* 12:109–120.

Glatzer, H. (1975). The leader as supervisor and supervisee. In *The Leader in the Group*, ed. Z. Liff, pp. 138–145. New York: Jason Aronson.

Glover, E. (1955). *The Technique of Psycho-analysis*. New York: International Universities Press.

Goldberg, C. (1980). Utilization and limitation of paradoxical interventions in group psychotherapy. *International Journal of Group Psychotherapy* 30:287–297.

Goodman, M., Marks, M., and Rockberger, H. (1964). Resistance in group psychotherapy enhanced by the countertransference reactions of the therapist. *International Journal of Group Psychotherapy* 14:332–343.

Kadis, A., and Markowitz, M. (1973). Countertransference between co-therapists in a couples psychotherapy group. In *Group Therapy 1973: An Overview*, ed. L. Wolberg and E. Schwartz, pp. 113–120. New York: Intercontinental.

Kernberg, O. (1965). Notes on countertransference. *Journal of the American Psychoanalytic Association* 13:36–56.

Langs, R. (1976). *The Bipersonal Field*. New York: Jason Aronson.

Liff, Z. (1975). The charismatic leader. In *The Leader in the Group*, ed. Z. Liff, pp. 114–122. New York: Jason Aronson.

Little, R. (1951). Countertransference and the patient's response. *International Journal of Psycho-Analysis* 32:32–40.

Mullan, H. (1970). Transference and countertransference: new horizons. In *Group Therapy Today*, ed. H. Ruitenbeek, pp. 121–132. New York: Atherton.

Mullan, H., and Rosenbaum, M. (1962). Transference and countertransference in group psychotherapy. In *Group Psychotherapy*, ed. H. Mullan and M. Rosenbaum, pp. 215–241. New York: The Free Press.

Ormont, L. (1980). Training group therapists through the study of countertransferences. *Group* 4:17–26.

Racker, H. (1957). The meaning and use of countertransferences. *International Journal of Psycho-Analysis* 26:303–357.

Schafer, R. (1983). *The Analytic Attitude*. New York: Basic Books.

Schwartz, E., and Wolf, A. (1964). On countertransference in group psychotherapy. *Journal of Psychology* 57:131–142.

Sharpe, E. (1947). The psycho-analyst. In *Collected Papers*, ed. M. Brierley, pp. 109–122. New York: Brunner/Mazel, 1978

Spotnitz, H. (1976). *The Psychotherapy of Pre-oedipal Conditions*. New York: Jason Aronson.

Chapter 11
Acting Out

Some therapists use the term *acting out* to refer to any behavior that substitutes for verbal communication. There is disagreement, however, about whether the term denotes only behavior exhibited during the therapeutic session or if it also includes behavior in everyday life; whether the concept suggests pathology or if such behaviors indicate responses to an unempathic therapist or an unempathic environment. Acting out is a common occurrence in both individual and group therapy, but it may be more frequent in group because of the many opportunities available to "act out." Also, peer pressure and an emotional group climate result in temporary regressions which may then be displayed in acting out.

An individual or a subgrouping of members may act out, either within the group session or outside the group. Although acting out has traditionally been thought of in terms of individual patients, there may also be acting out by the group as a whole and on the part of therapists. Group members may act out in response to a therapist's countertransferentially acting out.

Members may not realize that they are acting out, but rather may believe that the behavior is a *reaction* to others in the therapy group or just "doing one's own thing." Although the person may be aware of an action, he may not be aware of its origin or meaning. Feeling like a victim, the group member might blame the action on the therapist, a group member, or the group-as-a-whole. Acting out can be recognized as resistance when the group member objects to examining the behavior. Nevertheless, it must be dealt with in the group; otherwise it may expand, with one member stimulating others also to act out, perhaps to join him in taking sides against the therapist or against other group members.

Spotnitz (1973) considered acting out a normal phenomenon, used occasionally by everyone. It could function as a safety valve to prevent psychosomatic illness or psychic disorganization, or it could be an effort to master a traumatic event. For Spotnitz, the therapeutic focus for this "human phenomenon" was on its intentionality—whether it was being used for better or worse adaptation.

Acting-out behavior is sometimes difficult to distinguish from participation in the group. There is no doubt, however, that the group is used as an emotional outlet for members to satisfy various needs. Weiner (1984) and Yalom (1985) urge that the group therapist distinguish between interactions that arise from group participation and those behaviors that are repetitive, symbolically determined, and serve as resistance to change. The latter are symbolic communications and contain a signal that something has gone awry. Grotjahn (1973), as well as Foulkes and Anthony (1957), noted that relationships in a therapy group readily lend themselves to the dramatization of conflict, which, according to Rosenbaum and Berger (1975), in turn lowers defenses and fosters acting out. However, as previously pointed out (Fenchel and Flapan 1985), resistances to verbalization must be accepted and understood by group therapists, like any other form of dynamics encountered in group therapy.

THE PSYCHOANALYTIC LITERATURE

The term *acting out* first appeared in Freud's essay (1914) "Recollection, Repetition and Working Through." The technique of psychoanalysis is based on the idea that for change to occur, the past must be remembered and experienced in the present. When such recollections are not forthcoming, either due to repression or to the fact that such experiences occurred during a preverbal period, affects are discharged in motoric action.

In 1968, Anna Freud surmised that Freud's original definition might no longer fit since the theoretical shift to ego psychology and emphasis on aggression focused on the inevitability of expression by action. In a similar vein, Rangell (1968) defined acting out as a resistance to obtaining meaningful insight into mental content. He, as well as Vanggaard (1968), cautioned that not all actions represent acting-out phenomena; rather, there may be trial actions arising from successful analysis. On the other hand, strict prohibitions by the therapist might lead to inhibitions and obsessional paralysis. When acting out occurs, Rangell believed, it is the only available means of communication, and he encouraged patients to "think out" and "feel out" their behaviors, which might be "experimental recollections."

According to Grinberg (1968), acting out can occur only in an object relationship, and the essential roots of the acting out are often associated with object loss and separation that were not worked through. In the same context, Winnicott (1968) perceived acting out as an abortive form of playing. During the discussion session of the 1968 International Congress of Psycho-Analysis, Segal (Laplanche 1968) distinguished "normal" acting out that permits the expression, development, and symbolization of the transference from "pathological" acting out, which destroys the analytic relationship or becomes self-destructive, or both.

Acting out, then, is a cohesive piece of behavior, not experienced as bizarre by the patient. It is an ego-syntonic repetition of a piece of the past, in a distorted form as wish fulfillment, that only the therapist considers strange. The dramatization connected with acting out tends toward the symptomatic side. But one must be careful not to inhibit it too strongly, since doing so can hinder the process of trial-and-error learning. Because verbalization is inhibited during the early years of life, acting out contains information about early infantile conflicts that are expressed in action. Acting out within the therapeutic situation is necessarily part of the transference, whether it is directly connected to the person of the analyst or shifted to other persons. As Rangell stated, it sometimes *is* the transference.

Therapists form their own individual notions about acting out according to their own theoretical positions. Nevertheless, we should not lose sight of the complexity and special nature of this means of communication; a word is often an action, or even an acting out, and an action can be an eloquent communication.

The Group Therapy Literature

Etiology of Acting Out

Slavson (1964) likened acting out to catharsis, noting that its form and shape were determined by (1) the individual's life history, (2) the intensity of the external stimulus, and (3) the health of the ego. Whereas Rosenbaum and Berger (1975) thought of acting out as a motor discharge within the context of transference, Saravay (1975) and Wolberg (1983) believed that acting out occurred because of a shift in identifications. Using psychoanalytic structural theory as a model, Saravay suggested that group members had to forego some of their past beliefs and values in order to accommodate themselves to others and that this resulted in rearrangement of psychic structures, with temporary ego regressions. Wolberg, addressing masochism in the borderline patient, observed that such patients repeated their identified role in the original family and had great difficulty seeing themselves and behaving as if they were not victims: " . . . This system is a function of group dynamics as these operate in the family over time." (p. 47)

Not all interactional behavior can be viewed as acting out. Kadis and colleagues (1974) warned that unless the behavior is repetitive, it may not be "true acting out." True acting-out behavior always functions in the service of resistance and is, at the time it occurs, not amenable to introspection. Both Yalom (1985) and Spotnitz (1973) stated that acting out is tension alleviating; and Spotnitz thought it originated from unpleasant emotions during the preverbal period of development. Because it is not always possible to determine the function of such discharges, Yalom suggested that such determination be made in retrospect.

Classification of acting-out behavior was attempted by Abt (1965) and Spotnitz (1973). Abt proposed three modalities: (1) aggressive-destructive, (2) aggressive-controlling, and (3) passive-resistive and assertive-dependent; whereas Spotnitz thought that acting out must be differentiated from compulsive and impulsive acts.

Sexual Acting Out

Group therapists are as much concerned with sexual acting out as with aggressive acts. Strict prohibition of sexual acting out was advocated by Slavson (1964) because he thought that easy gratification made it impossible to examine the impulse. Both Mullan and Rosenbaum (1962) and Rutan and Stone (1984) considered sexual acting out a "group emergency" and perceive it as the most serious acting out because of the envy and distrust it arouses in other group members.

Control of Acting Out

Bry (1953) and Munzer (1966) believed that acting out was a diagnostically valuable form of communication; and Bry observed that it frequently facilitated socialization and consolidated therapeutic gains. In contrast, Ziferstein and Grotjahn (1957) maintained that such actions represented resistance to the exploration of oral and oedipal dynamics. Rosenthal (1978) described it as "immature" behavior.

To minimize destructive behavior, Spotnitz (1973) suggested five principles of maintaining a therapeutic atmosphere in groups:

1. The therapist must control the degree of excitation.
2. The group must be firmly conditioned to verbalize; they are free to do as they wish provided it does not interfere with the standards set for the group.

3. The therapist must focus early in treatment on the verbalization of aggression.
4. The group and the therapist must accept responsibility for
   maintaining the functioning of the group.
5. The group therapist must study all factors that engender
   internal and external resistances and enlist the cooperation
   of the group.

Similarly, Rey (1975) believed that group members can understand the meaning of a behavioral act and reflect it back to the
one who is acting out so that it can be understood. However,
Weiner (1984) cautioned that the observing group members must
have sufficient ego strength to integrate relevant information.

Most recently, Rutan and Stone (1984) addressed lack of impulse control and aggressive acting out, stating that while resistances can be worked through, the temporary or not so temporary loss of control cannot be worked on. For example, the
expression of violent rage necessitates the setting of limits and
the promotion of ego controls before interpretations can be
made. If these fail and the patient is unwilling or unable to live up
to the group contract, then the temporary or permanent removal
of the person from the group must be considered.

Individual Acting Out

The motivation for acting out is unconscious or otherwise not in
the patient's control; the person is aware of the action, but at the
moment unaware of its cause or meaning. The acting out is
usually rationalized by the patient and may even be experienced
as ego-syntonic.

Which behaviors do we recognize as acting out? Besides sexual
intimacy, group patients may break their therapeutic contract by
not paying fees, repeatedly arriving late, remaining silent, engaging in aggressive behavior, being absent, failing to reveal
what has gone on in alternate sessions or in their outside lives,
leaving the therapy room, terminating prematurely, threatening
suicide, or hinting that a breakdown is imminent.

Acting out may be an expression of anger or of fear, a provocation, a testing, a resistance, or a transference reaction. It has diagnostic value for the therapist and can also serve as a basis for working through with the patient.

Handling Acting Out

If acting out by a group member is not handled by the therapist or the group, the member may become more provocative and may act out even more—to test the limits. Or, the member may withdraw from active participation and ultimately leave the group. In intervening, the therapist must take care not to become a punitive figure; it is important that the therapist retain a position as ego support and object of identification.

The therapist's choice of intervention will be influenced by an assessment of the situation, as well as by the therapist's own values, needs, and previous experience. The decision may also depend on *who* is acting out, the *current status* of the group, and the potential *consequences* of the intervention. These considerations affect *when* and *how* the therapist intervenes.

The therapist may want to postpone an immediate response in order to allow time to become more clearly aware of what is happening in the group, to examine the possible causes and meanings of the acting out, and to consider various ways of handling the behavior, as well as the possible outcomes. It is important to differentiate between unconscious acting out and conscious "testing out" or fighting for control of the group. It is also advisable that the therapist be cautious not to overinterpret milder forms of acting out; the therapist may recognize the acting out but decide not to focus on it at that moment.

How is the group therapist to deal with acting-out behavior? Rather than prohibit acting out—much of which is unconsciously motivated—the therapist observes it and then decides whether at a given moment to point it out and interpret it. By drawing attention to it, the therapist can communicate the purpose it serves, so that the group members themselves ultimately understand the nature of acting out and begin to recognize it in other members of the group and in themselves.

At times, group members may confront one another's acting-out behavior by raising questions, making interpretations, or challenging one another.

A few months after a new female member entered the group, Carol and Tricia began meeting for dinner before the scheduled session and then coming in together about ten minutes late, after the group members were already involved in lively interaction. This went on for several weeks, until George, a veteran in the group, confronted them directly with their lateness and questioned them directly about whether they were reacting to having another woman—and an attractive woman at that—in the group. At first they denied any connection between their behavior and the entrance of Lorraine. But when other members supported George's observation and interpretation, both Carol and Tricia admitted that they had been angry about having a new member, especially since she was both young and attractive.

Fenchel (1978) observed that acting-out behavior is either therapeutically usable or nonusable. If the behavior cannot be addressed therapeutically, the therapist must trust the group members to deal with it.

Joan was not able to sit in the group when the men talked about women. She felt narcissistically hurt and would run out of the group, coming back later. All the therapist and members could do was to ask why she had run out; she would respond that she couldn't tolerate listening to the way the men were talking about women. This was not interpreted. There could be no interpretation because of the patient's weak ego. However, the group accepted her behavior, helped her to understand that these were certain members' opinions and not personalized feelings about her, and helped her get some distance from the interaction of the men.

If the behavior is minimally pathological, the group therapist must interpret it supportively while remaining an object of identification.

Flapan (1978) stressed the importance of the group therapist's self-examination to discover whether acting-out behavior has been caused by the therapist's subjective stance. She also points out the importance of distinguishing between acting out, testing out, and fighting for control.

In order to determine how and when to intervene, the group therapist must determine (1) the *mode* of acting out (sexual, aggressive, or other), (2) *who* is acting out, (3) the current *developmental stage* of the group, and (4) possible *consequences* anticipated as a result of the intervention. Related to this, Bernstein (1978) cautioned therapists against taking a prohibitive and moralistic stance. "Excessive zeal in enforcing the rule against acting out generally signals an acting out on the part of the analyst of panic, guilt, neurotic anxiety, or self-interest" (p. 10). Along similar lines, Wolf and colleagues (1954) believed that one should respond to acting out with the warmth and understanding the patient did not receive from the original family, with the hope of channeling the behavior into a constructive therapeutic experience.

Although patients are aware of their behavior, they may not be aware of its meaning; as a consequence, they may try in various ways to justify the behavior and make sense of it. At times, the acting out may be ego-syntonic, helping the individual avoid intolerable feelings carried over from an earlier life situation. Alternatively, the acting out may occur when a person is unable to ask directly for what is needed. In fact, at times a patient may not be able to identify what is wanted, but just "feels" deprived, ignored, frustrated, or angry. Then the acting out is a call for the therapist and group to "do something!" The patient provokes a response since *any* response is better than *no* response. By provoking a response, the patient is no longer ignored and receives the desired attention.

Acting-out behavior may be conveniently categorized into the following descriptive and functional diagnostic terms: (1) it is symptomatic, (2) it is characterological, and (3) it is a reaction to real events. In the classical sense, when we speak of a symptom, we are talking about anxiety stimulated by an *active* conflict at a given point in time. Such symptoms usually contain live transferences that have been stimulated. In such an event, either displayed by individual group members or the group-as-a-whole, the therapist proceeds with the usual technique of confrontation, clarification, and interpretation. Where individual members are concerned, it might be helpful if the assistance of other members is sought to clarify what is going on. For example, if a young woman is attracted to an older man in the group and takes on the role of a sexy, bright daughter-helper, oedipal dynamics can be assumed. If a young man consistently searches out depressed, helpless women (and if his history validates this) a similar intervention concerning a mother–son transference may be made. When the entire group exhibits resistance and communication blocks because of anxiety aroused by a particular topic, the therapist would do well to make group-as-a-whole interventions to elicit the transference towards himself. The therapist might also explore intermember feelings in an effort to break up the resistance.

Characterological acting out, such as chronic lateness, cannot be dealt with in the same way. In this case, there is no active conflict and symptom formation. Rather, we are dealing with dormant transferences and conflicts that have become amalgamated into character and identity. The individual is either unaware of any conflict or feels helpless to change his behaviors. Since anxiety is minimal in characterological behaviors and since it protects self-esteem and identity, it cannot be used as leverage. Also, confrontations are liable to be experienced as assaults on personality, causing narcissistic wounds and retrenchment.

Group may have such diverse actors as the monopolizer, the detached, the masochistic character, the borderline, the passive-aggressive, and the hysterical and narcissistic characters. We have found it helpful to involve group members in describing how they respond to such characteristics—how they feel *experientially*—without attacking the person's character armor. In effect, the therapist has to take care to guard the defenses of such persons until sufficient libidinal investment has been made in the group. The time needed for this to occur differs from person to person, from group to group, and in some instances may only be a therapeutic goal, never to be completely achieved. If such investment does occur, however, and the person feels accepted by the group despite his character, a loosening of defenses will then bring about transference issues that can be analyzed.

Sexual Acting Out

When Bob joined the group, he was angry and sullen; he did not participate except to offer sarcastic and negative comments. Female group members were attracted to him because of his good looks. Time and time again, Jean, the most outgoing woman in the group, attempted to engage him. After such maneuvers to welcome Bob and assimilate him into the group failed, Jean was sexually intimate with him "to afford him entry into the group." Of course, this was ineffective, and Jean and Bob became antagonistic toward one another.

Roots of the Acting Out.   Jean needed a "loving family" to validate her. It was difficult for her to allow for differences and separations. She could not tolerate a group member who did not love the group. Jean had attempted (in vain) to keep her family of origin together by performing services for each one. With men, Jean was accommodating and then disappointed when they left her.

Intervention.   While the group acknowledged Jean's "good intentions," they questioned the effectiveness of her behavior. Members elicited from Bob the acknowledgment that although he did not especially care for Jean, he took her up on her offer when she pressed it on him. The therapist, remaining neutral, commented that still another attempt on the part of the group members to involve Bob had failed.

Mullan and Rosenbaum (1962) primarily addressed aggressive behaviors. Although they set limits, they cautioned therapists to examine their own anxieties and not to intervene prematurely. The therapist cannot strictly prohibit acting out, but the recommendations for handling such behavior differ with each therapist.

Later, Rosenbaum and Berger (1975) stated that if the transference is pointed out immediately after the motor discharge of an act, the patient can begin to acquire control over his previously blind behavior. Rutan and Stone (1984) believed that rigid rules place therapists and patients in a no-win position. By pointing out a problem, the therapist has discharged his duty, and the responsibility then lies with the patient.

Acting Out Aggression

Charles, a rather schizoid person, habitually came 15 minutes late to group meetings. When he first entered the group, he had explained that he tended to become overinvolved in his job, which is a challenge to him and represents an avenue for recognition and acclaim. Group members had become irritated about this lateness pattern, feeling that Charles was giving them short shrift by making his work more important.

Finally, one day when Charles was 25 minutes late, a recent group member, Bill, challenged him provocatively. Charles explained in a very controlled voice that he had "many hassles" in his life and did not want any more from the group. Ignoring his admonition, Ruth began "harping," with a cutting tongue, on his asocial behavior. Charles became red in the face and, exercising the utmost control, told Ruth how he would like to beat her up, pummel her, and push the words back into her mouth. He warned her that she'd better shut up because he could not guarantee his behavioral control.

Roots of the Acting Out. Charles had an intrusive mother and a dictatorial father. While compliant on the surface, he had separated himself emotionally from both. Although he appeared mild-mannered, he was unable to tolerate complaining, intrusive women, or dictatorial men. He harbored murderous, hidden fantasies. Bill saw in Charles an aspect of himself—the rebel who wanted special attention and recognition and could not submit to the rules that govern everybody else. Ruth responded to Charles as if he were her husband, with whom she had chronic, long-standing battles for control.

Intervention. After Charles's outburst, a silence settled over the group. The therapist praised Charles for exercising control over his motor discharge. He told Bill and Ruth that it was understandable that they wanted more from Charles but questioned whether their method of addressing him could be successful. He asked whether Ruth was aware of when her harping became too much for another person. He interpreted then the incident's transferential meaning for each person. After this incident, neither Bill nor Ruth again provoked Charles in this manner. Nor did Charles have another crisis like this. However, the group remembered the crisis and often spoke about it.

Acting Out by Irregular Attendance

Lola, a group member of long standing, participated in the group on a surface level, and any attempt to deepen her involvement met with passive-aggressive resistance. She also took irregular vacations that did not coincide with scheduled group vacations. Although the group and the therapist pointed out to her that her statement of how much she needed the group for support did not appear congruent with her behavior, she had always been able to defend herself by rationalizing and citing extenuating circumstances.

One day, when there was a silence during the session, Lola again announced that she would be away on vacation. The group was stunned. Joe, who had persistently attempted to help Lola, exploded. He told her how annoyed he was that all his attempts to get her to become more involved and to be there for him had failed; the outcome was always the same—she left and had no feelings of regret.

Lola was silent for a moment. Then she remarked that announcing her trip during the middle of the group session instead of in the beginning had again put her into a masochistic position. She resented Joe's telling her when she could take a vacation and would not accede to anyone's controlling her life. Further, Joe reminded her of her older brother, who had shirked his responsibility of taking care of five siblings and shoved this onerous task onto her. She stated that she did not want that responsibility now; she wanted to be free.

Roots of the Acting Out. Lola, the oldest girl of six siblings, resented her brothers for having more freedom than she and her sisters had. Her parents could not handle such a big family, so her mother had assigned the task to Lola, who was an obedient child. Lola resented this bitterly, but because she needed family support, she could not openly oppose her mother. Lola had never married and tended to discourage a suitor when it appeared that she would have to accommodate to his life-style.

Joe resembled her older brother, whom she "wanted to kick across the football field." He came from a working-class family and had one younger sister. His mother, who had suffered from a serious illness, had emotionally removed herself from him; his father had been unable to give him support; and his sister was sassy, not accepting his overtures. Joe felt that any involvement with a woman was death; in the end, they left and were not there for him. Nevertheless, he continued to become emotionally involved, needed their love, and tended to become something of an older brother or a father figure for them, trying to reform them but unwilling to "play."

Intervention. No intervention on the part of the group therapist was necessary. These senior members were aware of each other's character and engaged it. The transferential material was spontaneously elicited and available for exploration.

Acting Out by Lateness and Late Payment

In preliminary interviews, Terry, a new group member, was informed about the meeting time and about when the fee should be paid. After the first group sessions, during which she was anxious and constricted, a pattern developed. She arrived on time, she arrived late; she paid on time, she paid late. Although the group members addressed her tardiness, Terry had good excuses. However, she also complained that group members "made too much of it." During sessions, she looked out the window, did not participate, and spoke only when spoken to. From time to time, the group therapist would mention that she had come late or paid late. Terry would blush and ask why she was being "picked on." It was suggested that her lateness was a way to be noticed. She denied this, insisting that nothing was more uncomfortable for her than being in the limelight. Her way of dressing and sitting belied this, however. She projected the image of a pretty picture that had been composed with care. After the therapist pointed this out to her, she admitted wanting the therapist's attention more than she wanted to join the members in their discussions. The group experienced Terry as thinking that they were not worthy of her attention. But because she had an appearance of fragility, they treated her kindly. They told her that she could avoid being "picked on" by coming on time and paying on time.

Roots of the Acting Out. Terry was the only child of immigrant parents. Her mother stressed appearances; her father was a feared authority. During adolescence, she revolted, wishing to be more like her schoolmates. She learned to be secretive and lead a double life. Terry could never oppose her father, except by running away. At the expense of emotional involvement, she made several life decisions to enhance her status and narcissism. She did not want to be given orders and rules, but sought an environment in which she was admired for her looks and good intentions and where she was left to her own devices.

Intervention. The group therapist thought that the group was fooled by Terry's apparent fragility. He therefore decided to take a more active stance to evoke transference, and for a while purposefully called on Terry in every session. Her lack of involvement in group discussions, her sitting posture, and other nonverbal behaviors were called to her attention. This resulted in her admission that she both wanted attention from the therapist and feared him as an authority. She acknowledged that she had a hard time following rules and essentially did not want to be bothered with them. After several discussions of her transferences, the group therapist left her alone. She subsequently became more integrated into the group, and her behavior seemed less constricted.

Depending on the individual and the context, acting out may be a symptom, a resistance, a characteristic interpersonal style, or a nonadaptive defensive maneuver to guard the integrity of the self. Obviously, in each instance and with each individual case, the intervention has to be tailor-made and appropriate.

Before intervening, the therapist must reflect on whether a particular acting-out behavior has become a neurotic symptom arising in the course of therapy and is therefore the container of specific transference feelings, or whether it is determined by anxiety arising from narcissistic wounds and a danger to the identity the patient has or wishes to establish. Such consideration should be emphasized throughout the range of acting-out behaviors. In addition, when patients near the end of their therapy, acting out may represent healthy trial actions that are colored by the fear of separation.

For example, Jean's attempt to "love" Bob and to integrate him into a loving group family represented identity formation in an attempt to cope with anxiety. Jean did not easily tolerate differences and aggressive behaviors. Her wish to be seen and to see herself as a loving, assertive person was dependent on external validation and climate. Disruptive influences in this ideal picture caused disruption in her psychic harmony. Thus, an oedipal interpretation would have missed the mark and have caused further anxiety and disruptiveness. Validating her good intentions and helping her to deal with Bob's negativism without causing harm to her self-picture was the correct intervention *at that time.*

Although Charles's chronic lateness and schizoid withdrawal contained transference elements, they were not available for introspective observation. Here, as in Jean's case, by making a late entrance, his behavioral message was that he was important and that he was powerful enough (in a passive-aggressive way) to ward off the group members' criticism. This message was important *at that particular time.* Later, Charles was able to verbalize that he needed to assure himself that he "had balls."

On the other hand, entering the group and starting out with late arrivals and late fee payments, Terry exhibited a symptom caused by the anxiety of entering and having to be involved with a cohesive analytic group that might pierce her mask of "a beautiful picture." Because it was a symptom that contained resistance to group integration, the group therapist decided to address it as he would other symptoms—with confrontation, clarification, and interpretation.

ACTING OUT BY THE GROUP

At times, an entire therapy group may act out. Such behavior may be a response to a too-passive therapist *or* to an overcontrolling therapist. Or, if the group therapist abdicates leadership and participates as another member of the group, becoming pseudodemocratic, the group-as-a-whole may react. This reaction could include such behaviors as ignoring (that is, eliminating) the therapist or engaging in nontherapeutic behaviors like joking with one another during the session or becoming involved in trivial socializing.

At times, the entire group might unite in resistance against the therapist. For instance, in one group led by an inexperienced therapist, the group spent the first half hour of each session discussing baseball scores and the ranking of teams. At other times, there may be expressions of aggression against the therapist.

Kadis and colleagues (1974) referred to group resistance as a *G response* and believed that it was caused by unresolved feelings that disrupt the group homeostasis. It may be due not only to leadership style but also to members' leaving or entering the group or other disruptive events.

One group lost one of its most disturbed, acting-out members, Carol. She tended to argue with group members who tried to help her with her flamboyant, masochistic behaviors. In a short time, she would have the whole group embroiled in fights with her; and she became a help-rejecting complainer. This Gordian knot could not be resolved, and Carol quit therapy. The group was saddened by her leaving and berated themselves and, implicitly, the therapist for not being able to help Carol.

When there seemed to be no resolution to the group's inability to mourn and separate, the group therapist decided to put two new group members into the group – a young man and a young woman – as replacements. For months the group ignored them, but when the young man tried to assert himself, senior male group members attempted to squash him. This situation was handled with group-as-a-whole interventions, the therapist interpreting the group's feelings toward the therapist. Murderous feelings of rage surfaced, with an attempt to make the therapist feel as impotent and depressed as the group felt. After several months, however, the climate changed.

ACTING OUT BY THE THERAPIST

Not only group members and whole groups, but also group therapists, act out. Some therapists act out by shying away from addressing patients' acting-out behaviors. Some are overly "nice" because of their fears of confronting angry members and may even try to placate members rather than interpret the behavior. Other therapists may unconsciously stimulate acting out by the group members.

Therapists act out when they enforce the "rules" with excessive zeal. This behavior may signal their anxiety, guilt, or panic. But such excessive zeal may at times precipitate premature termination by group members.

Some therapists act out by giving too much gratification to group members, while others act out by becoming personally involved with particular patients. Sometimes therapists act out their own insecurity, anxiety, panic, or guilt. Alternatively, especially with less experienced group therapists, the acting out may evidence the therapist's vulnerability, feelings of inadequacy, weakness, or intimidation.

The therapist's acting out may come out in being overactive, overprotective, or overcontrolling. Or, a therapist who does not feel in control of a situation may become defensive, self-protective, and more involved with her own reactions than with the group members', resulting in impulsive or irrational reactions.

A therapist's countertransference may exacerbate acting out by individual members or by the group-as-a-whole. Viewing this acting out from a moralistic point of view or trying to prevent group members from acting out may emphasize the therapist's countertransference—which may then invite further acting out.

As Rutan and Stone (1984) mention, a therapist's acting out may also proceed in more subtle ways. Admitting a patient to a group that may be inappropriate, forcing the patient and the group to stay together, or letting such a patient be scapegoated out of the group may all indicate a group therapist's countertransferential acting out.

When individual member reactions or group-as-a-whole responses are caused by the therapist's style or anxiety, we would suggest not addressing them as transference. If, upon reflection or consultation, the group therapist validates the behavior ascribed to him by group members, then the reality has to be acknowledged and changes made. When, for example, the therapist has admitted an inappropriate member to the group for his own irrational reasons, he may have to examine with the group and the patient why the therapeutic setting is maladaptive. He will subsequently have to plan, in conjunction with the patient and the group, the separation of this person from the group.

A group therapist may be accused of "playing favorites," with a resultant divisive effect on the group. If this is validated as a perception that has not been distorted, the group therapist would have to examine with the group the reason for this behavior and seek changes. Similarly, when group members are not allowed to express affects because the therapist is too reality oriented, this style may need to be examined and more flexibility achieved.

Although the responses just described can be viewed as symptomatic, they are also a reaction to *real* events within the therapy group and are not derived from infantile conflicts.

Acting out has been examined both intrapsychically and interpersonally. It is seen as symptomatic in the sense that it signifies a communication block because of unverbalized emotions, thoughts, and messages. As such, the disguised communication must be deciphered in order to understand the meaning of the behavior and to render it susceptible to examination.

Acting out may occur by an individual, between patients, by subgroups, by the group-as-a-whole, and by the therapist. The etiology and meaning will differ depending on the origin of the anxiety and the function and intentionality of the act.

Patients will often act out symptomatically because infantile conflicts have been stimulated in the present; that is, the behavior contains unverbalized transference messages. In this instance, the message must be explored with the help of the group and the therapist. The patient is then advised that acting-out impulses can be linked to specific feelings and dynamics; should they be repeatedly experienced, the patient is advised to verbalize the feelings instead of discharging them into motor behavior.

At other times, during successful therapy, patients may act out in the form of trial actions arising from the need to test out newly developed abilities. In such cases, encouragement and appreciation of these achievements, rather than addressing of the transference, are in order.

Patients with serious character pathology may act out continuously in the way they integrate or resist integration into a therapeutic group. Although, theoretically speaking, hidden transferences are at work here also, the patients experience no intrapsychic conflict, but rather feel in conflict with the environment. Acceptance by the therapist and the group helps such a person to be more at ease and elicits his cooperation in understanding what the externalized conflict is about.

Group-as-a-whole acting out also signifies that something is amiss. This can include resistance to a painful group theme, reaction to an event in the group, or reaction to external events that resonate with an intragroup event. Or, such responses can be a reaction to a style of therapeutic intervention that the group considers inappropriate, preventing further exploration and ventilation. Such group-as-a-whole responses are indicative of a disturbed group climate and are a threat to the group's functional integrity.

Group therapists may inadvertently act out for several reasons. Group events or members may have stimulated countertransference of which the therapist is not aware. Certain events may have clashed with the group therapist's personal value system and philosophy of life. Or, the therapist's style may not suit the group at a particular phase of the group's development.

In handling acting-out behaviors, moralistic attitudes and prohibitions on the group therapist's part will be counterproductive. The emphasis is on decoding messages, achieving insight into acting-out behaviors, and therapeutic honesty.

REFERENCES

Abt, L. E. (1965). Acting out in group psychotherapy: a transactional approach. In *Acting Out*, ed. L. E. Abt and S. L. Weissman, pp. 173–182. New York: Grune & Stratton.

Bernstein, A. (1978). The fear of acting out. In *Group Therapy Monograph #5*, pp. 7–16. New York: Washington Square Institute.

Bry, T. (1953). Acting out in group psychotherapy. *International Journal of Group Psychotherapy* 3:42–48.

Fenchel, G. H. (1978). The concept of acting out. In *Group Therapy Monograph #5*, pp. 3–6. New York: Washington Square Institute.

Fenchel, G. H., and Flapan, D. (1985). Resistance in group psychotherapy. *Group* 9:35-47.

Flapan, D. (1978). Acting out, acting in, acting up: synthesis and
implications. In *Group Therapy Monograph #5*, pp. 50-56. New York:
Washington Square Institute.

Foulkes, S. H., and Anthony, E. J. (1957). *Group Psychotherapy: The
Psycho-analytic Approach*. Baltimore: Penguin.

Freud, A. (1968). Acting out. *International Journal of Psycho-
Analysis* 49:165-170.

Freud, S. (1914). Further recommendations in the technique of psychoanalysis: recollection, repetition and working through. In *Collected
Papers* 2:366-376. London: Hogarth, 1949.

Grinberg, I. (1968). On acting out and its role in the psychoanalytic
process. *International Journal of Psycho-Analysis* 49:171-178.

Grotjahn, M. (1973). Selected clinical observations from psychoanalytic
group psychotherapy. In *Group Therapy 1973: An Overview*, ed. L.
Wolberg and E. K. Schwartz, pp. 43-54. New York: Intercontinental.

Kadis, A., Krasner, L., Weiner, M., Winick, C., and Foulkes, S. H.
(1974). *Practicum of Group Psychotherapy*, 2nd ed. New York:
Harper & Row.

Laplanche, J. (1968). Reports on discussion of acting out. *International
Journal of Psycho-Analysis* 49:224-230.

Mullan, H., and Rosenbaum, M. (1962). *Group Psychotherapy*. New
York: The Free Press.

Munzer, J. (1966). Acting out: communication or resistance? *International Journal of Group Psychotherapy* 16:434-441.

Rangell, L. (1968). A point of view on acting out. *International Journal
of Psycho-Analysis* 49:195-201.

Rey, J. H. (1975). Intrapsychic object relations: the individual and the
group. In *Group Therapy 1975*, ed. L. Wolberg and M. Aronson, pp.
84-101. New York: Stratton Intercontinental.

Rosenbaum, M., and Berger, S. (1975). *Group Psychotherapy and
Group Function*, rev. ed. New York: Basic Books.

Rosenthal, L. (1978). Acting out in group psychotherapy: group destructive aspects. *Group Therapy Monograph #5*, pp. 39-44. New York:
Washington Square Institute.

Rutan, S., and Stone, W. (1984). *Psychodynamic Group Psychotherapy*.
Lexington, Mass.: Heath.

Saravay, S. (1975). Group psychology and the structural theory: a
revised psychoanalytic model of group psychology. *Journal of the
American Psychoanalytic Association* 23:69-89.

Slavson, S. R. (1964). *A Textbook in Analytic Group Psychotherapy*.

New York: International Universities Press.

Spotnitz, H. (1973). Acting out in group psychotherapy. In *Group Therapy 1973: An Overview*, ed. L. Wolberg and E. K. Schwartz, pp. 28–42. New York: Intercontinental.

Vanggaard, T. (1968). Contributions to the symposium on acting out. *International Journal of Psycho-Analysis* 49:206–210.

Weiner, M. F. (1984). *Techniques of Group Psychotherapy*. New York: American Psychiatric Press.

Winnicott, D. (1968). Reports of discussions of acting out. *International Journal of Psycho-Analysis* 49:224–230.

Wolberg, A. (1983). Further thoughts on projective identification and group therapy. In *Group and Family Therapy 1982*, ed. L. Wolberg and M. Aronson, pp. 43–59. New York: Brunner/Mazel.

Wolf, A., Bross, R., Flowerman, S., Greene, J., Kadis, A., Leopold, H., et al. (1954). Sexual acting out and the psychoanalysis of groups. *International Journal of Group Psychotherapy* 4:369–379.

Yalom, I. (1985). *The Theory and Practice of Group Psychotherapy*, 3rd ed. New York: Basic Books.

Ziferstein, I., and Grotjahn, M. (1957). Group dynamics of acting out in analytic group psychotherapy. *International Journal of Group Psychotherapy* 7:77–85.

Chapter 12
Group Contacts without the Therapist

Over the past 30 years, there has been much controversy regarding the consequences of group patients' having contact with one another outside the regularly scheduled sessions (at which the therapist is not present).

The arguments by those practitioners who follow what they perceive as a classical Freudian tradition extend not only to what might be construed as extragroup social interactions, but also to the so-called alternate session (Wolf and Schwartz 1962), a regularly scheduled session not attended by the group therapist. They are convinced that the potential dangers of such contacts outweigh whatever good may emerge. Hannah (1979), in a brief review, cogently presents their arguments. What, then, are they?

Traditionally, analysts have claimed that only analysis of resistance and transference can be considered analytic therapy and that whatever remains unanalyzed increases resistance or encourages acting-out behavior, or both. Contacts without the therapist present – that is, whatever cannot be analytically scrutinized, whether in alternate sessions or as extragroup socializing – would, of course, fall into this category. The second argument centers around Mahler and colleagues' paradigm of

separation–individuation (1975). According to this view, alternate sessions, without the therapist, as well as any social contacts
outside the group, are a way of escaping the painful feelings of
separation and therefore prolong dependency and do not encourage separation–individuation. The third argument stems from
the belief that contacts without the presence of the therapist are
representative of Alexander's position (1948) that cure can be
obtained from a "corrective emotional experience." Clinicians
who see themselves as classical analysts vehemently oppose this
view, holding that change can come about only through intrapsychic reorganization.

In responding to the first argument, our experience has shown
that there is resistance whether or not contact between group
members occurs without the therapist; this resistance can be
dealt with in the regularly scheduled session. In most instances,
whatever interaction occurs in the therapist's absence, whether
resistance, transference, or acting out, is sooner or later brought
into the regular group session and discussed in the presence of
the therapist. The group members will often recognize the acting
out of one another's transferences to the therapist and point it out
in the regular therapy session. In addition, some forms of acting
out cannot be avoided in the group modality even when the
therapist is present, because it is an action-oriented approach, as
contrasted with an introspective one. One thus has to decide
whether to view *all* acting out as *only* resistance or whether
some acting out may also contain growth-promoting elements.
Some writers (Abt 1965, Fried 1979, Grotjahn 1976, Kadis 1956,
Mullan and Rosenbaum 1975, Munzer 1966) believe that certain
kinds of acting-out behaviors may also represent communications
or attempts at mastery.

Therapists who use alternate sessions do not usually conceive
of themselves as doing *individual analysis* in the group setting.
Rather, they tend to see group process and group dynamics, as
well as relationships between members, as important to the
therapeutic process, and to use these in working with their group
therapy patients.

Concerning separation–individuation issues, one has to be
aware that Mahler's is only one of many analytic paradigms. It

can be argued that keeping the patient always under the therapist's scrutinizing eye may even hamper individuation and contribute to continued dependence on the all-powerful therapist.

It would seem that those who forbid member contact without the therapist present both prefer to have complete control over what happens among group members and tend to be more authority oriented. It is a more traditional orientation to assume that the therapist is not only the central figure but also the most important person in the group, and that the most valued interaction is that between the therapist and each patient. This view implies that only one person (the therapist) knows how to be beneficial to each member or knows what the best interests of each member are, that group members have no beneficial effect on one another, and that the only one who can understand what is happening in the group is the therapist. Therefore, it is essential for the therapist to have complete control over intermember interactions, perhaps to "protect" some of the more fragile members, or to maintain a certain focus or orientation, or to regulate the pace of the group.

Another implication is that each patient will "bring out everything" and be completely honest in the presence of the therapist, so that contact with only peers will bring out nothing different or nothing additional. Obviously, different behaviors *will occur* when the therapist is not present than when the therapist is present. Some patients will be more relaxed and less defensive when only their peers are present. Some may feel freer in the therapist's absence to criticize the therapist or to express other negative feelings about him. For others, because of their negative transference feelings toward the therapist, it may be easier to "open up" to other members outside the group session and then, having discussed it in a "safe" situation, to bring the transference feelings into the regular *group* session.

Those who forbid contact without the therapist present may assume that the therapist is the *only* or the *most important* transference figure. But other members are often related to as "father," "mother," or sibling.

In addition, it is also often a positive experience for group members in the alternate session to see that the group is able to function without the therapist present. Such experiences may result in less focusing on the therapist and more focusing on the other group members, and in fact may contribute to increasing group cohesiveness in the regular sessions with the therapist present. Through some of the alliances that emerge outside the regular session, members may feel *less* anxious in bringing difficult material into the regular session because they anticipate support and understanding from other members.

The third argument, questioning the value of corrective emotional experiences, is more tricky. Inherent in Alexander's view is the belief that contact alone may have mutative effects on psychic deficit and conflict. Even the classical analysts see themselves as having a benign mutative effect, although they reserve this position exclusively to themselves. As traditional an analyst as Greenacre (1954) called attention to a "basic transference" in all people. Tarachow (1963) discussed a compelling "object need" that occurs in all human relationships. In other words, when a patient meets with the therapist over a period of time, there occurs a longing to be closer to the therapist. If it occurs with the therapist, it certainly can also occur with the group members over a period of time.

In group therapy, when conducted as an interactional modality, we cannot shut off, at the end of the hour, what has been experienced and what has been happening. When we encourage patients to interact and to explore how they feel about one another and about themselves (as we do when we place a patient in a group), how can we rationalize that it is benign only when it occurs in the therapist's presence but becomes destructive with the same peers without the therapist's presence?

Grunebaum and Solomon (1982), who at first considered the group members' dining out together a resistance, were forced by events to assume a different view—that extragrouup socializing might be accepted as a developmental phenomenon. They did not feel that it constituted a hazard against individuation, because the final relationship would be determined by mature interests. Indeed, we have known very few patients who continued for long their relationships with one another, either while still in group or after leaving the group. Once the therapeutic task has been accomplished, people tend to form other friendships.

Although we are aware that there are therapists who strictly prohibit, at the risk of being expelled from therapy, extragroup contacts and sexual alliances, we cannot go along with their position on several grounds. For one, it is very difficult to set up prohibitions, with the threat of expulsion, unless you can, and are willing to, enforce these prohibitions. Even if we were willing to terminate treatment each time a patient "broke" the rule prohibiting extragroup contacts, it is doubtful that such a position would be therapeutically helpful. In contrast to the analytic position of maintaining a neutral stance, the therapist, in forbidding extragroup contacts with the threat of expulsion, is in reality assuming the position of the parental authority and reacting in a moralistic, punitive fashion. This stepping into a superego role, in our opinion, repeats the omnipotent, intrusive power position originally occupied by the preoedipal mother. It is as if once again the parental figure dictates to the child how life should be lived, the parental values instead of the individual's own life experiences being the guideposts. This position is alien to ego psychology, in which the therapist allows and encourages the patient to do as much of the therapeutic work as possible in order to achieve a sense of autonomy and identity in the process of adapting and developing.

In all our groups, therefore, we have alternate sessions. We believe that a continuity exists between what happens to a person during the therapeutic hour and what happens outside the therapeutic setting. And our position has particular significance to group therapy inasmuch as it is an "in-action" treatment modality.

It can be expected that in *every* therapy group, sooner or later, some extragroup socializing will occur. Even if outside contact is forbidden by the group therapist, it will at some point take place. But because it is forbidden, it will take place surreptitiously and therefore will not be dealt with therapeutically since it will not become a topic for group discussion and analysis. Our concern is that under such conditions, there may then be temporary blocking of the entire group's therapeutic progress.

On the other hand, anticipating and accepting that extragroup contact is likely to happen, we can establish the basic ground rule, which is that *any* contact between group members outside the therapy setting is considered "group property" since it involves members of the group and will affect what happens in the group. Therefore, information about the contact is to be shared with the entire group and the therapist during group sessions.

Group members are thus treated like respected adults who are expected to abide by the rules, rather than like children who are forbidden certain actions and who then do not report these actions because they expect to be punished or, at the least, reprimanded "in public." In order for group members to be completely open and honest in reporting extragroup contacts, they must believe that they will not be judged, criticized, or attacked for their actions, but rather that they will be accepted and that an attempt will be made to understand the underlying dynamics of their behavior—just as would be the case with any other group behavior. The members must feel that they can trust the group *and* the therapist, and must have some confidence in the therapist's handling of what is revealed, no matter how difficult the situation.

Extragroup socializing may have either positive or negative effects on the individual members, as well as on the group-as-a-whole. But even the negative effects can be temporary and can become positive if the action is openly discussed and examined within the group setting. The behaviors exhibited in extragroup socializing are dealt with in the same way any other material is dealt with in the group—by searching for the meanings and significance for those involved.

Positive Aspects of Extragroup Socializing

Maintaining Continuity and Cohesiveness

The out-of-group contacts of members can at times aid in maintaining the continuity and cohesiveness of a therapy group during difficult periods. Members may informally—over the telephone or in personal get-togethers—persuade a resistant member to attend group sessions and to discuss difficult topics.

In one group, Ralph became so furious with Betty, who was confronting him with her feelings about his "macho" attitude, that he abruptly stood up in the middle of the session and left the group. During the week, two of the other group members called Ralph and spoke to him about how they had perceived the interaction and emphasized how important it was for him to return to the next session and try to deal directly with Betty. In complying with their suggestion, Ralph was able to begin to get a better idea of how he came across to women, not only in the therapy group but also on the outside, and to see his own role in provoking women.

Facilitating Exposure in Group

Extragroup socializing often facilitates more "exposure" in the therapy group.

Chuck had often offered to drive various women home after group, and from time to time some had accepted. After some months, however, he settled down to driving Selma home regularly since she lived near him.

Then, in one session, Selma brought up the fact that Chuck would give her a ride home but then expect her to feel obligated to him. When she mentioned this in group, the other women stated that they had also felt that he was nice to them in order to evoke a positive response or to ensure their support in group. After first objecting to this characterization, Chuck later said that he had thought about it and recalled that women outside the group had accused him of treating them like whores – expecting favors in exchange for his gifts or kindnesses. This was the initial opening up of a basic dynamic, which was followed up over many months in group.

Indicating Dynamics in Group

Another positive aspect of extragroup socializing is that it can provide an indication of some of the less overt dynamics that are occurring within the group.

Fred and Bill appeared to be of different generations, although the age difference between them was less than ten years. On every issue they opposed each other or had differing views. Fred, at the age of 27, seemed still to be part of the college generation and was intolerant of conservative dress and attitudes. Bill, at the age of 36, saw himself as a middle-aged man, dressed accordingly, and was moralistic in disapproving modern styles and customs. Yet after being in the same group for a couple of years—always on opposite sides of each issue—they began to go out for dinner together (which they mentioned weeks later in the group situation). Their pairing on the outside had *anticipated* their pairing within the group, where each began to support the other, especially in confronting the women in the group.

What gradually came out in the group sessions was that Bill sympathized with Fred's loneliness and depressed feelings after Fred separated from his wife; and Bill, who was a bachelor and often ate alone, had suggested that Fred join him and enjoyed introducing Fred to his favorite restaurants. On the other hand, Fred, who was feeling "miserable" and abandoned, welcomed Bill's overtures and accepted the companionship that was being offered outside of group. This contributed to Bill's positive feelings about himself for having helped Fred. Later, when Fred was no longer overwhelmed by the separation, he became more active in social activities and established some new friendships, and there was a tapering off of his extragroup socializing with Bill, who in turn was developing a relationship with a middle-aged woman outside the group.

Substituting for Social Relationships

This pattern of tapering off extragroup socializing frequently occurs as members become involved in outside relationships. It appears that the out-of-group socializing is sometimes used as a substitute for other social relationships, and perhaps even as an *opportunity for practicing social relating*. Thus it can frequently serve as a transitional period for those in the group who have no close relationships outside group and have not been successful in trying to establish such relationships.

George used going out for beer after the alternate session with two of the female group members as a rehearsal for going out with other women. And as he began to date on weekends, he felt less need to go out with the women from group. It had not only given him practice in talking to women, but becoming familiar with these two group members had also aided him in overcoming some of his fear of women.

Being Accepted More Quickly in Group

Occasionally a new member will use extragroup socializing as a means of being accepted more quickly as one of the group.

Soon after her entry into a therapy group, Carol, an attractive woman approaching the age of 40, joined Wilma and Sam a few times in going out for burgers after the alternate session. Once they were comfortable with her in the extragroup situation and began drawing her into the group during regular sessions, she stopped going out with them, with the excuse that she had a long trip home to Brooklyn and that going out after group made it more difficult to get up the next day.

Improving Group Relationships

Extragroup socializing is sometimes used by group members to improve their relationships within the group.

In a group composed of three women and four men, one of the women reached successful termination after several years. The two remaining women, Sally and Ruth, immediately started going out together after the alternate sessions—although they had been together in group for at least one year with no outside contact. Gradually, they became mutually empathic to each other during group sessions and for a while had an alliance in group. Once they had become better acquainted with each other, felt comfortable with the similarities and differences between them, and had accepted the loss of the third woman, they stopped going out after group, and it was less necessary to cling so much to each other in group sessions.

Helping Members over a Life Crisis

Sometimes, these out-of-group contacts are used to help a member over a life crisis.

Fran had been dating a man for a year and a half and had often used the group to talk about her ambivalent feelings toward him—how attractive she found him and how much she enjoyed being with him, and her fear of being engulfed by him or being pressured to give up her career and her separate life in the city, including group therapy. With the group's help, she had finally reached a point of being able to handle this, so that she was living with him in the suburbs, continuing her freelance career, and commuting to the therapy group. One evening, she happily informed the group that she was planning to get married in the spring.

Fran did not attend group the next week; a message was left by her sister that Fran's fiancé had suddenly died of a heart attack the day before the group session. Most of the session was spent discussing the shock and feelings about the fiancé's sudden death and the effect this would have on Fran. Group members wanted to contact her to offer their sympathy and to ask if they could help in any way. Because she had been living with her fiancé, however, no one knew the telephone number, nor even the last name of the man, so they could not reach Fran.

After the group session, one member, Max, managed to track down the telephone number of Fran's mother, called her, and found out how to reach Fran. He then called her, gave support and sympathy, and then, with her permission,

called as many of the group members as he could find
telephone numbers for, so that he could give them Fran's
telephone number. Everyone he contacted then called Fran.

The following week when Fran came to group–a week
after the death–she talked about feeling strongly supported
by the group and feeling she would receive understanding at
the group session. She expressed her appreciation for the
telephone calls, indicating that she had somehow anticipated
them, even though she knew that no one had her telephone
number at her fiancé's house. She trusted the group to the
extent that she was able to spend most of the session talking
about her feelings about her fiancé's death and about the
events following his death, involving his mother and children. She talked about her earlier ambivalence and about
the tremendous loss she felt now that she had reached the
point of wanting to marry him. Group members expressed
sympathy to her but also carried the topic further by discussing their feelings about deaths of those close to them, as
well as some anticipation of their own deaths.

Clarifying Transference

Extragroup contacts may also serve the purpose of clarifying
transference reactions.

> Terri had been frightened of Julia for a long time. With
> much caution, and with support from some other members
> and from the therapist, she was able to say that she saw Julia
> as arrogant and overwhelming and that she was afraid to
> open up in group for fear of being criticized by Julia. Then,
> due to external circumstances, they unexpectedly shared a
> taxi going home a couple of times after group. In that
> situation, they talked more easily and began to see each
> other differently. They could then start to separate the
> transference reactions they were having to each other in the
> group setting from their reactions outside group. Their own
> transference reactions thus became more obvious to them
> and became an open subject for group discussion.

NEGATIVE ASPECTS OF EXTRAGROUP SOCIALIZING

Extragroup socializing may have negative as well as positive effects. These negative effects must be dealt with by the therapist and the group in order to have some therapeutic outcome.

Subgroups

Subgroupings within therapy groups may result from extragroup socializing. Those members who are not included in the out-of-group socializing may feel envious and resentful. Being rejected by those in the subgroup may feed into feelings of being "less than" or "not worthy." It may become symbolic of status—who belongs to the "in-group" and who is in the "out-group." Though it may not be immediately discussed, someone will eventually express feelings about what is happening.

Such subgrouping repeated childhood and high school experiences for Warren. For some time he was less active than usual in group and looked sullen and depressed, until, through questioning by some of the other members, he was able to bring out his very strong negative feelings about himself and about the subgroup.

Manipulating a Group Member

In some instances extragroup socializing facilitates manipulation.

In one group, a male member, Stanley, became a father for the first time. Freda, who often went out after group sessions for a snack with Stanley and Mary, suggested to Mary that the two of them buy a baby gift together and take it to the new baby. Mary accepted the idea, although without much enthusiasm since she was less involved with Stanley than Freda was. However, she even agreed to shop for the gift on her lunch hour since it was more convenient for her than for Freda—as Freda had pointed out.

After Mary had bought the gift and arranged with Stanley for a visit to the baby, Freda backed out of the arrangement, and Mary felt compelled to make the visit herself and to present the gift herself, as *her* gift to the baby. Other members of the group did not know about this until some weeks after the episode had occurred; and many sessions were then spent in dealing with Mary's feelings of betrayal and of being trapped by Freda into a situation that Mary would not have initiated.

Extragroup contacts can also offer other possibilities for manipulation of one member by another.

In another group, Sarah, who had been in the group for a couple of years, made a point of cultivating out-of-group friendships with *each* new male member. After a man had attended a couple of sessions, she would suggest eating or drinking together after the alternate session. Then she would exchange telephone numbers with the person and call during the week "to chat." She would sometimes even arrange to meet during the week between group sessions. This assured her the support of the new member in group – at least until another new member entered the group, at which time Sarah would shift her attention to him. After this had happened with three successive men, they began comparing notes in group and then joined forces to confront her with what they felt she had been doing to each of them. In this instance, each one felt he had been "had" in some way, and what had started as a supportive relationship became a suspect one, with the three coming together to question Sarah's motives and her sincerity in pursuing each of them.

Acting Out Defiance of Authority

Some members use extragroup socializing as a way of acting out their feelings of defiance toward the authority figure. They share secrets "behind the back" of the therapist and enjoy feeling that they know more about one another than the therapist knows about each of them.

Robert and Debra would have conversations in the car on the way home, and these conversations were not brought back into the group. Instead, they tried to help one another deal with problems in work situations and in interpersonal relationships; then, having thought of a "solution," they did not feel it necessary or desirable to discuss it in group. Only much later, when Debra felt that Robert was making unreasonable demands on her for sympathetic understanding and that he had expectations of her that she was unwilling to meet, did she bring the matter up in group to search for the meaning of what had been happening.

"Special" Relationships

Out-of-group socializing can also be used to develop "special" relationships between group members.

Eileen used the group session itself as a "warm-up" and did not get into her deeper feelings until the alternate group sessions. However, this resulted in other members' eventually confronting her in the group with their feelings of resentment that they were being asked to give *so much* to her after the group session itself was over, rather than her using the group session to understand her feelings and needs.

When the pressures of participating as an equal in a group are too much for a member to tolerate, extragroup contacts may be sought to compensate for the narcissistic affront of *not* being special. Such a member wants to be in the limelight and will engage in sadomasochistic behavior in the group to achieve this goal, provoking other members and then feeling misunderstood when they respond to the provocations. The idea of needing help can be a threat to self-esteem, while at the same time other group members are experienced as being insensitive. A member who feels no special relationship with one person may experience the group as an unpleasant reality. When the cumulative effect of all these traumas becomes too much, such a member may seek extragroup contact to create a milieu to protect his need to be special and to avoid therapeutic scrutiny.

So it was with Sidney. He would invariably ask female group members to go out with him after the alternate session. If the woman refused to go with him, he took it as a personal rejection. If the woman joined him for food or drink, he felt "special" and would brag about it in the next group session. He wished to form narcissistic alliances with the women, expecting them to support him in group sessions, where he aired long lists of grievances, and to be his backup in any group confrontation, so that he could emerge as the "victor." Thus, Sidney used extragroup contacts to do what he felt unable to do in the group itself. When the therapist and other group members, particularly other males, were excluded, he felt more confident in his ability to "win over" the women; such alliances then served to protect his own grandiose, special, and generous self-image.

Sexual Acting Out

Extragroup socializing sometimes leads to sexual acting out. This therapists seem to feel more intensely about than they do about nonpayment of fees, irregular attendance, or other kinds of acting-out behavior. We favor Grotjahn's view (1976), based on long experience, that sex between two consenting adults never hurt anybody as long as it could be talked about in group.

Different theories have ascribed various motivations to sexual alliances. For those who are group centered, the nature of the act has been explained in terms of narcissistic, magical expectations. Boris (1970) thought of sexual alliances as an attempt to reinforce an idealized group image. More individual interpretations of many forms of acting-out behavior are found in the writings of Freud (1949) and Eckstein (1965), which seem to assume that we are dealing with repetition compulsions and attempts to master certain developmental arrests. The following is an example of a repetition compulsion in which a talented, attractive young woman attempted to recreate her relationship with her father, who had indulged her during the early years of her life.

For a long time, whenever a new man came into the therapy group, Jane, a young woman in her 20s, would manage to have a brief sexual relationship with him. Eventually it would be brought back to the group by the man when he felt that Jane was trying to use the extragroup sexual relationship to manipulate him in group and to get him to favor her over the other female group members. It had reached the point at which the group would "warn" any male newcomer about Jane. There were some attempts to explore the meaning of the sexual acting out, but Jane resisted all questioning and all interpretations by the other members.

Finally, one night, in the midst of actual sexual intercourse with a male member of the group who was nearing 50, Jane suddenly had the *feeling* that he was her father. This caused her to leap out of bed abruptly and run into the bathroom, where she experienced much anxiety. This was reported back to the therapy group and was followed up by open discussion of this episode, as well as the earlier ones, by the group. With somewhat more self-understanding, Jane was then able to exercise more control over her sexual behavior, so that it was no longer necessary for her to have sexual experiences with the male members of the therapy group.

Ziferstein and Grotjahn (1957) have emphasized the basic oral affects propelling such behaviors. It is not unlikely that heterosexual alliances in particular allow the participants, in a magical way, to ensure themselves a strong position within the group context. The man and woman who start an alliance during their early phases of group therapy may be compensating for deep-seated feelings of low self-esteem. Thus, by subgrouping in this way, they appear to form a reciprocal support system with the hope that it will raise their group status and elicit respect from their peers. Sexual alliances may have various explanations, and interpretation will have to depend on exploring and understanding the status of the participants' psychological development, as well as the group's stage of development.

Three members of one group formed a triangle – Bill, Jack, and Sophie. Bill had more education than the other two and was older and more cultured. He often presented himself as "better" than everyone else. Jack was a blue-collar worker whose major interest was in playing the role of macho man vis-à-vis the women. Sophie was a single, young professional woman who was not satisfied with her achievements and tended to latch on to people who she felt were "further up the ladder." Within the group, Jack had fulfilled a brotherly role toward Sophie, who was the only female group member he had not been sexually intimate with at one time or another. Bill related to Jack in a brotherly, supportive way and made no overt flirtatious overtures toward Sophie, although he often expressed a sympathetic attitude toward her. In contrast to Jack's macho attitude, Bill recited over and over his harmlessness to women, since he had a chronic symptom of fluctuating impotence. Sophie rejected Jack and put him down as a "male chauvinist pig." She was fascinated by Bill's charm, suaveness, and "man-of-the-world" quality and wanted to talk him out of his impotence.

One day during session, Sophie and Bill announced to the group that they had spent time with each other and intended to become sexually involved. Far from being dismayed, the group supported their position and "rooted" for Sophie to cure Bill's impotence. It was obvious that they preferred Sophie in the role of a magical Venus than in her usual role of depressed, whining baby. It also seemed clear that they could not deal with Bill's deeply ingrained characterological defenses and had assigned Sophie the task of overcoming them in order to make Bill a more benevolent and integrated group figure. Sophie's intentions were to elevate her own status in the "group family," as well as to elevate the total family by magically transforming Bill from a depressed, bitter man to the Prince Charming of her choice.

When we look at the intentions of the participants, we are struck by the observation that no true object relationships existed. Both Sophie and Bill were acting out a repeated life pattern. Bill dared not examine his own responsibility for his pattern of impotence and a seeming inability to form lasting relationships with members of either sex. He assumed a passive role, throwing his fate into the lap of a more powerful "mother" figure and demanding a solution to his problems. Sophie, picking up the challenge, insisted on a magical transformation of herself via her transformation of another.

As one could anticipate, even if successful, such triumph could only be temporary. And indeed, although both Sophie and Bill celebrated Bill's successful sexual act with a bottle of champagne, the relationship soon ran afoul when each party rejected the demands of the other. Sexual success could only have been maintained if there had been very little investment besides the organ pleasure, or if the sexual enjoyment could have been integrated within the context of mutual enjoyment of each other. As soon as Sophie demanded that Bill leave his wife and daughter and spend more time with her, she retransformed him from the Prince Charming to the haughty, rejecting, bitter father figure. As soon as Bill objected to Sophie's temper tantrums and whininess, Sophie changed for him from the powerful, accepting, sexual mother to the demanding, rejecting, preoedipal witch. The group, then, underwent a period of disappointment and found it difficult to accept that they had not found a more potent magic. After working through this reaction, however, the group was able to deal more effectively with Bill's untamed aggression and Sophie's passive-aggressive role.

HANDLING EXTRAGROUP SOCIALIZING

As already indicated, many individuals give up the extragroup socializing on their own when they see its destructive aspects—

such as the potential to be exploited or taken advantage of by another group member. Some stop the out-of-group contacts when they begin to feel that too many demands are being made on them. For example, in one group, Oscar stated his feeling that to give in to *any* of Harriet's demands outside the group was to open himself to further demands and to a dependence on him that he could not handle.

Others will stop out-of-group contact when they feel it is taking too much time outside the group session and interfering with their other activities. Still others will stop when they feel that the extragroup relationship has become too intense and they cannot cope with the feelings—either their own or the other participant's. They recognize and acknowledge within the sessions that they need the therapist and other group members to be present as a safeguard and as a limiting environment.

It appears that the more dependent, needy, and isolated members are more likely to socialize with other group members outside the sessions. However, their hopes and expectations of the extragroup contacts usually are not fulfilled in a satisfying way. They then "outgrow" this type of behavior when they begin to have more gratifying relationships of their own in the "real" world.

The effect of out-of-group socializing depends to a large extent on how the situation is handled within the group by the therapist.

> Richard and Fern became acquainted with each other in a therapy group at a time when each was on the verge of breaking up with a spouse. Each was looking for an immediate intimate relationship, and each experienced feelings of physical attraction to the other that were apparent to the group members.
>
> Several weeks later, Fern called the therapist and said that she was thinking of leaving the group. When questioned about her reasons, she mentioned—almost incidentally—that she and Richard were "dating" and "had gone to bed together," and she did not want to talk about it with the group. The therapist explained how important it was to look at the relationship within the group setting in order to understand

its significance as well as its meaning, that it was pertinent
to the entire group, and that, if there was a firm basis for the
relationship, it could withstand the group's scrutiny. Fern
agreed to continue with the therapy group "for the time
being" and said she trusted the therapist's judgment and
would talk about her relationship with Richard at the next
group session—which she did.

Fern was defiant in presenting the situation to the group,
stating that her seeing Richard was *her right* and that she
intended to continue the relationship no matter what the
group said. The men in group were especially sympathetic
with Richard's position. Questions were raised in terms of
how Richard would feel in group when Fern talked about
dating other men, as she had done previously and probably
would do in the future. Group members, both men and
women, pointed out how Fern had used what Richard had
said in the group—about his loneliness, low self-esteem,
difficulty meeting women, admiration of Fern's gregarious-
ness, and problem of always needing to please a woman—to
get him involved with her. They also recalled Fern's talking
about some of her own problems in starting to date again;
Richard was a known quantity, readily available, and easily
manipulated. The sexual interaction was lightly touched on
since the other dynamics seemed more important to the
group members.

Richard had only one more date with Fern. He was
uncomfortable with the idea of their relationship's being
discussed in the group. And Fern had used her ability to
relate to Richard as a stepping-stone to a deeper and more
permanent involvement with another man outside group,
which eventuated in marriage after two years.

Other types of extragroup contact must also be dealt with by
the therapist. For example, extragroup contacts may be used by
both males and females to create situations charged with eroticism. Although they may engage in similar behavior, however,
the parties involved may have different aims. A man who is
insecure about his masculinity may want to impress a female

group member with his car, perhaps without consciously thinking that the closed, intimate space sets up seductive possibilities. The woman may respond to the offer of a ride for the sake of convenience, without consciously recognizing that she is engaging in a seductive scenario. Should these invitations be repeatedly offered and accepted, the frequency of contact will intensify the suggestive interplay, with the possibility that the man will finally make a sexual advance. The woman may then stage her own scenario by denying any responsibility and putting the blame on the man.

Alan, Rose, and Penny had been together in a group for over a year. Alan frequently offered the women rides home because the three lived in the same general direction. One evening, as each woman got out of the car, Alan kissed her passionately—or at least this was what was reported to the group by the two women. The therapist asked the other members for their reactions, and they immediately began to focus on the women rather than on Alan. As the group questioned the portrayal of Alan, what became obvious was that both of the women had been seductive with him, and he felt he was being responsive. He had previously been reticent about participating in group and had spent more time listening than talking, while each of the women was quite an active group participant. Alan had frequently expressed his admiration of each woman's ability to be open and to reveal her feelings to the group. In their discussion, group members pointed up this difference between Alan's shyness and the two women's assertiveness. As the emphasis shifted from Alan to Rose and Penny, the women accepted responsibility for their own actions and faced their own needs to see men as aggressors who take advantage of "innocent women."

A different approach was taken by the therapist when established group members used their extragroup socializing to solidify their subgrouping and to keep the new members outside the group.

Nancy, Gordon, and Fred were regularly going to a

nearby restaurant after sessions. They used this extragroup contact as a way of excluding other members from their more intimate feelings and thoughts. Within the group session itself, they would banter with one another and refer to their "serious" talks at the restaurant. In this way, they maintained an "exclusive" relationship with one another and addressed other group members from a superior position.

As soon as it became clear that this was happening, the therapist questioned the meaning the subgroup had for the three who were having "secret" conversations about themselves and other group members, and questioned the meaning for those who had been excluded from the secrets. Resentment and anger were openly expressed by those excluded for being considered less worthy than "the three," and indignation was expressed that the group itself was not being used in a therapeutic way. The members of the subgroup expressed their own feelings of closeness with one another and their fears of revealing themselves to other members and of becoming intimate with them, since to do so would carry the risk of breaking up the threesome. After this had been openly discussed for an entire session, two of the threesome became more open in the next session of the group, talking about some of their personal experiences and feelings. Gradually, those who went to the restaurant after sessions became a more shifting population, open to anyone who wanted to join, and not always including the same three. There was a noticeable change in the group members' interactions during sessions, and much more serious consideration was given to the feelings aroused within this context. At the same time, the postsession at the restaurant became less regular, occuring only once or twice a month, and with the participants unpredictable from one month to the next.

It should be pointed out that, rather than rigidly prohibiting extragroup socializing, the stated rule of discussing such socializing within the group session usually eventuates in the material's being dealt with therapeutically—both for those involved in the extragroup socializing and for the group-as-a-whole.

REFERENCES

Abt, L. E. (1965). Acting out in group psychotherapy: a transactional approach. In *Acting Out,* ed. L. E. Abt and S. L. Weissman, pp 173–182. New York: Grune & Stratton.

Alexander, F. (1948). *Fundamentals of Psychoanalysis.* New York: W. W. Norton.

Boris, H. (1970). The medium, the message and the good group dream. *International Journal of Group Psychotherapy* 20:91–98.

Eckstein, R. (1965). General treatment philosophy of acting out. In *Acting Out,* ed. L. E. Abt and S. L. Weissman, pp. 162–172. New York: Grune & Stratton.

Freud, S. (1914). Further recommendations in the technique of psychoanalysis: recollection, repetition and working through. In *Collected Papers* 2:366–376. London: Hogarth, 1949.

Fried, E. (1979). Narcissistic inaccessibility. *Group* 3:79–87.

Greenacre, P. (1954). The role of transference. *Journal of the American Psychoanalytic Association* 2:671–684.

Grotjahn, M. (1976). A discussion of acting out incidents in groups. In *Group Therapy 1976: An Overview,* ed. L. Wolberg and M. Aronson, pp. 180–186. New York: Stratton Intercontinental.

Grunebaum, H., and Solomon, L. (1982). Towards a theory of peer relationships. *International Journal of Group Psychotherapy* 32:283–307.

Hannah, S. (1979). An argument against the use of the alternate session in analytic group therapy. *Group* 3:147–152.

Kadis, A. L. (1956). The alternate meeting in group psychotherapy. *American Journal of Psychotherapy* 10:275–291.

Mahler, M., Pine, F., and Bergman, A. (1975). *The Psychological Birth of the Human Infant.* New York: Basic Books.

Mullan, H., and Rosenbaum, M. (1975). *Group Psychotherapy: Theory and Practice.* New York: The Free Press.

Munzer, J. (1966). Acting out: communication or resistance? *International Journal of Group Psychotherapy* 16:434–441.

Tarachow, S. (1963). *An Introduction to Psychotherapy.* New York: International Universities Press.

Wolf, A., and Schwartz, E. K. (1962). *Psychoanalysis in Groups.* New York: Grune & Stratton.

Ziferstein, I., and Grotjahn, M. (1957). Group dynamics of acting out in analytic group psychotherapy. *International Journal of Group Psychotherapy* 7:77–85.

Chapter 13
Terminations

Terminations of group members and of therapists are inherent in group therapy. Any termination will have an effect on the group-as-a-whole, as well as on the individual members, and must be dealt with prior to as well as after the termination. The basic dynamics of termination are the same whether the person leaving the group is a group member, the group therapist, or a cotherapist.

All separations are mixtures of sadness and joy, and all leave behind a temporary vacuum. In everyday life we experience such losses when a person to whom we were psychically close goes out of our lives. In groups, where there are established relationships of intimacy, a person can become psychically significant to others, and they may in turn become similarly meaningful to that person.

Within the framework of a "significant other," fantasies evolve and affects are exchanged. The reciprocal meaningfulness of each person involved becomes incorporated into the other's self-systems over time. This is particularly evident when a family member or a good friend dies and the work of mourning begins. The grieving period is a slow process during which past memories are decathected and the bonds are slowly dissolved.

THE PSYCHOANALYTIC LITERATURE

Freud (1937) was skeptical regarding a lasting "curative" outcome of an analysis. In his paper "Analysis Terminable and Interminable," he took a practical position that the analyst sets a termination date, which has two meanings: (1) visits to the analyst are discontinued, and (2) no further change could take place if the analysis were to be continued. He cited three factors as responsible for the success or failure of treatment: (1) influence of early traumas, (2) the constitutional strength of the instincts, and (3) the alterations in the ego. The purpose of the analysis was to secure the best possible conditions for the functions of the ego.

A similar view was expressed by Reich (1950), who was curious about the fact that, until her presentation, only two papers had appeared on termination—one by Freud (1937) and an earlier one by Ferenczi (1927). She found Freud too pessimistic but accepted his propositions. Reich quoted Ferenczi as laying down two preconditions for termination: (1) analysis of character traits and (2) analysis of hidden distrust of the analyst. Addressing the idea that analysis did not make people perfect, Reich thought that it could free patients of anxiety and symptoms, and make them capable of having adult object relationships and of adjusting to their reality. If only partial help could be given, termination should be brought about when it was least painful.

In the context of terminating treatment, Greenson (1967) emphasized that prolonged and intense hateful reactions toward the analyst should emerge before termination is considered. It was his view that it was just as important to analyze transference hate as it was to analyze transference love.

A more pragmatic and detailed focus on termination is found in Menninger and Holzman's primer (1973). They emphasize that reason and intellect should be available to the patient toward the end of analysis. Patients must have a clearer vision of their self-defeating tendencies, want to love and be loved, and hate and fight effectively in self-defense. In addition, they must be able to bear guilt without the emergence of symptoms and to endure failures with regret.

There is a progressive shift from infantile passivity to adult activity, from the assumption that love is something to be taken to the realization that love is also something given, from the passive expectation of being loved for one's own sake to the active satisfaction in giving love without the requirement of a "quid pro quo." [p. 167]

Schafer (1983) remarked that during termination, the analyst and the analysand express the belief that they have shared a profound experience. He hoped that the terminated patient would be free to deal with conflicts, to develop and independently affirm important insights, and to make important life choices.

THE GROUP PSYCHOTHERAPY LITERATURE

As in the analytic field, the issue of termination appears problematic in the group therapy field. Grotjahn (1972) saw the goal of successful treatment as "modified self-acceptance." He questioned whether all psychic structures could be changed even in prolonged group treatment, but emphasized that the patient had to feel comfortable with the kind of person he was and with the kind of life decisions that were made to accommodate that unique personality.

Four possible types of unforeseen termination were distinguished by Kadis and colleagues (1974): (1) enforced by the therapist, (2) circumstantial, (3) premature, and (4) vacation from therapy. It was suggested that terminations enforced by the therapist are brought about when continued treatment does not serve the best interest of the group or the patient. Circumstantial terminations occur because of a change in life circumstances. Premature "dropping out" may reflect seasonal endings such as school vacations, at which time remaining "in the same class" denotes that one has been held back. Temporary vacations from therapy may come about when both patient and therapist agree that there are still problems to be worked on, but that other circumstances—financial limitations, for example—make it impossible to continue.

Kadis and colleagues provide indicators for assessing termination requests. Is the patient able to express warmth, tenderness, and love? Does the patient negotiate life situations with ease and derive satisfaction from everyday activities? Can the patient tolerate the inevitable frustrations of social, home, and work life? A sign of emotional health is the patient's increased freedom from free-floating anxiety, compulsion, and rigidity; the patient becomes more reasonable, more discriminating, and more positively involved with others. When patients are ready to terminate, they are less preoccupied with their own thoughts and more interested in considering the needs of others.

A date for termination is set in the group, but the working through of this end phase may take as long as a year. Both the patient and the other group members are urged to "feel through" the anticipated loss generated by the process of separation and the possible sense of abandonment. When a member terminates, the group inevitably changes and has to restructure itself.

Focusing on such restructuring, McGee (1974) wrote about therapists' terminations. Terminations in group therapy are radically different from terminations in dyadic therapy. Many training institutions have therapists and cotherapists in groups for limited time periods. McGee thought that groups could benefit from such events, however, becoming more cohesive and stronger after working through the separation and loss. The operation and maintenance of the group must be given high priority in order to maximize the therapeutic potential of the group. Interventions must be addressed to the group-as-a-whole, and the departing therapist should not involve group members in subsequent therapeutic relationships.

Kauff (1977) applied Mahler's separation–individuation paradigm to terminations of group patients. She stated that termination is usually seen as an isolated event – the end point of working through – and not as a process with unique characteristics of its own. During terminations of group members, themes of abandonment, anxiety, rejection, and narcissistic affront prevail. According to Kauff, it is the nature and outcome of early separations from the mother that will determine the adult reactions to termination. The terminating patient is usually experienced by the group as the abandoning mother.

According to Weiner (1984), the process of growing up involves leaving those whom we loved and valued and depended on earlier in life in order to make new attachments and to incorporate what we have learned. Termination is built into therapy from the very beginning. However, there exists no single criterion.

Caligor, Fieldsteel, and Brok (1984) suggest that termination assessments should be made in terms of the ongoing therapeutic process rather than cure. They observe that the issue of termination is not widely written about and still presents a problem, in particular since "symptom analysis" has changed to "character analysis." Whereas the disappearance of the symptom used to be considered a resolution of a particular conflict, it is now believed that the underlying character structure must be explored to afford more permanent change. The authors appear to think that it need not take longer than a month to explore a group member's termination request.

According to Caligor, Fieldsteel, and Brok, patients in combined therapy usually terminate their individual treatment first and exit through the group. These authors focus on one specific psychic capacity that patients need in order to terminate group therapy: They must be able to leave – that is, to separate, without destroying the loved object or risking being destroyed. The loss of a group member will activate anger toward the group therapist and will change the group configuration. But when a patient has completed the therapeutic task, there will be no problems with separation, and it becomes inappropriate to continue work in the group.

The highly individualized nature of termination was addressed by Yalom (1985). He accepted Freud's definition of a productive life as being able to love, work, and play. For patients, it means that they are able to love others, to let others love them, to be flexible, to trust their own values, and to use the environment favorably. Yalom observed that termination is at hand when a patient behaves the same way in an alternate session as in the group session when the therapist is present.

TERMINATION OF A GROUP MEMBER

Termination in group therapy is a more complicated process than in individual therapy because it affects not only the person terminating but also each of the other members of the group, the group-as-a-whole, the alliances within the group, and the therapist.

In part, the reactions will be affected by the reason for termination—that is, by whether the member is terminating because certain goals have been attained and functioning has improved, or whether the terminating is a form of acting out, an expression of resistance, or a way of avoiding conflict, or even interaction, with another member.

Before an individual enters a group, the therapist, in one or more individual sessions, should set forth the norms regarding termination. Such norms include achieving certain goals, announcing one's intention to leave group, and setting a date sufficiently in advance of leaving so that the group members have a few weeks to process the termination. The therapist's attitude in this preliminary session, as well as the attitude expressed in the group situation whenever a member terminates, will affect the attitudes of group members.

Some therapists may specifically state the criteria to consider in deciding to terminate the therapy group, possibly presenting these in terms of the individual's having dealt with the problems that existed at the time of entering the group; having improved ego functioning, as observed by the other members; and/or having achieved symptom relief and more positive self-feelings.

When new members enter a group, a "working contract" is established, whereby they agree to explore themselves within the group in cooperation with other group members and the therapist. Although this contract is open-ended and can be terminated by either party, it provides that verbal notice be given of the intention to leave the group and that this notice allow sufficient time to explore the reasons for terminating. Group members may periodically attempt to break the therapeutic contract, however. Such attempts are recognized as resistance by the therapist and are explored within the group.

Because the appropriateness of termination is difficult to assess, the therapist must analyze whether the decision to leave the group is a valid one. The therapist's assessment is to some extent influenced by her view of successful treatment, as well as by the goals of the particular patient. In addition, the therapist must consider whether "unfinished business," inevitable in any treatment, would be harmful for this patient if it remains unfinished. However, the therapist's goal might not coincide with that of the group member, who might experience further self-exploration as a hindrance to a more productive life.

Terminations have various meanings, depending on the unique needs and problems with which each member enters the group. We can distinguish those who at the outset are withdrawn and in pain, not in control of their lives, and seeking relief from their discomfort, from those who enter the group in a state of conflict and proceed to project the conflict onto the group. Other members enter group therapy for a circumscribed, stated problem, such as lack of success in a career or difficulty in interpersonal relationships.

Patients who enter the group with circumscribed conflicts will work to improve these external areas and may demonstrate little insight and understanding of their own personalities. Their goals for termination might be set by external achievements. Members who enter group because they are in pain and who lack specific goals will slowly evolve goals as their self-esteem improves and as they are able to expend more energy toward getting their lives in order. As their feelings of discomfort lessen, they will also create a more comfortable environment for themselves. Patients who enter the group with raging internal conflicts will have different goals and will involve the group in their projected dramatizations. For these patients, even though they may be in conflict, there is less emphasis on external achievements and more emphasis on the acceptance of their own needs and lifestyles.

At times, patients may terminate because of outside conditions, such as being transferred to another state by an employer, moving to a different geographical area, or developing an illness that prevents continuing in therapy. Under these circumstances, it is usually possible for the departing member to take time to discuss with the group the reasons for leaving and to allow group members to express their feelings.

In contrast, some patients suddenly and unexpectedly leave group, abruptly announcing either during a session or in a telephone message that they are terminating. Often this is an expression of anger at the therapist, at another member, or at the group-as-a-whole. Abrupt termination may be due to frustration, exasperation, or disappointment. Alternatively, the patient may fear going further in therapy or feel hopeless about the group's not meeting certain expectations or needs. Or, there may be a strong negative transference, as in the following example.

Maria had been in group for several years. When she entered, she presented a hard, brassy persona. She was critical of all the men and denigrated the women for being "soft." When anyone commented on her behavior, she attacked in a strident voice. One male characterized her as being "like sandpaper." Over a couple of years, some of Maria's defensiveness lessened, and she was able to interact more calmly. Then Mike entered the group.

Mike's appearance, voice, and interactive style reminded Maria of her older brother. When Mike spoke to her, she would huddle in the corner of the sofa, crying and looking frightened. Other members questioned her behavior, since they did not feel that Mike had attacked her. It was clear to the therapist and to the other members that a strong negative transference had developed and would have to be dealt with. They pointed this out to Maria and were supportive of her feelings.

Despite this support, Maria suddenly announced in the midst of a session that she was not coming back; this was to be her last session. She could not stand to be in a group with Mike, whom she experienced as attacking and critical. Other group members tried to point out that she was being irrational and self-destructive. Maria began crying hysterically and had difficulty catching her breath to speak. Mike sat silently while other members pointed out that although he had questioned some of her behavior in previous sessions, he had not attacked her. In fact, William and Gail had seen Maria as more critical of Mike than he had ever been of her. Furious, Maria exclaimed that Mike was just like her brother–self-centered, omnipotent, and superior. Again the other members disagreed with her; some of them had found Mike quite likeable and helpful. It seemed to them that Maria's extreme reactions might have more to do with her brother than with Mike.

Most of the session focused on Maria, with Jane being supportive and helpful, Gail being more confronting, and Sally siding with Mike. Although William and Sam sympathized with Maria, they also recalled Maria's having made similar accusations about Richard. The group expressed their concern for Maria and their desire for her to continue in group therapy since she had made so much progress. She agreed to come to *one* more session.

Maria announced the following week that she had decided to continue in group "for a while." In thinking over the session, she realized that she was having feelings similar to the ones she had *always* had toward her brother. Maybe the group was right; perhaps she should stay and try to better understand her relationship with both Mike and her brother.

For the next few months, Maria said little, observing Mike's interactions with the other women in the group. Then she began one session by complaining about how badly Mike had been treating the other women. The women were puzzled by Maria's reaction. Mike, having some understanding of her transference, expressed sympathy. She would not let herself accept this from him, but she did say that she had decided to continue in the group and *try* to deal with her intense feelings.

Patients can only go as far in therapy as their self-esteem permits. Deeper exploration of disavowed wishes may create too much anxiety and stress.

Stan had been in group therapy for about two years. The first indication that he might be considering termination was his irregular attendance. After attending two or three sessions, he would call on the evening of the group meeting, usually 30 to 45 minutes before the group was scheduled to begin, and leave a message with the receptionist that he was not feeling well or that he had to work late. By calling so late, Stan avoided having to talk to the therapist and possibly having to explore his motivations or feelings. Then, at the next group session, he would apologize to the other group members, who would usually question his reason for missing the session and wonder about his diminishing commitment to group therapy. Various members would point out his need for therapy, including his difficulties in relationships with his wife and with his boss. Stan would agree and promise to attend group regularly; then after two or three sessions, he would skip another time.

Finally he announced to the group that "tonight is my last session"; and after a meaningful pause, "unless you can show me the value of group therapy." Everyone then focused on him, trying to persuade him to continue. Some pointed out how much he had changed over the past two years, during which he had been using the group in a positive way. Others emphasized the changes that were yet to be made. As the evening progressed, it seemed that Stan had settled in again as a group member, participating actively, agreeing with others' interpretations of his behavior, and even questioning his own motivation for leaving. At the end of the session, however, he reaffirmed his decision to "give up group therapy" and said that he would not return.

It seemed that he really was giving up. He had made some superficial changes in his external behavior and had improved somewhat his relationships with his wife and boss. But he now realized that he was at a point at which more basic problems had to be faced and dealt with—his competitiveness with his six-month-old daughter for the position of the "baby" of the family; his dependence on his boss, who was also his uncle and who felt some responsibility for keeping him on the job; his feelings of inadequacy and low self-esteem; and his frequent reliance on drugs to escape his problems.

For the next couple of sessions, in order to integrate and come to terms with the loss of a member, there was much discussion of Stan—disappointment that he had not continued in the group; recognition of much of what he was evading; regret that he was no longer a member because he was so likeable and because he had often helped other members with his questions and interpretations. At the same time, group members mentioned that Stan had never let himself become completely involved in group, that he had always been defensive and self-protective, and that he had shown much ambivalence about whether or not he wanted to change.

Terminations evoke ambivalent feelings. The natural tendency of group members is to try to persuade a departing member to stay and save the group from the pain of separation. At the same time, they identify with the departing member in the hope that they, too, will some day complete their therapeutic work. Similarly, departing members may not wish to participate in the painful process of leaving, yet feel the time has come "to stand on their own." Unless the group therapist is alert to both sides of the ambivalence, collusion may result. The therapist may side with one feeling without being aware of the other and find himself, for example, trying to keep the member from leaving.

Under some circumstances, the group may not only approve of a member leaving, but may even encourage the person to terminate, as was the case in the following example.

Sylvia informed the clinic group that she was thinking about terminating. She had been a member for many years, during which time she had separated from and divorced her husband, had changed jobs and developed a successful new career, and had become involved in a satisfying relationship with a man, but with no immediate plans to marry. The group members voiced approval of her leaving and com-

mented on the changes they had seen take place in her in
group interaction over the past few years. She set a final
date to leave the group in two months, to allow herself time
to work out any remaining feelings.

The week before her termination, William said he wanted
to celebrate her success at the next session; others spontaneously endorsed the idea. A proposal to celebrate had
never before been made in this group. But everyone knew
how much Sylvia, the senior member in the group, had gone
through, and they wanted to celebrate her "graduation." It
gave them a feeling of satisfaction and hope that they, too,
would some day leave.

On her last night in group, Sylvia talked about how she
had seen herself when she first came into the group and
contrasted this view with her current behavior. She had
been unable to talk or participate in group interaction for
almost the entire first year, and had sat huddled in a corner
of the couch, much of the time with her back turned to the
group. Now she saw herself as an active group member, having positive relationships with almost every member. At the time she entered group, she had been unable to
hold a job for long; now she had been with a large, national
organization for over a year and had become head of her
department. For a long time, she had tolerated an un-
satisfying and conflictual relationship with a husband who
lacked a regular job with a predictable income. During her
years in group, she had separated from and then divorced
him and was currently in a mutually loving relationship with
another man. During all this time, she had gone through long
periods of intense transference feelings, toward the therapist and various members, which were eventually resolved.

Group members responded to Sylvia by elaborating on her
growth and expressing their good wishes for her, while at
the same time stating how much they would miss her. They
had decided to use the group session to deal with their
feelings of loss *and* satisfaction and to take her out after the
group session to celebrate her success.

In some instances, external circumstances make it difficult for a patient to attend group sessions. Instead of accepting the reality, they continue to hang on, creating disruption for the therapy group.

Nancy had been in the group for several years and had been able to use it to advantage. She had changed from an aggressive, belligerent young woman who "scared off" men, to a competent, successful executive in a national organization, involved with a caring man.

Her achievements at work had been recognized, and she was rewarded by being promoted to a new position with much higher pay and more responsibility. The position was in a new location, however, and involved a commute of about 90 minutes each way. She began to arrive late to every session, which other members found disruptive. She would often be 60 to 75 minutes late, so that she did not know what was going on in the group and could not participate meaningfully. Instead, she would wait for the first pause and then plunge in with her current problems on her new job and the difficulties of commuting.

Group members soon began to resent her behavior and voiced it to her; she would apologize but explain that she could not get there any earlier. She also mentioned her intention to move to the town where she now worked but stated that she had not yet found an appropriate living place.

Taking into consideration the effect on the group of the weekly disruptions, as well as the fact that Nancy would ultimately be terminating, the therapist decided that termination must be sooner rather than later. Since Nancy was in group therapy only, the therapist stated her opinion in group one night after Nancy had arrived with only fifteen minutes left in the session. As the therapist explained why termination was indicated, Nancy began to cry and quickly left the room, grabbing her coat as she went. Group members were concerned about her, and the therapist told them she would call Nancy immediately after the group session

and arrange to meet with her in an individual session to
discuss the situation.

They met the next day. The therapist pointed out that
Nancy was actually no longer a member of the group, since
she did not know what was going on and was just using the
group for support in her new job. Nancy agreed, admitting
that she realized that she was going to continue in group only
a short time longer and could understand how disruptive her
late entrances had been. She was quite calm and much more
in control than she had been the night before. She then asked
the therapist to relay to the group her positive feelings for
them and her understanding of why it was necessary to
terminate now. (Since she could only arrive very late – even
for the final group session – and since her arrival had always
been disruptive to the group, she preferred that the therapist inform the group that she would not return rather than
come to one more session just to say goodby.)

The group, on the other hand, expressed relief that Nancy
would no longer be interrupting each session with her late
entrances. They expressed interest in her and asked the
therapist to give them any future news of Nancy – and then
began to discuss their own concerns.

When it becomes evident that a group member must leave
because his work is finished, the other members, during the
mourning process, will usually review with the departing member how much progress has been made. At the same time, the
members will experience a sense of loss, which may then remind
them of previous losses. The departing member may also experience and express guilt feelings for leaving those who have
helped him. And with this historical review, the mourning process commences.

Even before the departure, the group will reorganize, partially
ignoring the departing member. As the new organization is
formed, affect is discharged and the group renews its cohesiveness. By the time the departing member leaves, most of the
grieving has been accomplished, and the departure is perceived

as a hopeful anticipation that such accomplishment is also possible for other group members.

A member's departure evokes a variety of feelings. Even when the group approves of the termination, there may be feelings of loss and sadness. In addition, it may reactivate feelings about separation, abandonment, and death, as well as feelings of envy and competitiveness or even rejection and hurt; all of these must be dealt with in the group. On the other hand, there may also be hope: "If she can complete group therapy, maybe I can, too."

If members experience the departure as disruptive, they may be angry at the departing member and at the therapist for allowing it to happen. Such feelings have to be dealt with in the subsequent sessions. Therapists occasionally make the mistake of putting into group a patient who is not appropriate for group therapy; this can have a disruptive effect on the group.

Mary, a borderline patient who had been in individual therapy for several years, indicated an interest in combining individual with group therapy. The therapist saw no reason to oppose this and prepared both Mary and the group for the entrance. From the first session, however, Mary took over the group, acting as if everyone was there only to help her with her problems. She monopolized the sessions with reports of her abuse by her parents, was furious when members wanted to talk about their own problems, and verbally attacked them if they tried to point out what she was doing. Her early termination was abrupt and emotional, and it took the group many weeks to recover from the stormy assault.

At times, a remaining member who has had a "special," positive relationship with the departing member may try to hold on to the departing member, feeling personally rejected. Some terminations may be threatening to the group-as-a-whole, especially if the departing member had played a central role in the group. In such instances, the group may go through an extended period of mourning.

The therapist may also experience a variety of feelings upon a member's termination. If the termination was unexpected and sudden, the therapist may experience feelings of helplessness and failure. Such dropouts may occur when a new member has been in the group a short time and begins to foresee having to "give" or expose more than anticipated. Precipitous termination may also evoke anger at the disruption of the group. The therapist may even feel hurt at being personally rejected, or other countertransference reactions may be evoked. On the other hand, if the termination occurs after the member has worked through basic problems in interpersonal relationships, the group and the therapist can share in the feelings of satisfaction of the departing member.

TERMINATION OF THE GROUP THERAPIST

Therapists may terminate for many reasons, including illness, pregnancy and childbirth, geographic relocation, or career changes. The therapist's announcement of intention to leave the group may stimulate various fantasies in the group members, as well as a range of negative feelings, such as resentment and anger, feelings of rejection and abandonment, and possibly a sense of guilt for having "caused" the therapist to leave (whether this is rational or not). There are differences when the therapist departing is a *cotherapist*, and this will be discussed separately, in the next section.

The intensity of the members' reactions varies with the cohesiveness of the group and the abruptness of the therapist's departure. A more cohesive group can deal in a more positively therapeutic way with the loss; and the group can deal more effectively with the loss if given sufficient time to discuss it before the therapist leaves. The varied reactions must be openly dealt with by the group.

Anticipation of the therapist's leaving may precipitate terminations by some group members, who may prefer to be the one leaving rather than the one being left. On the other hand, members may give one another support during this period and in this way contribute to group cohesiveness.

It is helpful if the departing therapist encourages the members to talk about their feelings, both current and historical, regarding loss and separation. As individual members and as a group, it is important that they deal openly with their feelings about the "abandonment," as well as their feelings of loss. Such discussion may require many sessions, both before the therapist leaves and after the therapist has gone and a new therapist has joined the group. It is essential that the group continue to work through their feelings after the therapist has left.

The group may tend to split with regard to the departing therapist and the incoming therapist, with idealization of the former, "good" therapist and devaluation of the latter, "bad" therapist. The members' reactions will, of course, be affected by their previous feelings toward the departing therapist.

The therapist must prepare the group for the departure, setting a date far enough in advance to allow time for the group to discuss their reactions. If little notice is given to the group and the departure is abrupt, the effect on members can be destructive. In cases of sudden emergency, death, or unexpected illness, however, there may not be time to prepare the group.

Whether or not the group has been given advance notice of the therapist's departure, the therapist may be seen as the "bad," rejecting mother. Many feelings, including hostility, frustration, and anxiety, may be expressed *after* the therapist has left, all of which must be dealt with by the new therapist.

Ideally, the incoming therapist should enter the group before the departing therapist leaves, so as to ensure the continuity of the group process. The incoming and outgoing therapists can discuss plans for changing the leadership and can set a timetable that is mutually acceptable and that will be least disruptive for the group. We prefer that both therapists attend at least two, and preferably four, sessions so that the incoming therapist can get a sense of what has been happening in the group and of the leadership style to which the group is accustomed. This gives the incoming therapist an opportunity to observe the outgoing therapist's style, as well as the relationships between the members and the departing therapist; the incoming therapist is thus better prepared to take over the group. Such a plan also has the advantage of allowing the members to become somewhat familiar with the new therapist before the outgoing therapist leaves.

The departing therapist may experience feelings of loss, guilt, and anxiety, as well as feelings about separation, all of which may stimulate memories and feelings about earlier separations. While reassuring the group that it will continue to function, the therapist may experience some feelings of hurt that the group *can* still go on.

TERMINATION OF A COTHERAPIST

A group therapist's termination is less traumatic if there has been a cotherapist in the group. A remaining cotherapist provides continuity and increases the likelihood of continued stability and cohesiveness.

The reactions of the members and the remaining therapist will vary widely, depending on whether the departing therapist is a cotherapist-in-training who had joined the group for a specified period of time, in which case the group will have anticipated the departure from the beginning, or a senior therapist who had been with the group for a long period before leaving. In a training situation, the institution usually determines how the group is informed that a therapist-in-training will be entering the group, when it is to happen, and how termination will proceed. The institution also determines the length of the cotherapist's tenure, which may range from several months to a few years. We have usually required training therapists to remain with a group for 40 weeks, which generally coincides with an academic year. This allows time for the student to observe the experienced therapist for a while before becoming actively involved with the group, to become an active group therapist, and to handle the process of terminating in a way that is not traumatic to the group members.

Although some group members may express negative feelings about "being used for training purposes," we have found that, more often, the group welcomes having a second person to contribute observations and interpretations. Group members may develop a positive attachment to the trainee and may exhibit new behaviors in response, as was the case with Warren.

After Karen entered a clinic group as a cotherapist, Warren began expressing previously unverbalized feelings about being overweight. He was more open in talking about his overeating habits and his difficulties in exerting control. In supervision, Karen talked about her own problems in having been overweight and in now maintaining her proper weight. Although she did not talk about this in group, her attitude of acceptance and understanding had encouraged Warren to reveal his "eating problem."

It had been made clear to the group from the beginning that Karen would be there as a cotherapist for 40 weeks. Warren, knowing that she would have to leave, used to advantage the time she was there. Having revealed himself to the group during that period, he was able to continue his openness after Karen left.

Knowing that the cotherapist is only semipermanent, some group members will not let themselves become "too involved," preferring to direct themselves mainly to the senior therapist and more or less ignoring the trainee. In no instance, however, have we seen group members act in a hostile way to the cotherapist. We attribute this to the way in which the senior therapist has presented the fact that a training therapist will be entering the group, with emphasis on the value of having an additional person to offer observations and interpretations.

A few weeks before the trainee is to leave the group, either the senior therapist or the trainee will remind the group that the termination date is near. A process of preparing for separation can then ensue, which may evoke feelings about other separations in each patient's life. After the trainee has left the group, the senior therapist continues the process of "working through" with group members feelings about being rejected or abandoned, as well as feelings about other separations. The senior therapist may also have some feelings about the trainee's leaving.

When a senior therapist departs unexpectedly, leaving the cotherapist to lead the group, the cotherapist may have feelings of competitiveness with the former therapist and a need to prove his own competence. In addition, the less experienced therapist may experience anxiety, inadequacy, and a wish to be accepted by the group, as well as some resentment at *having* to be responsible for the group.

Whether it is a member or a therapist leaving the group, the remaining members will experience feelings of loss. It is as if there is now a hole in the group, and the interactions of those remaining will increase to fill the empty space. At the same time, the loss will stimulate old feelings about previous losses in the lives of the group members. It is important that the therapist recognize and acknowledge these feelings and enable the group members to face them and work them through over whatever period of time is necessary. In fact, the group may return from time to time (over months or even years) to the discussion of a particular departure, and in these discussions recognize and deal with feelings that were not discussed at the time of the termination.

REFERENCES

Caligor, L., Fieldsteel, N., and Brok, A. (1984). *Individual and Group Psychotherapy*. New York: Basic Books.

Ferenczi, S. (1927). The problem of termination of analysis. In *Final Contributions to the Problems and Methods of Psychoanalysis*, pp. 77–86. New York: Basic Books, 1955.

Freud, S. (1937). Analysis terminable and interminable. *Standard Edition* 23:216–253.

Greenson, R. (1967). *The Technique and Practice of Psychoanalysis*. New York: International Universities Press.

Grotjahn, M. (1972). Learning from dropout patients. *International Journal of Group Psychotherapy* 22:306–319.

Kadis, A., Krasner, J., Winick, C., and Foulkes, S. H. (1974). *A Practicum of Group Psychotherapy*, 2nd ed. New York: Harper & Row.

Kauff, P. (1977). The termination process: its relationship to the separation–individuation phase of development. *International Journal of Group Psychotherapy* 17:3–18.

McGee, T. (1974). Therapist termination in group psychotherapy. *International Journal of Group Psychotherapy* 24:3–12.

Menninger, K., and Holzman, P. (1973). *The Theory of Psychoanalytic Technique*. New York: Basic Books.

Reich, A. (1950). On the termination of analysis. In *Annie Reich: Psychoanalytic Contributions*, pp. 121–135. New York: International Universities Press.

Schafer, R. (1983). *The Analytic Attitude*. New York: Basic Books.

Weiner, M. (1984). *The Theory and Practice of Group Psychotherapy*. New York: American Psychiatric Press.

Yalom, I. (1985). *The Theory and Practice of Group Psychotherapy*, 3rd ed. New York: Basic Books.

Index